SCHOOLING AND EDUCATION IN AFRICA

THE CASE OF GHANA

GEORGE J. SEFA DEI

Africa World Press, Inc.

P.O. Box 1892
Trenton, NJ 08607

P.O. Box 48
Asmara, ERITREA

Africa World Press, Inc.

P.O. Box 1892	P.O. Box 48
Trenton, NJ 08607	Asmara, ERITREA

Cover Design: Ashraful Haque
Book Design: Getahun Alemayehu

Cataloging-in-Publication Data is available from the Library of Congress.

ISBN: 1-59221-002-3 (hardcover)
ISBN: 1-59221-003-1 (paperback)

*To all the school children of Ghana and Africa,
knowledge is power and more.*

Table of Contents

ACKNOWLEDGEMENTS

As is always the case with most published works, one owes a great deal of intellectual debt. I know that I cannot do justice to all by mentioning every name. I hope I will be forgiven and remembered for saying that the intellectual, material, spiritual and emotional help that I received from so many people will never be forgotten as long as this work is read and responded to. Let me begin by singling out two individuals whose help has been instrumental to my ability to put this work out there. If there is any coherence in my thoughts as you read this text please give some credit to Beth McCauley and Dr. Margarida Aguiar. To Beth, your initial assistance in helping to organize my thoughts and presenting my ideas cannot be described and appreciated in mere words. I am extremely grateful for your devotion to the work, and in particular, your editorial, word processing and synthesizing skills. You and Dr. Margarida Aguiar have gone 'beyond the call of duty' in ensuring that my words fully represented my feelings on the topic and what I wanted to convey to readers. I am extremely grateful to Margarida, who has worked with me for so long along the course of my many research projects by providing and sharing intellectual guidance, support and inspiration. You have taught me in many more ways than you are aware. You have not just helped in the transcribing and analysis of my research data, you have been at the forefront of all attempts to present my research findings to the academic and community audience through conference papers, essays for publication in scholarly journals and other presentations at public forums. Your critical reading and commentary on my texts, advice and suggestions to sharpen my thoughts and ideas on this work will not go unnoticed. I thank you sincerely.

As an educator, I have learned a lot from my students. My graduate students at the University of Toronto have been my teachers and any success that I achieve in my academic pursuits cannot be told without you. I have also been blessed to work with many colleagues and staff at the university who have supported my intellectual work and I am honored to share their company

Furthermore, over the last few years I have presented many of the ideas at the heart of this text at scholarly international conferences. I am grateful for the critical comments received from the audience who have contributed to making this work presentable. Also, I thank Gurpreet Singh Johal and Christine Connelly of the Department of Sociology and Equity Studies of the University of Toronto (OISE/UT) for reading and commenting on some of my early working papers. Thanks go to Kristine Pearson, Cheryl Williams and particularly to Olga Williams of OISE/UT for her editorial assistance with my academic papers that have provided the springboard for this manuscript. Cheryl Zimmerman and Olga Williams were wonderful with the depth of their expertise in putting together a camera-ready copy for this work. I cannot repay that service for sure. I also acknowledge the assistance of Hyacinth Francis in completing the editorial work on the manuscript and John Okumu, and Stanley Doyle-Wood both of the University of Toronto for looking over the galleys and assisting in the author/subject index.

I am also grateful to Africa World Press for the decision to publish this manuscript and also for the editorial work that was put into making this book a reality. I acknowledge those anonymous readers of the manuscript including the copy editor for their constructive comments and suggestions. Throughout my research in Ghana I worked with a number of Canadian and Ghanaian scholars, educators, researchers and community members. I acknowledge the assistance of Dr. Bizunesh Wubie, Dr. Grace Puja, Dr. Leeno Karumanchery, Rosina Adjepong, Dr. Martha Donkor, Dr. Bijoy Barua, Alireza Asgharzadeh, Munya Kabba, Erica Lawson, Professor Njoki Wane, Professor Rose Baaba Folson, Ernest Dei, all from OISE/UT and Messrs Ferdinand Otigbo, Dickson K. Darko, K. Baah, Kofi Adu-Amankwah, Martin Duodo, Ester Dei-Danso, Master Bonsie, Wofa Yaw, Mavis de Souza, Samuel Amaning, Kuma Korante and

Paul Ofori-Atta,— all of Ghana—who shared intellectual ideas with me and further facilitated the conduct of my research work. Funding for my study leave project in Ghana was provided by the Spencer Foundation, U.S., and also the Social Sciences and Humanities Research Council of Canada (SSHRC) through the OISE/UT Small Scale pool. Finally, it is to my family that I offer my heartfelt thanks for their continued support and encouragement throughout the course of my academic journey. To my wife and partner, Nana Adwo Oku-Ampofo, and my children Prince Yeboah Dei, Opokua Biney and Kwasi Biney, I will always love you and cherish your care, attention and devotion. To my mother, Afua Donkor, my sisters, Helena and Joyce Dei, brothers Kwasi Manu, Ernest Dei, Atta and all the family members in Ghana—Grace, Adwoa, Abena Mene, Kwasi, Afua, Attah—thank you for being a family in the true sense of the word.

INTRODUCTION

Today the forces of globalization are ever more upon us and the images are frightening for a world secure in its sense of complacency and innocence. Across the many geographical spaces and borders within our global transnational community local peoples are contending with the political, economic, ideological, cultural and spiritual consequences of global change. Arguably this is a change that threatens to sweep every facet of life into an imposed imperial order. Nonetheless, while globalization continues to script us all in varied and myriad ways, to see those damaging effects of globalism as something that cannot be resisted and transformed is defeatist. How can communities make the best out of the emerging opportunities afforded by these changes? As a pedagogue I also work with a philosophy of hope. I continually tell my students to develop and cherish a philosophy of possibility just as we acknowledge our limits and limitations. Education has an important role to play in the search for genuine alternatives to human existence. As I note repeatedly in this book, my use of 'education' is in the broadest sense of the varied ways, strategies and options, through which we all come to know the world and act within it. We can allow ourselves to be informed by multiple knowledges if we uphold our collective intellectual and political agencies. There is the power of human, intellectual agency.

Such "agency" resides in and emerges from knowledge about ourselves, our worlds and our surrounding environments. It is the existence of such knowledges that allow a pedagogue to speak of multiple ways of knowing. Education can provide and build such human agency.

However, if education is to be able to provide this role, then it must be "relevant and responsible" education that clearly and forcefully addresses contemporary human needs and problems. It has to be an education that is truly transformative in the sense of becoming relevant and responsive to community needs, dreams and aspirations.

For far too long debates on African education have spoken at the theoretical level of a desire for relevance and responsibility. Such desire is embedded in a call for education that is neither imposed nor dominating. The desire is shared by many and has been felt across a broad spectrum of society. Breaking the existing trend of colonizing and imperializing education has not been easy. It is not just because of the lack of a political will. The problem, I believe, is the entrenched interests that defend the "status quo" for the benefits gained. The problem has equally to do with the failure on the part of leaders and the vanguards of society to develop a vision of education that neither confuses nor privileges short term therapeutic benefits with a deeper understanding of the long term deleterious consequences of "mis-education." Therefore, what is needed is a vision of education that promotes structural change informed by the lessons and resilience of local peoples' knowledge of their place in the world, and what is seen as the collective responsibility of everyone.

To cultivate the power to imagine, articulate and create new visions of our world, education must empower all learners to think and act critically. Alternative visions of schooling and education are needed that herald the power of individual and collective subjectivities and identities for political work to bring about change. Local struggles for education and educational change cannot be understood exclusively as questions about identity. There are fundamental and broader economic, political, symbolic and spiritual considerations that need to be taken into account in order to move beyond the conventional and dominant paradigms of schooling. By simultaneously emphasizing the issues of culture, identity, history and politics, critical education can assist learners to begin to understand

and appreciate why and how local peoples themselves must continue to be subjects and actors of change.

In the face of insurmountable threat to their existence through poverty, social misery, political domination and material deprivation, local peoples have still managed to effect change in ways that continue to preserve their cultural, political and moral integrity. In many community circles they are generating innovative solutions to daily problems, by looking to their cultures, languages, histories, social norms and values as well as to their and traditional notions of humanness. The acknowledgement of a dynamic relation between nature, culture and society, the sanctity of life as well as sacredness of activity have been powerful forces in the preservation of local communities and their cultures. If education is to be a crucial partner in this task of community survival and social viability then it must be education that responds to the needs of the times. It must be education that is not afraid to address local people's needs, concerns and aspirations as a necessary entry point to the integration of local communities in the global network of nations.

Despite some gains made during the periods after colonization, critical educators continue to deal with Western dominance over what constitutes "valid" knowledge and how such knowledge should be produced and disseminated locally and globally. The search for viable educational options and alternatives, particularly in Southern countries, is increasingly complicated by transnationalism, with its impact on knowledge, "nation," "culture" and the understandings of the "self" and group identities and collective politics. Within the academy, it is important for critical educators to explore ways of rethinking education to reflect the aspirations and desires of diverse peoples. For example, the spiritual development of the learner is an important dimension of effective education. Western dominance over what constitutes "valid" knowledge in formal schooling has been there for some time, but its presence is becoming increasingly noticeable as greater numbers of communities find themselves in the position of structuring and restructuring formal (or compulsory) schooling.

The preoccupation to restructure has been different in African countries which have emerged from colonial structures and struggled through nationhood and independence in the most recent past. The aim has been to establish systems of comprehensive schooling alongside a global economy of transnationalism. The threat of economic dependency looms large. This is, perhaps, one of the reasons educators are increasingly concerned about Western dominance over what constitutes "valid knowledge" and over the marketing of knowledge and culture, which runs the risk of homogenizing cultures globally. With systems of compulsory formal (primary) schooling in this era, what happens to the local learning processes of children in the community? How do school systems bring these ways of knowing into the mainstream of schooling along with economic development? These are not easy questions.

When I set out to write this book, I was preoccupied with one question: Given the current contexts of globalization and its techno-fix approach to human problems, how do we (that is all who share the politics of educational change being pursued in this project) articulate genuine educational options and alternatives for Africa in ways that recognize the African human condition, African histories, creativity and resourcefulness, as well as the challenges posed by local specificities? While there are powerful connections between education and national development that can be made and have, in fact, been historically assumed, the theoretical and practical underpinnings of this linkage have not always been interrogated or problematized. Thus, an important component of this book is to solicit ideas and further the discussion of educational change required for the development of the nation, specifically the Ghanaian nation (see Samoff 1996; Quist 1994).

Most, if not all, citizens recognize the importance of education. The question is, How much priority have governments and nation states given to education over the years? The "much talk" and no action backed with concrete commitment is itself part of the problem. It is argued here that education must be driven by the needs and aspirations of the local populace, rather than the dictates of external capital interests. We must have a system that truly propels the agency of subjects as capable citizens who are participating in a genuine and continuous creation/ acquisition of knowledge and collective power in a social context. Educational changes (e.g., current reforms) taking place in many countries are resulting in the privatization of schools, cutbacks and decreased access to education. Local peoples in most places are facing disturbing moves, by largely fiscally conservative governments, to undermine public schooling. Faced with choices in fighting budget deficits, economic recession and other monetary woes, national governments are not simply reneging on equity commitments; they are "favouring privatization, reduced government expenditures, user charges and difficult choices between sub-sectors in education" (Jones 1997, 373). Even in times of prosperity (as in the North), countries have not always found it appropriate to invest heavily in education and to address long-standing educational inequities (see Hatcher 1998 for Britain; Dei and Karumanchery 1999 for Canada).

Writing in a different context, Amalric (1998) has argued that in rethinking futures, it is important "to develop alternatives in order to re-animate political debates and counter the too often heard argument there is no serious alternative" (37). It is imperative that alternatives for future schooling and education in Ghana be discussed if, as a nation, Ghanaians are to promote and sustain social change that meets the needs and aspirations of all its people. Long ago, a noted educationist stated that "the effect of schooling, the way it alters a person's capacity to behave and to do things, depends not only on what is learned, but also on how and why it is learned and the environment within which it is learned" (Dore 1976, 8; cited in Nwagwu 1997, 94). Implicit in this reasoning is the power of understanding the contexts and politics of schooling in order to promote social change.

No one would dispute the connection between education and national development. There is, however, an assumption of a direct and immediate linkage between education and development that is not firmly understood and interpreted in social policy. To ensure that education meets the material and social needs of a nation, the universal definition of the parameters of the relationship between education and development should not simply be assumed but also explained and implemented in practical terms. This means that social policies for educational change must meet the practical and immediate needs and aspirations of a nation. So far, in many African contexts, the connection between educational policy and the immediate needs and concerns of a national polity is an evolving struggle that has encountered major obstacles.

The Challenge of Education: What Does Social Research Tell Us?

We know from existing scholarly research that there are many problems of education facing Ghana and other African countries.

Some of these problems are stagnating school enrolment, lack of textbooks and instructional materials, teacher training, constrained educational finances and inefficiency of educational administration and management practices. While many of these problems have been long standing, others can be attributed to the dismal failure of the post-colonial state to change the existing system so that it reflects changing times, circumstances and social realities (e.g., the problem of curriculum relevance and employment needs).

Today in Ghana, only a quarter of school-age children have access to basic education. Those fortunate enough to graduate from school barely gain employment. The great majority of the Ghanaian populace have yet to have basic educational and development needs met through formal schooling. While external interests have intruded in educational reforms in Ghana, it is evident much of this involvement is driven by the needs to serve the interest of international capital. Ghana needs an educational system that first and foremost addresses the immediate needs of local communities and its populace as a nation. Many of these needs are simply basic rights. Achieving these goals would then enable Ghana as a nation to insert itself into the global/transnational framework under its own terms and conditions. This is not rhetoric. It is a sad state of affairs that as a nation we continue to depend on external sources to manage our educational systems while local creativity and talents are underutilized. Education must be driven by the needs and aspirations of the local populace rather than the dictates of external capital interests.

Reforms from the State

Since the early 1980s, the introduction of structural adjustment policies (SAPs) and the ongoing challenges of globalization have constituted two external capital interests that have had and continue to have profound effects on Ghana. For genuine social development, we must have a system that truly ensures that all subjects are citizens able to participate in a genuine democracy of equal and unfettered access to knowledge and power. This book looks at how this is possible in Ghana and why it is so critical that Ghana and other African nations make grassroots educational reforms long lasting and effective for their populations.

Given the current emphasis on a global techno-fix society, there is great potential that technology will explode and exacerbate existing differences between the North and the South. Even as the reform rhetoric heats up, glaring educational inequities (e.g., access, outcomes) persist in African education. Local governments, educators, students, parents and communities yearn for "school improvement" in order to address a complex array of problems ranging from lack of basic materials (e.g., textbooks) and physical support (e.g., adequate building and technological facilities) to low retention rates in schools to irrelevant curricular and instructional practices. Dissatisfied with rote learning and regurgitation, many educators welcome a focus on developing the critical thinking skills that allow learners to harness their individual and collective creativity and resourcefulness. From this perspective, the pursuit of educational reforms should be rooted in some basic questions: How can schools effectively promote education for the good of society? How do schools promote effective learning outcomes among all students? How do schools ensure that education is defined contextually and that it is responsive to the local needs of ordinary peoples? What are the lessons of effective schooling practices in local contexts?

Today, education in Africa is often said to be in "crisis." This "crisis" is, to some degree, a colonial legacy of often misguided educational policies and practices (curriculum, texts, pedagogies) that failed to "speak" adequately to the variety of human experiences and the diverse history of events and ideas that have shaped and continue to shape social growth and development. But the problem facing African education is more than colonialism. The current educational policies and practices of governments in sub-Saharan Africa, for the most part, are not appropriately contextualized in local human conditions and social realities. Fortunately, in some communities, scholars interested in promoting education are pioneering new analytical systems based on indigenous concepts and their interrelationships (see Dei 1994; Lawuyi 1991). There are signs of cultural renewal and a revitalization of African cultural-resource knowledge that has the potential to address current social and educational problems.

Subject(ive) Location and the Personal, Political and Academic Project

In this work, I locate myself from within the perspective of my own learning in the local community of my birth, as separate from the formal schooling that I received in Ghana and abroad. I operate from a grounded and contextualized learning that is shared with individuals, families and community groups. There is a form of local knowing that is connected to the land, the people and the ancestors, all of which form a community with a past, a present and a future. For example, I was brought up to appreciate the geographic community and to know that we live in a land bestowed unto us by our forebears and that our ancestors still guard over us. They keep a watchful eye on everyday practice and social activity. The individual living subject could be punished for going against the wishes of the ancestors or for not looking out for the interests of the larger group or community. This is an important knowledge base that has, unfortunately, been corrupted over time (the corruption has had negative consequences). I grew up in a culture that respects the spiritual and the metaphysical as a way of life and a source of knowledge. I have also studied and taught in environments where the interactions of body, mind and soul have not always been duly acknowledged, leaving many students feeling disengaged in our/their school systems. I have observed that the material rewards of competition far outweigh the benefits of co-operation; as a result, there have been many "losers" or "casualties" in the de-spiritualized, competitive system of teaching and learning.

The separation of education from local communities has left many poor rural communities disenfranchised from schooling, both in access and in content. The separation of education from local communities in Ghana must be understood as the privileging of schooling over education. The schooling I refer to is purported to take place within formal institutional structures. It is indeed the formal school tradition that the various educational reforms have tried to change. In that context, children from poor rural communities were disenfranchised from opportunities for formal learning. Often their parents could not afford to send them to boarding schools because they needed them to work on the farm and they could not pay the costs. Those who did go "to school" were uprooted from their families, cultures and communities. Their formal learning was disconnected from the land and community to which they belonged.

I see myself as located and implicated in the struggle to affirm diverse knowledges as a way to transform schooling and education. Speaking from a personal educational history, I can say that formal schooling in Ghana for me was very Western and disconnected from the life of the community of which I was a member. Yet it is this education that has enabled me to pursue graduate studies in a Western academy and even teach in such an institution. It is this attraction of formal schooling that some of the Ghanaian students speak of today as desirable international cultural capital which they do not want the ongoing reforms to place at risk. Many speak about wanting to learn of local knowledges and experiences but also of wanting to earn degrees and diplomas that are "transportable" to other areas of the world. For students struggling in such educational contexts, there have been some losses along the way or, at best, their learning has moved along the parallel of two fragmented knowledge streams. As an adult pedagogue, I have located myself in the struggle to affirm a transformation of schooling and education that is inclusive of diverse knowledges and ways of knowing. I have further interacted with these knowledges in ways that inform, challenge and affirm the self, culture and community. I would assert that these pedagogical struggles and tensions occur on many educational fronts, one of which is spiritual.

I understand education in a broader context to encompass emotional and spiritual empowerment of the learner. Education is broadly conceived to mean the varied options, strategies and ways through which people come to know themselves and the world and how they act within this world. This conceptualization of education draws on the intersections of indigenous knowledges, spirituality, culture and identity in the learning process. Learning as an emotionally and spiritually felt experience is only possible by integrating educational and economic reforms with the spiritual sense of connectedness to the local community, culture and history within the goals, the curriculum, and pedagogical practices of schools. The tensions of learning the appropriate skills to function as an individual, as a collective member of a community and of a nation, and to function as a nation in these times is coupled with the need to understand the present not simply as connected to some "inevitable global market forces" but as connected to a past in a culture that continuously evolves through active engagement in the co-creation of knowledge grounded to local experiences of a material and social reality over time. These issues come through clearly in dialogue with Ghanaian educators, parents, students and community workers. Depending on how discussions were framed, responses focused on the tensions between education for employment and training or education for developing a sense of belonging to a local community with a history and a culture. It is apparent that these two contentions need to be brought together in the educational projects of African countries.

The Focus on Ghana's Education

Since the mid-1980s, I have been involved in Ghana in studies examining how local people utilize their own creativity and resourcefulness to address pressing human problems. This book is informed by field studies conducted in Ghana in the 1983-84, 1989-90, 1990-91 and 1997-98 school years. The studies in the 1980s were largely concerned with local economic and socio-environmental hardships (see Dei 1986, 1992). They looked at the effects of the SAPs. The later studies examined the effects of these economic reforms on education and identified how Ghanaians are developing their own strategies to off-set the ill effects of both sets of reforms. My field work for the 1997-98 study had as its focus on examination of actual school and classroom educational practices. More importantly, it entailed soliciting responses of students, school administrators, teachers/educators and parents to educational reform initiatives.

For the most part, this book is based on the ethnographic studies conducted in two Ghanaian school sites and local communities between July and October 1997. The study specifically explored the nature, contexts, consequences and impact of ongoing national educational reforms of the 1990s on local communities (Dei 2000a, 1999). The schools selected were a Senior Secondary School (SSS) and a Teacher Training College in the Eastern region of Ghana. The SSS is one of a number of science resource centres established in major regions of the country under the reform program of the 1990s. Being a second cycle institution, its graduates move on to post-secondary education, teacher training college or university education. The Teacher Training College (a tertiary institution), was chosen because it is the primary school in the country that trains post-secondary students as teachers in the vocational and technical courses of the Junior Secondary School (JSS) program, which was established under the initial reforms of the mid-1980s.

From these two sites, sixty students and eighteen teachers and school administrators were interviewed individually. In the case of the students, focus groups were also conducted. The interview sessions were supplemented with additional interviews with ten university trained educational theorists and practitioners and twenty-five parents. The criteria for the selection of participants included the need to reflect gender, ethnic, cultural, religious and language differences in the school population. Study participants were asked for their perceptions of and views on the continuing school reform initiatives as well as their expectations regarding the search for genuine educational options. Other research questions explored the participants' understanding of inclusive education, issues of minority schooling and the challenge of dealing with difference and diversity at school.

Interviews were conducted using interview guides. All interviews were taped and transcribed verbatim in order that the analysis be directly connected to the data. Study participants spoke about the many different aspects of the reforms, e.g., school facilities, classroom texts, teacher training, working conditions and instructional practices, school fees, boarding and day education, parental involvement and the challenge of celebrating difference and diversity. Participants were encouraged to speak on issues from their different social positions. Analysis of the individual perspectives reveals general patterns as well as differing opinions, depending on the participants' standpoints.

Through these in-depth individual interviews and student focus groups, study participants were asked for their perceptions of and views on the continuing school reform initiatives, how they saw the connections of these initiatives to national development and to describe their expectations regarding the search for genuine educational options for Africa and for their individual and local needs. Interviews were also supplemented with classroom and school observations in order to better examine teaching and instructional practices and social arrangements. Included as well was a study of published work on educational change in African contexts.

Four key research questions shaped the overall study: First, how do schools/educators take into account students' home and off-school cultures in the teaching, learning and administration of education? Second, how do schools/educators deal with difference and diversity among the student populations in classroom relations, instruction and other educational practices? Third, what particular educational practices deal with issues of identity and representation in knowledge production? Fourth, how do schools seek out and incorporate African-centred and local resources in the curricular and teaching practices? The more specific questions asked of study participants were: How do students, teachers, educators and parents/guardians understand the nature, effects, implications and limitations of the educational reforms? What do students and educators like about their schools and why? What changes do they want to see effected in the school system? What specific teaching, instructional and curricular practices enhance learning for a diverse student body? How do educators and students make the link between home, family, culture and schooling? What is the connection between identity, schooling and knowledge production and how do schools tap local cultural knowledges to effect learning and education in schools?

The study has used participants' words to describe the situation and to bring forth the tensions, struggles, contradictions and ambiguities in subject(ive) accounts on the educational reforms. The importance of "voice" in educational research cannot be overemphasized. Voices convey personal feelings, thoughts, desires and politics. Voices allow readers to bring their own interpretations to the data. By infusing the actual voices of participants the text moves beyond an abstract, theoretical discussion of inclusive schooling. In fact, the voices of different subjects (students, teachers and community educators) reveal a nuanced interpretation of what inclusive education means. For a critical researcher, the careful analysis of voices can offer detailed insights into specific situations, including the past and present historical contexts that have contributed to the standpoint knowledge of the participants.

The Coding

With the help of graduate assistants all files of the taped transcriptions were coded and entered into the Ethnograph, the program for qualitative data analysis. Before systematically entering the coded transcripts into the Ethnograph program, there were various stages of revision to the coding process. The processes informed one another and an effort was made to maintain some consistency. From the perspective of qualitative analysis, the number of transcripts posed challenges to the effort of keeping the number of codes manageable while not losing the detail of similarities, differences, stories, patterns and emerging themes. Also, the diversity in the subject positions of the persons interviewed (e.g., secondary school students from different socio-economic backgrounds, regions and of both genders, secondary school teachers, parents of both genders and of different income and educational backgrounds, students at a teacher training institute and teacher educators) meant that it was particularly important to tease out the tensions and contradictions in subject narratives. The different processes of coding helped provide a more systematic analysis of the excerpts within this research context.

We first hand-coded all the files with primary key codes and sub-codes, according to how individual blocks of transcripts (i.e., high school students, teachers, parents, and students at a teacher training institution) appeared to have certain classifications, sub-classifications of emerging themes. After going through all the transcripts individually in this form, we developed a sense of some common classifications across the different participants which needed to be worded more uniformly in the initial hand-coding. We made the decision to develop the more uniform terms examining the transcripts of the high school students. This draft system of codes was then tested across the other blocks of transcripts. Taking the approach of developing a code list from the perspective of high school students was a conscious decision based on the fact that they would be the more vulnerable constituent population interviewed for this research to be directly affected by the reforms. From this initial process, we added information emerging from other files to the list of code words. It was as if we were working our way through the rims of a circle beginning with the students, moving out to the teachers, the parents, the student teachers and then teacher educators. This in-depth process of data analysis was possible because after the tapes had been transcribed with the help of various graduate assistants it was necessary that one researcher (Margarida Aguiar) along with the principal investigator (author, George Sefa Dei) get an in-depth sense of all the transcripts and codes before the transcribed tapes and codes would be ready to be entered into the computer program, again with the help of various graduate assistants. Limiting the number of persons working on the development of preliminary hand-codes facilitated the work of seeking to achieve consistency in the coding across the different blocks of transcripts. The use of interview guides at the data collection stages also contributed towards the process of seeking to obtain and maintain a consistent system for analysis. These two decisions in the research process were particularly critical not only due to what was a large number of interviews but, as mentioned earlier, due to the variety in constituent populations interviewed (students, parents, teachers, teacher educators). In-depth qualitative text analysis requires time for close examination of the texts. It is, therefore, important when planning for this kind of research that the work involved at the different stages in the process be clear. There are definite personnel needs to assist with interviewing, transcribing and entering the data into the computer. But there is also the need to frame the research at the beginning of data collection through the use of interview guides and to plan for the design and development of a consistent system of coding at the analysis stage before entering the transcripts and codes into a computer program. The researchers involved in this process need to be or become intimately familiar with the body of data to be analyzed.

It is also important to note here that throughout the data analysis we made notes in the transcripts highlighting issues of theoretical and practical significance. Critically examining significant issues noted in the transcripts (as separate from the actual codes) provided additional insights on issues not coded because they didn't show up repeatedly. We also flagged interesting discussions or comments on some of the issues so that the analysis includes not only the frequency of a critique or issue (commonality) but also an issue presented in an interesting, insightful or comprehensive way. We also looked for concrete examples of *critical issues* and *cases* flagged in the transcripts.

Following the various preliminary stages of hand-coding, we examined the use of the Ethnograph program. It has a built in structure of a code book that included family code trees with parent files and child files. This suited our purposes and structure of coding which was not a limited linear list of codes. Once at this stage, we made minor changes and adaptations which the computer facilitated. New codes were developed along the way as we rethought and re-examined the transcripts in the process of entering the material into the program. (For a table of the system of codes used see Appendix 1.) It is important to highlight here that for qualitative in-depth text analysis the computer can be and is a useful tool but it is the lenses of the researchers that are critical to the process.

Discursive Framework for Anti-colonial Education

My discursive approach to the study of educational options in Africa has been to examine how state reforms compare to grassroots initiatives taking up the agenda of reforms. For example, understanding at the levels of theory and practice seeks to bring out and interpret how grassroots educators are combating corporatization in Ghanaian education and how Ghanaians are resisting this re-colonization of their school system. Consequently, this book uses an anti-colonial discursive framework(see also Dei and Asgharzadeh 2000) to explore questions of culture, social difference, identity and knowledge production in an African context. "Colonial" is conceptualized not simply as "foreign" or "alien" but rather as "imposed" and "dominating." The anti-colonial framework is a theorization of issues emerging from colonial relations. When employed as a methodological approach, it interrogates the configurations of power embedded in ideas, cultures and histories of knowledge production and use (Fanon 1963, Foucault 1980, and Memmi 1969). It also recognizes the importance of locally produced knowledge emanating from cultural history and daily human experiences and social interactions. Certainly, the creation of knowledge begins with "where people are at." This means that knowledge must be understood to emerge from multiple sites and sources—formal and informal learning cultures. Knowledge is socially and politically relevant if it fits in with peoples' aspirations and their lived experiences and daily practices. The anti-colonial approach helps one see marginalized groups as subjects of their own experiences and histories and presents local communities as valuable sources of knowledge in theorizing and practicing educational reform and change.

The generation, interrogation, accumulation and application of new knowledge about the learning experiences and lived practices of marginalized groups can contribute to a meaningful transformation of educational processes in Africa. The anti-colonial discursive approach questions institutionalized power and privilege and the accompanying rationale for dominance in schooling. This approach draws on a critical analysis of the structures for delivering education: that is, the structures for teaching, learning and the administration of education. It acknowledges the role of the school system in producing and reproducing racial, ethnic, gender and class-based inequalities in society. It also acknowledges the pedagogic need to confront the challenge of social diversity and the urgency of creating an educational system that is more inclusive and capable of responding to varied local concerns about formal schooling. The anti-colonial approach to understanding and dealing with educational reform problematizes the marginalization of certain voices and ideas in the school system as well as the delegitimation of the knowledge and experience of subordinate groups. The approach views schools as one of the institutional structures sanctioned by society and the state to serve the material, political and ideological interests of the state and economic/social formation. But it is not limited to a critique of schooling. Rather it recognizes the role of the school as a critical public institution and seeks to transform it into one that reflects the needs and world views of the communities and societies in which it is located. Thus, strategies designed to respond to issues of schooling need to examine local knowledges and their roles in instituting viable and alternative ways of educating youth and adults.

An important component of meaningful and genuine educational change is the application of indigenous knowledges to address human concerns, needs and aspirations. By indigenous, I mean knowledge consciousness emerging from an awareness of the intellectual agency of local subjects and their long term occupancy of a place. This agency is rooted in knowledges about traditional norms and social values, as well as in the mental constructs which guide, organize and regulate African ways of living. Indigenous knowledges differ from conventional knowledges. Indigenous knowledges are used by local peoples to make sense of the contemporary world in ways that are continuous and consistent with traditional world views and principles. In other words, indigenous knowledges are distinguished by an absence of colonial and imperial imposition. This contrast is instructive. The notion of indigenousness highlights the power relations and dynamics embedded in the production, interrogation, validation and dissemination of global knowledge (Dei 1999). The search for genuine educational options needs to incorporate indigenous knowledges about local learning, teaching and instruction.

Within Euro-American/Canadian contexts, educators continually struggle to provide inclusive education to meet the needs of a diverse student body. Similarly, African schooling is not immune to this concern. Among many things, Africa must confront the challenges of post-colonial education for celebrating differences within its peoples and geographic regions. Among the pressing questions are: How do we theorize education within the context of pre-colonial, colonial and colonized relations and their aftermath (Prakash 1995; Harding 1998)? How do the experiences of migration, agency, resistance and the reclamation of multiple identities and representations inform our understanding of the colonized subject (Fanon 1963)? And how do differences, multiplicities, ambivalences and contingencies inform educational practice? While the investigation of these questions is crucial, this book specifically examines the extent to which local subjects utilize their knowledge and cultural resource base(s) to ensure that education responds to local needs and concerns.

My argument is that the struggle for educational change in Africa is being conducted along two battlefronts. First, educational change is being addressed/problematized in terms of equity and social justice. Second, reform is being conceptualized in terms of developing critical consciousness in learners that challenges mental subversion and allows students to use their creativity and resourcefulness to solve pressing and immediate social problems. By the development of critical consciousness, I am referring to work in the tradition of Kincheloe and McLaren (1994) (cited in Brock-Utne 1996), which conceptualizes learning as a process not of transmitting knowledges to oblige assimilation but of considering how the social construction of human consciousness is a political process shaped by power. Equity, social justice and critical conscientization are powerfully linked. (See also Asante 1988, 50-1 for a discussion of oppression consciousness; and Ndulu et al., 1998 for a discussion of transformative possibility at the nexus of social, economic, political and cultural dynamics in the face of globalization demands).

Furthermore, African education is not alone in its need to take up these two crucial strategies for educational change. Many local communities in both the North and the South face disturbing moves by primarily fiscally conservative governments to undermine public schooling. In Africa, Asia and the Caribbean, faced with budget deficits, economic recession and other monetary woes, national governments are reneging on equity commitments. They are "favouring privatization, reduced government expenditures, user charges and difficult choices between sub-sectors in education" (Jones 1997, 373). Similar developments can be recounted in the North even in times of prosperity. For example, Hatcher (1998) recounts events in Britain where the current discourse and practice of "school effectiveness and improvement" has sidelined equality and social justice concerns. Equity issues remain peripheral to educational policy developments despite the fact that there continue to be "profound inequities... affecting students from ethnic minority backgrounds" (287). As already noted, Dei and Karumanchery (1999) also discuss similar problems for Canadian contexts in terms of how a "corporate managerialist model of education" (Hatcher 1998, 268) is being strenuously pursued by some provincial governments in order to respond to the requirements of global market competition. In the current economic scene, governments have begun to view and speak about education through the metaphor of the market. When examining this discourse, one needs to ask the question, Who is deciding the educational agenda and why? In a post-colonial context, whereby former colonized nations and other national and local governments have been seeking to transform local and national governments into more representative governing structures, why is it that their powers are being eroded systematically by this global market competition? What are the colonizing interests and tools in this era? The tensions visible in the post-colonial challenges of African school reform as seen alongside the pressure of this global market context provide an opportunity for critical insights.

Inclusivity

There are many problems afflicting African schooling and education. Without a doubt there are genuine concerns, ranging from the shortage of trained teachers, lack of basic materials, decaying physical infrastructure, fiscal, administrative, bureaucratic mismanagement and inefficiencies, curricular irrelevance, school indiscipline, academic standards as well as ethnic, cultural, linguistic and gender disparities and imbalances in education. These issues were discussed by all the study participants and have been disseminated in the African diaspora through African community newspapers (*African Connection*, Toronto: March 1, 2000, May 5, 2000). However, beyond these difficulties there are cases of educational achievements and success stories that not many hear about.

The discussion of an anti-colonial framework for education must include a focus on the challenge and possibilities of inclusive schooling. This focus is complicated because there is a weak and pervasive understanding that issues of social difference (i.e., race, ethnicity, gender, class, culture, language, religion) constitute important sites of unequal power and differential power relations. Furthermore, terms, concepts and conceptualizations such as race, ethnicity, culture, class and language, which are essential to a theoretical discourse on minority education, are themselves usually subjected to different interpretations and analyses. This is usually the case with the use of conceptual and analytical categories that are themselves social constructs (Samuels 1991, 2). This book uses the notion of inclusivity as evoked in the North American contexts (see Hilliard 1992; Anderson and Collins 1995). That is, education that is capable of responding to complex and nuanced concerns of a diverse school body (McCarthy and Crichlow 1993). These forms of education also draw on the accumulated knowledge resources and capabilities of its constituent members (Asante 1987; Mazama 1998). Explained in these contexts, the connection between inclusive schooling and minority education becomes clear: minority education is education targeting the needs and concerns of those subjects minoritized and disadvantaged as students.

The notion of inclusivity brings to the fore certain key questions. It calls for a broader understanding of learning, teaching and administration of education and of its relation to social development. Inclusivity also means focusing on both the process and content of educational delivery that produces differential outcomes (Dei and Razack 1995). In other words, inclusivity involves hearing voices of different actors and subjects. This includes asking about: What students learn, how and why? What educators teach? Who is teaching, how and why, alongside the issue of educational relevance. In order to deal with certain questions, the place and role of qualitative studies on/in schools becomes paramount. We need to understand the experience of students, parents, local communities and educators and their perceptions and understandings of difference.

Dealing with the Problems Today

Today, African educational systems are being privatized as the state cuts down on its subsidies for social services (health and education). Private and public schooling have become contested terrains for the delivery of education. As more costs are shifted to parents, the poor are finding it extremely difficult to provide for their children's education. The most affected are rural populations and, in particular, women and young girls who are often passed over for boys if parents have to make a financial determination as to which child to educate (Dei 1993; Gordon, Nkwe and Graven 1998; Mbilinyi 1998; Otunga 1997). Thus, local subjects are dealing with the rising costs of education in the face of intense poverty. Schools, colleges and universities are themselves facing the unavailability of material and human resources (Kwapong and Lesser 1989). All this is occurring alongside a public discourse on educational reforms that identifies as one of its primary goals the crucial importance of extending the provision of basic education as compulsory to all the children of Ghana. In addition to financial cutbacks and shifting the costs to parents, the over-dependence on external finance capital is perpetuating the cycle of subordination through unequal power relations between African and Northern countries (see Banya 1993; Banya and Elu 1997; Lindsay 1989; Salmi 1992; Samoff 1992). This, too, is occurring alongside a public post colonial discourse of asserting Ghana's development as an independent nation in the world, educating its people and reaffirming the histories and cultures of its peoples.

Within pluralistic contexts, educators are continually struggling with the challenge of providing inclusive education to meet the needs of a diverse student body. African schooling is not oblivious to this reality. Among many things, Africa must confront the post-colonial challenge(s) of education, that is; education in an era celebrating difference and diversity. The post-colonial challenge brings forth such questions as: How do we theorize education in the aftermath of the context of colonial and colonized relations? How do experiences of migration, agency, resistance and the reclamation of multiple identities and representations inform our understandings of the colonized subject? And, how do differences, multiplicities, ambivalence and contingencies shape educational practice?

This book explores what Ghanaians are doing to reclaim and revitalize their education through reforms at the grassroots community level. Chapter 1 provides an overview of the educational reforms pointing to aspects of structural adjustment policies with implications for education. The discussion examines how one Ghanaian rural community adapted to the challenge of educational reforms in the early and late 1990s.

Chapter 2 directs the reader's attention to broader theoretical and philosophical issues and problems plaguing the educational reforms. These are contextualized in the narratives of the students, teachers, school administrators who discuss the strengths and weaknesses of the reforms. It points to some of the grassroots initiatives being pursued in response to the problems and challenges of reform.

Chapter 3 introduces the concept of "critical teaching" and raises ontological and epistemological questions about educators' teaching methods and methodologies relating to African education. The chapter also identifies particular teaching strategies that make for the creation of relevant and resisting knowledges on and about Africa. The learning objective is to highlight grassroots initiatives to underscore the power of critical teaching for transformative change in

Ghana and Africa.

Chapter 4 focuses on how parents/guardians, educators, students and local communities see the dynamic relations between home and community in youth education. The chapter redefines home/community interrelations highlighting the strengths of not making a distinction between the home and off-school cultures of students. This chapter also takes up culture and local language and their roles in schooling and education. The discussion sees teaching culture and history as central to effective schooling education. Culture and history also have relevance for understanding questions of identity and the reclaiming of a pedagogy that is locally contextualized.

Chapter 5 is devoted to a discussion of spirituality, the individual and the self as a learner and how Ghanaian students and educators perceive the self as an important entry point to learning and for the schooling of youth. This centering of the self is relevant in order to understand the forces that propel students to act politically for change on the basis of received and acquired knowledge. This chapter discusses the importance of spirituality in African education and highlights the challenges faced by learners in the engagement of culture and spiritual knowledge. The discussion also stresses how learning for some can be an emotionally felt experience by drawing on the interface of body, mind and soul in the learning process.

Chapter 6 focuses on how indigenous knowledges are claimed in Ghanaian contexts and the role and significance of this knowledge base for schooling and education. The chapter highlights indigenous knowledges as important ways of knowing about ourselves, local environments and social surroundings. Such knowledge is appropriately contextualized in local land, history and culture and serves to provide Ghanaian students, educators and local community members with a shared sense of collective identity and destiny.

Chapter 7 examines difference and schooling in the Ghanaian context. It points to the power of inclusive schooling and the specific grassroot initiatives being undertaken in schools to ensure that all students can effectively be engaged in the learning process. The chapter introduces the concept of anti-racist education and its relevance in an African context.

Chapter 8 looks at indigeneity and African education, and examines in particular the role of Indigenous knowledges in African schooling and education. A particular interest is the broader questions of how Ghanaian [and African] schools take up local knowledges in

teaching about oneself, culture and history and its possible liberating
effect in challenging dominant Western forms of knowing. Schooling
and education must seek to harness the multiple ways of knowing and
interpreting our worlds. Educators must work with the idea of
collective, collaborative and multiple dimensions of knowledge and
knowing. The educational objective is not to posit local/Indigeneous
knowledge as separate and distinct from Western and other forms of
knowing. Rather, the objective is to stress the relational and dynamic
components of all knowledge systems and how local contexts, history
and culture, position different learners to know differently. Through
such critical teaching and learning practices, students can be
empowered to affirm their own understandings of their environments
and use that knowledge as a starting base and location to interrupt
dominant and hegemonic knowings.

Finally, Chapter 9 summarizes the participants' responses to the
reforms and focuses on the role of the nation in creating a blue print
for educational change in Ghana and suggests implications for Africa
as a whole. This is a crucial and pertinent discussion given current
forces of globalization and the search for genuine educational
alternatives and options for Africa. The African states cannot shirk
their responsibilities to their citizenry. They must address key
questions of accountability and transparency in the pursuit of
educational reforms. They have a responsibility to lead the way in
carving out real and meaningful educational reforms that allow
learners to become relevant to their communities by defining
individual responsibility to a larger citizenry and diverse community.
The chapter does not attempt to provide final solutions to these
problems and concerns. In many ways the discussion marks a
beginning and a desire to resist intellectual and academic closure on
the pursuit of meaningful educational praxis for change.

Chapter 1

From SAPS[1] to Globalization: An Economic Overview of Educational Reform

Sardar (1999) in his excellent critique of "development" has rightly argued that the issue at hand is the definitional power of the West in its control of the discourse about "development". Okolie (2002) also offers a poignant observation that perhaps the greatest significance of the role of the World Bank in African development is its domination of the development discourse rather than the money it provides or fails to provide for development (although both are related) [Okolie 2002: personal communication]. Such observations are important because they reinforce a longstanding critique of the conventional development discourse and practice and also raise questions about who controls the discourse of development and why (see also Dei

1998; Sardar 1999; Tucker 1999; Munck 1999; O'Hearn 1999)? These insights are also relevant because they maintain that in order for meaningful and sustained development to begin we must interrogate the power of ideas to bring about social change. The international financial community's domination of the development discourse ensures that African governments gear their domestic economic and social policies to suit the prescriptions of the West and those of international finance capital. We should wonder aloud if development can result from the mere cancellation of African debts, from the pursuit and tinkering of structural adjustment policies underway since the mid-1980s or from a rethinking of the discourse on development. What are the consequences of designing futures for others? This question of who controls the discourse and why is significant especially when we begin to interrogate education sector reforms under the structural adjustment policy in Ghana.

Since the early 1980s there has been a powerful discourse of development propagated foremost [but not exclusively] by the World Bank and the IMF that has successfully linked poor economic performance in Africa to crisis in governance. This discourse has also attributed Africa's economic problems solely to domestic policies hugely ignoring fiscal imbalances in African countries that are due largely to inequities within the global economy. While I would not ignore domestic implications of Africa's woes, it is important to reiterate that, by far, this discursive lens of minimizing external complicities and accountability has propelled the structural adjustment policies of the World Bank and IMF.

The literature on Structural Adjustment Policies and Programmes (SAPs) in Africa is very extensive and this discussion will not attempt to broach the subject in any detail (see Panford 2001; Sandbrook 1993; Pickett and Singer 1990; Sahn 1994; Gyimah-Boadi 1991; Hussain and Faruqee 1994; Weisman 1990; Adepoju 1993). Suffice to say that SAPS have generally been seen as an attempt by the West and particularly the G7 countries (now the G8) to respond to calls for assisting poor countries to service their official debt and in particular to accede to the request for debt forgiveness for African countries (see also Easterly 2001). The international financial community identified structural imbalances and weaknesses that characterised African economies as the root causes of African development problems. Marking a shift away from state intervention in domestic economies structural adjustment allows market forces to "allocate resources whenever possible" (Engberg-Pedersen, et. al., 1996, 3). Initially implementing a stabilization phase through initiatives and the directions of the IMF "to reduce public expenditure, raise interest rates and allow the local currency to reflect its market value," SAPs have proceeded with a long term adjustment phase under the auspices of the World Bank "intended to boost economic performance" (Djokoto 2002, 37; see also Engberg-Pedersen et al., 1996).

The arms of SAPs have been far reaching. As Olukoshi (2001, 2) notes, "coming into the developing countries under the rubric of International Monetary Fund (IMF) and World Bank structural adjustment programmes, the neo-liberal polices that were promoted encompassed virtually all aspects of economic and social life, with the attendant [deleterious] consequences." Indeed, SAPs were about the promotion of a market-driven economic system alongside the retrenchment of the state and the curtailment of state intervention in national economies. SAPs affected everything from "exchange rate, prices, interest rates, subsidies, the entire trade regime and industrial policy regime, the budgetary framework and public expenditures, investment policy, taxation and revenue mobilization, infrastructure development, or in such areas as social policy (encompassing health and education), labour market policy, and the management of public enterprises" (Olukoshi 2001, 2).

Today the limitations of the neo-liberal philosophical and policy underpinnings of IMF/World Bank structural adjustment have been laid bare. In fact, it has been noted that "rather than being 'adjusted' the continent has been seriously maladjusted" (see Olukoshi 2001, 5). Okolie (2000, 74) also argues that SAPs "were not simply a free market alternative to the regulation of African economies by African governments but are themselves a different form of political regulation which have, however, failed to produce the promised economic recovery for Africa." He goes further to point out that the problems of SAPs arose from the manner in which the world economy has been regulated historically, including the manner of Africa's insertion into the world economic system. While SAPs made contradictory demands on African states, the states themselves lacked the capacity and resources to fully implement the adjustment programmes. The international financial community has not been accountable to the people whose lives and futures SAPs have administered. Such lack of accountability coupled with a desire to ensure the interests of multilateral corporations, the pursuit of reckless lending policies, and the unfairness and inequities inherent in the global economy means the World Bank and the IMF (and indeed the West) bear a heavy responsibility for any perceived development malaise of Africa (Okolie 2000). After all, domestic policies in nation states are tied to shifts in the world economy and politics of pursuing global development.

Stiglitz (2001) is correct in pointing out that one of the challenges of development "is the recognition that transformation requires changes both in ways of thinking and in society's institutions" (3). Social change is about altering social, political, economic, and cultural institutions and structures to be in line with the process of development. In this context, development is seen as a transformation of society and not just an increase in physical and human capital. A basic failure in development initiatives in Africa is the lack of recognition of the importance of culture and social values in promoting change. SAPs as an approach to development heavily focussed on financial and capital market liberalization and the efficient allocation of resources. Local understandings of the necessity for change and the role that such knowledge about society, culture and history would play in the process of development was largely forgotten. With SAPs there was no pluralism in policy and structural adjustment programs basically failed to take into account the specificities of each context (see also Chandrasekhar 2001, 3).

Many writers have discussed the success and adverse effects of SAPs in Ghanaian populace (see Cornia et al., 1987; Hutchful 1989, 1995, 1996; Rothchild 1991; Abbey 1990; Alderman 1994; Leechor 1994; Sowah 1993; and Gyimah-Boadi 1991; Ninsin 1991; Djokoto 2002). Despite wrecking untold havoc on local people, Ghana has been showcased as a success story of SAPs in Africa. In fact, as Djokoto (2002) notes, a relatively recent Newsweek article states this about Ghana and SAPs:

> While the program has caused inevitable social and economic dislocation, it has made Ghana a star performer in Africa and the developing world. Despite the painful nature of the transition to a market-driven economy, the country and its people have persevered in carrying out the onerous remedies prescribed by international agencies. According to the World Bank, the country's adjustment programme "is by any yardstick one of the more successful in Sub-Sahara Africa." (Newsweek magazine November, 1994: 2, cited by Djokoto 2002, 3)

For the purpose of this book the focus is on SAPs impact on education in terms of the reforms carried out as part of the educational sector adjustment.

In his review essay on educational policies in sub-Saharan Africa, Dan Thakur (1991) highlights Africa's educational problems in the post-independent era. Alex Kwapong (1992) also addresses similar concerns. Among the problems identified are student attendance and dropouts, declining quality of education due to lack of textbooks and instructional materials, the poor quality of teacher training, decreasing educational finances and inefficiency of educational administration and management practices. Even before the World Bank and the International Monetary Fund (IMF) inspired Structural Adjustment Policies and Programs (SAPs) in a number of countries, a few scholars (Psacharopoulos 1986) have blamed the decline in formal education in post-independence Africa partly on shrinking national educational budgets, a political economic reality that could greatly restrict the possibilities of national post independence projects in Africa. And it is an economic situation that would be further aggravated by the increase in population and the Structural Adjustment Programs (SAPs).

In this chapter, I examine the impact that SAPs have been having on primary education in Ghana, from the individual accounts of parents, teachers and community leaders. Specifically, I look at how changes in basic primary education, such as the introduction of the Junior Secondary School program in rural communities, have affected local peoples already reeling from the effects of severe national economic hardships that can be attributed to both internal and external conditions. It is undeniable that, since the 1960s, the Ghanian economy has been in decline. Eboe Hutchful (1989) has pointed to certain internal contradictions within Ghana's modernization and industrialization policies of the post-independence era as generating severe problems in the national political economy. The contradictions centre on the "big push" to industrialize, which emphasizes import substitution and a less open economy, as well as state political and economic mismanagement that has led to the neglect of local food production, agricultural development and the dependence on expensive and inappropriate foreign capital. There has been an accelerated decline in the nation's exports and domestic production levels, as well as a growing imbalance between state revenues and expenditures. Hutchful (1989, 1990) identifies three crises in Ghana's economy that have been identified in the post-independence era: first, a structural crisis characterized by a combination of high domestic demand and a severe industrial and agricultural recession; second, a fiscal crisis caused by rising domestic and external debt and budgetary problems resulting from the inability of the state to reproduce its traditional source of export earnings (cocoa) and to generate additional sources of income; third, a crisis involving a marked level of political instability resulting from frequent changes in government and frequent policy revisions (Hutchful 1989, 1990).

It was in the context of seeking to reverse a further deterioration of ordinary living conditions that the then ruling Provisional National Defence Council (PNDC), in the mid-1980s, pursued a national economic recovery programme through the SAPs. Inspired by the international financial community, major reforms have been carried out in Ghana and other African countries, largely with an eye to trimming national budgets and improving creditworthiness.[2] By late 1988, at least thirty African countries had adopted SAPs. At the general level, the adoption of SAPs embraced the World Bank/IMF doctrine of market-oriented reforms of economic liberalization, external openness to trade and capital flows, and rationalizations of the public sector (Campbell and Loxley 1988). SAPs emphasized retrenchment in the public sector, social services, privatization and fiscal discipline. The management of a transition from colonial economy to a post-independence economy became closely tied to external market forces dominated by powerful economies of "the North."

Loxley (1989) noted that, in the Ghanaian context, the specific policies driven by and carried out through the SAPs have involved a reduced role for the state in the local economy, the improvement of local conditions for economic growth through fiscal, monetary and exchange rate incentives and trade liberalization policies. The SAPs have resulted in repeated devaluations of the local currency (cedi), internationalization of domestic price structures, restraints on wages and government expenditures and a reduction of state budget deficits through cutbacks or removal of state subsidies on social services (e.g., education, health, public transportation, agricultural inputs). In a study that examined the impact of the SAPs on rural economies, I noted that the state has actively promoted cash crop production for export and the wholesale privatization of state enterprises, or at least their rationalization, by requiring good management and incentives for performance and accountability (Dei 1992).

In its eighth year of SAPs, Ghana was presented as a showcase for the "success" of World Bank/IMF policies in Africa because of the gains in Ghana's GDP. In West Africa (December 1991) some World Bank economists expressed a feeling that Ghana could rival even those achievements of Indonesia, Korea, Taiwan, Malaysia and China. To do so would require a political commitment to vigorously pursue export promotion and undervaluation of the local currency, and a willingness on the part of Ghanaians to pay for large investments in the education and health care infrastructure.[3]

Very few in government would admit that part of the deal Ghana reached with the World Bank/IMF for assistance in restructuring the national economy called for reforming the nation's educational system and reducing the costs traditionally borne by the state. But it is also fair to say that this idea of reforming the nation's education system itself is not new. Throughout these discussions it has never been a question of whether or not there was a need for educational reforms but rather what directions the reforms would take. The political economic realities and the need to expand access to basic education which included the expansion of basic infrastructures for the provision of educational services for all children in all regions and sectors of Ghanaian society posed challenges around the issue of funding/financing. It has always been a contentious issue, a thorn in the flesh of political rulers, particularly reforms in the state's financing of education (Asobayire 1988). Various discussions on educational reforms have carefully avoided a thoughtful examination of who should actually be paying for the cost of educating Ghanaian children.

Arguably, problems afflicting Ghana's educational system have been long standing, some of which are colonial legacies. Others can be attributed to the dismal failure of the post-colonial, patriarchal state to alter the existing system to reflect changing times and circumstances, greater equity and access as well as other contemporary realities. One such contemporary reality is the high rate of population growth and its impact on the nation's limited resources for the provision of education for all citizens. The projected steep rise in Ghanaian population from 6.7 million in 1960 to over 15 million for the early 1990s has added stress from the increased number of school-age children (George 1976). In fact, the population growth rate was projected at over three percent per year (Ghana Statistical

Services 1984). In 1960, the number of students enrolled in academic institutions at all levels of schooling was 696,000. By 1983, the figure was over two million. In the 1985-86 school year, 1.2 million children were enrolled in primary schools, and in the 1989-90 school year, 1.6 million children were enrolled (Ghana Statistical Services 1991). The Ghanaian situation is no different from that of other sub-Saharan African countries.[4]

Other long standing problems afflicting education in Ghana include issues of curriculum relevance, lack of material support from both state and the local community for education reform, official corruption and embezzlement of public education funds, administrative bottlenecks, duplication of educational services, lack of jobs for trained school leavers, and the unwillingness on the part of school leavers to serve in the rural areas. These issues along with the specific needs and aspirations of the post-independence project and the projected and very real rise in student population should have flagged the importance for educational planning to take into account the need to redirect and increase educational expenditures that could meet the articulated goal of access to basic education for all Ghanaian children. Economic policies that focused on reducing expenditures in education would appear to contradict the stated goals and compound the problems.

Historical Overview of Educational Reforms in Post-Independence Ghana

In presenting a brief historical overview of educational reforms in post-independence Ghana, I want first to highlight a few of the works that have identified the problems and challenges in African schooling. I do so in order to contextualize the discussion on Ghana. Generally the extensive literature on education in Africa focuses on specific themes such as curriculum, policy, language, teacher education, culture, science and development (see Blakemore and Cooksey 1983; Nyerere 1974; Zymelman 1990; Jolly 1969; Thompson 1984; George 1976; Uchendu 1979; Sifuna 1992; Obanya 1995; Samoff 1993). To varying degrees, other authors have sought to relate the discourse on educational reform to social development and change (Bray 1986; Nyerere 1979, 1985; Mwingira and Pratt 1967; Callaway 1973; World Bank 1988; Samoff 1992; Carnoy 1986; Carnoy and Samoff 1990; Craig 1990; Jones 1992; Foster 1985; Psacharopoulos 1989, 1990;

Banya and Elu 1997; Jones 1997b. These works point to the historic problems in education that African countries face. As already noted, these include stagnating school enrolments, lack of textbooks and instructional materials, inadequacy of teacher-training, diminishing educational finances, and inefficiency in educational administration and management practices (Thakur 1991; Craig 1990; Kwapong 1992; Kwapong and Lesser 1989; Banya 1991; Ntiri 1993; Alexander 1994). While many of these problems have been long standing, others can be attributed to the 'post-colonial' state's dismal failure in altering the existing system to reflect changing times, circumstances and social realities (e.g. the problem of curriculum relevance and employment needs).

To redress these above-mentioned problems, educational researchers and theorists have endeavoured to account for the decline in formal education in post-independence Africa and then, on the basis of their conclusions, have suggested a rethinking of the schooling process. Fafunwa (1982), Jegede (1994), Betts and Tabachnick (1998), Bledsoe (1992), Johnson (1995), Kinyanjui (1990), AALAE (1990), Banya (1991, 1993), Tedla (1995), Folson (1995), Dei (1994a & b) and Brock-Utne (1996), among others, have critiqued conventional African educational processes, suggesting ways of moving beyond the colonial and paternal discourse that has traditionally characterized interrogation of the field. In particular, these authors question the suitability of applying foreign ideas and institutions uncritically to Africa. They suggest an understanding of the continent on its own terms: that is, within the context of local culture, language, history and politics. Further, these authors locate their critiques in the lessons they have gleaned from countries which have attempted to implement educational reforms with the objective of maximizing social returns (Craig 1990; Psacharopoulos 1989, 1990; Eshiwani 1990; Galabawa 1990; Achola 1990; Maravanyika 1990). It is clear from a critical review of the literature that in identifying the important role education plays in African development, research must focus on the strategies, options and ways through which local peoples come to know their school and educational systems and how they perceive the place of educational reforms in social change. Without doubt such knowledge has implications in the search for viable educational options for Africa.

Within the context of Ghana's education and reforms of the school system, the literature attests to the challenges and possibilities of educational change that can emerge for a critical analysis of local conditions and knowledge and how structural processes implicate the struggle for social change and development (see Foster 1965; George 1976). Folson (1995) has provided a more detailed review of the history of formal education in Ghana by touching on pre-colonial through colonial to post-colonial reforms. She has looked at the historical basis of the national educational system portrayed as a criticism of the colonial educational system and the socio-political forces and changes that propelled a series of reforms since the 1960s. Her work is valuable in the identification of the specific problems inherent in Ghana's educational system and the consequences and implications for national development.

Throughout Ghana's history a series of committees have been set up by successive governments to examine the nation's educational system and recommend reforms. In fact, in the decade following Ghana's independence, seven different reports came out of such committee work (see also Folson 1995). They included the Botsio Report (1960-61), Ammissah Report (1963), Kwapong Report (1966-67), Cockroft (1966), Busia Report (1967), Russell Report (1969) and the Dowuona Report (1970). These reports have placed varying emphasis on particular segments of Ghana's educational system and made recommendations ranging from complete state financing of education to total divestiture of the state in the provision of services for university education (see Asobayire 1988). For fear of political repercussions, many of the recommendations for educational reforms were shelved.

The need to reform Ghana's educational system has long been recognized by the Ghanaian public. In the mid-1970s, there was concern about the elitism that the post-independence system of education inherited from the colonial experience and about the heavy emphasis on academic work which was very far removed from national socio-economic development and human power requirements (see also Foster, 1965). It was felt that the country's educational system was not serving the needs of individuals, communities or the nation at large.

In March 1972, the Ministry of Education submitted proposals on a new structure and content of the country's education for public discussion. The government appointed a national committee (the Dzobo Committee) to collate public comments and suggestions. Out of the committee's deliberations came a new educational structure that the military government of Colonel I. K. Acheampong accepted in July 1973. The basic principles or ideas underlying the new structure and content of the nation's education were summarized in a publication by the Ministry of Education (1974). It included proposals for all Ghanaian (pre-school) children to have between eighteen to twenty-four months of preparation and pre-disposition before the start of their formal education. Formal education, extending to nine years, was to begin at age six. It was to be free and compulsory. The new system also stressed that, throughout the entire pre-university education, emphasis should be placed on the "development of practical activities and the acquisition of manual skills, the development of qualities of leadership, self-reliance and creativity through the promotion of physical education, sports, cultural and youth programmes, as well as the study of indigenous languages, science and mathematics" (Ministry of Education 1974, 1).

Generally, except for a few experiments in a handful of schools in the Ghanaian capital, the proposals for restructuring Ghana's education in the 1970s were not implemented. The Dzobo recommendations were nothing more than an exercise on paper. Among the many reasons for this were national political instability, lack of political will on the part of national leaders, bureaucratic bottlenecks and the high cost of providing infrastructure and skilled personnel in practical and vocational subjects. By the 1980s many of the problems afflicting the nation's educational system still prevailed (see also Folson 1995).

By 1983, it was widely perceived that the educational system, as much as the Ghanaian economy, was in serious trouble and required immediate national attention. In a keynote address at a national seminar on the educational reform programme, the Deputy Secretary for Education lamented the severity of the state of the nation's educational problems in the 1980s. He pointed to the exodus of significant numbers of trained and highly qualified teachers to other countries, which necessitated the recruitment of untrained teachers in primary and middle schools. Most schools, particularly in the rural areas, were without textbooks and stationery items due to severe foreign exchange constraints. Much of the infrastructure of the schools, such as buildings, furniture and equipment, had deteriorated due to lack of replacement and repair. School enrolment was declining in proportion to the size of the school-age population and there was a dropout rate of about 30 percent at the elementary school level in some communities. This declining demographic school reality was occurring alongside an increase in population growth and alongside a public discourse that spoke to the national, social and economic need to expand the provision of access to education and to increase the levels of educational attainment of Ghanaian school children at all levels (pre-school through to University). In addition, nearly two-thirds of the nation's adult population were classified as "illiterate." Education officials recalled that successive Ghanaian governments had cut back on educational funding over the years, and the effect on educational quality was clearly being manifested in the failure rates of Ghanaian school children at competitive international examinations, such as those conducted by the West African Examinations Council.

Compounding these woes was the virtual absence of data and statistics needed for national educational planning.[5] The Ghanaian government, under the encouragement of the international financial community, saw the introduction of SAPs as an opportunity for implementing some of the major educational reforms. At this juncture, it is critical to reiterate here that government cuts in social spending (particularly in health and education) were themselves part of the conditions imposed by the international financial community to "help" restructure Ghana's economy and "improve" the nation's creditworthiness.

The Educational Sector Adjustment Program of the mid-1980s

The general policies of SAPs in Ghana embraced educational reforms as a way to address some of the problems within the nation's educational system. The educational SAPs aimed to privatize educational services and reduce, as was then stated, the "intense pressure on public sector budgets which jeopardises education, its quality, relevance and cost effectiveness" (see Jones 1992, 172). A major objective of the SAPs was to increase cost-effectiveness and cost recovery through the "effective use" of education funds and through involving parents, communities and private business groups in funding education (e.g., provision of buildings, furniture, tools and equipment for workshops for the schools' infrastructures).

The emphasis was placed on improving "quality" by reforming education to meet the needs of the labour market by decentralizing management to save bureaucratic costs and improving the distribution of educational resources between the primary and tertiary sectors. These objectives were to be achieved, in part, by decentralizing the national educational system at both the district and regional levels (see World Bank 1988, 1989). Active local participation in the development and delivery of educational programs that seek to better reflect and address past and present local realities is critical. However, this did not seem to be the thrust of the reforms initiated through the assistance of the SAPs. Rather the thrust appeared to be in the direction of devolving national public responsibility for the financing of education by downloading this responsibility onto local communities without consideration of the inequitable distribution of wealth across regions and within communities.

The national education agenda was to focus on the immediate training of skilled Ghanaians to support the agricultural and industrial sectors of the economy. A primary goal of formal education was to promote self-employment (World Bank 1989). The structure of the national educational system was to be changed from seventeen years of pre-university schooling (i.e., six years of primary, four years of middle, five years of Junior Secondary and two years of senior secondary school education before entering the university level— 6:4:5:2) to twelve years (i.e., six years of primary, three years of Junior Secondary and three years of Senior Secondary education—6:3:3). It was felt that this five-year reduction in schooling would allow more resources to be released for improving access to education, especially at the basic level, and for improving the "quality" of education. The reduction in the number of years of pre-university schooling was to be compensated for by extending the length of the school year itself to forty weeks from thirty-five, an increase of five weeks per year.[6]

Furthermore, the state was to promote the development and use of textbooks written by Ghanaians and the development of a curriculum more relevant and consistent with the country's social, cultural and economic needs, while catering to a diversity of individual talents and skills. Invitations would be extended to private publishing houses to tender for manuscript development, publishing and printing of required textbooks.[7] The schools were to place emphasis on the teaching and learning of the core subjects of Health, Education, Agriculture, Industry, Science, Technology, Mathematics, English, Ghanaian Languages, Environmental Studies, Physical Education, and Arts and Crafts.

The educational SAPs also called for renewed progress toward the long-term goal of universal primary education. Theoretically, the structural adjustment policy upheld the importance of continued state support, including the necessity of redirecting funds to primary education from cuts to post-secondary funding. The policy sought to reduce the unit cost of education through a "better utilization" of primary school teachers, revised construction standards, and reductions of school drop-out and repetition rates (see World Bank 1988, 133-42; Jones 1992, 173).

Some aspects of the educational sector adjustment and reforms were well meaning and, in some instances, long overdue. For example, the notion of reducing the number of years of education was basically sound. Ghanaians had already drawn attention to the excessive length of the system. However, students who were lucky to get into secondary school did not have to complete the full four years of middle school. Although the reduction in school years had been called for by many sectors, the extent of the reduction (five years) has been strongly criticized by the majority of participants in this study and the critique has continued to be a part of ongoing local and national discussions. A forum has formally recommended that the reduced three year Senior Secondary School Program be extended by one year to four. The recommendation "has yet to be accepted by cabinet and approved for recommendation by parliament" (*Daily Graphic*, Accra March 21, 2000). Along with what had seemed to be the not so contentious issue of reducing the number of school years, the reforms also approached the more contentious issues around the financing of education, which included introducing user fees for primary school services, for parent-teacher associations, for equipment and laboratories (e.g., health service fees, sports and recreational fees, textbook and stationery fees) and introduced room and board charges for institutions of higher learning. The state was to cut down on recurrent expenditures on staff, staff training, and textbooks. These measures could not be implemented without creating hardships for people and without compromising many of the stated national objectives of the post-independence project.

Educational reforms and policies contained within the SAPs blamed the nation's educational problems on administrative inefficiencies and the increased involvement of the state in running the educational system. Cost-sharing among parents, the corporate sector, and the state was seen as an important step in addressing problems in the national educational system. Inadequate attention was given to the deplorable national economic conditions and widespread poverty, which partly accounted for the educational problems.

As Asobayire (1988) has pointed out, from an ideological viewpoint, the educational sector adjustment was a diversion as it sought to remove the traditional responsibility of financing education from the collective (i.e., the state) to the individual. With the educational sector adjustment policies, the state committed itself to the privatization of the education system, particularly the post-secondary levels, by making parents contribute more toward their children's education. The state also actively promoted a "culture of sponsorship" by urging the private corporate sector to contribute toward the establishment of a national educational fund. Given the increasing impoverishment of ordinary Ghanaians in the 1980s, such measures as the cuts in national educational funding were bound to have social implications, particularly in terms of educational equity and accessibility. Throughout the 1980s, the role of the state and international finance capital in the reproduction of the social and economic relations in Ghana ensured that the school continued to be a site for reproducing societal inequalities. The relations of power between the international financial institutions and the Ghanaian state were unequal. Internally the relations of power between those who have and those who do not have are not equal. Therefore, it should not be surprising that policies premised on greater privatization and fees for services would produce greater inequalities of access to material and cultural capital/resources.

Educational Structural Adjustment Policies at the National Level

My argument is not that SAPs are responsible for the problems within Ghana's educational system in the 1980s and 1990s. The existence of the long-standing internal structural problems in the Ghanaian economy cannot be denied. The downturn in the economy during the transition to the post-independence period and the increase in population had meant that social inequities were becoming more pervasive. The policies of the SAPs further aggravated a deteriorating condition, thus contributing to what was coming to be known as the current crisis in education in Ghana. By adding to the economic hardships of many Ghanaians, SAPs particularly incapacitated rural parents and their communities and denied them the purported benefits of implementing educational reforms, originally aimed at serving the needs of local peoples. The existing literature on Structural Adjustment Programs in Africa in general shows their damaging effects on national social programs, particularly in the provision of education, health and nutritional needs of the local population (see Elabor-Idemudia 1991 and Herzfeld 1991). All over Africa, especially among the countries that have adopted SAPs, education budgets have been cut. In fact, in sub-Saharan Africa, the overall percentages of the GNP going to education fell from 4.9 per cent to 4.5 per cent between 1980 and 1988.

In Ghana, national education expenditure per capita has also fallen, as has education's share of the total budget expenditure. Repeated budget cuts have only exacerbated the ongoing erosion in the standard and quality of education in the country that began in the late 1970s. Budgetary statistics show that education took up 30 per cent of total national expenditure in the 1970s. In 1984 the figure dropped to 20 per cent and has continued to decline in the 1980s and 1990s. The World Bank itself acknowledges that in the 1970s per capita expenditure was $20 in US funds, but in the 1980s and 1990s it has been less than $1. In 1976, education spending was 6.4 per cent of GDP. In 1985 it was 1.7 per cent. It is impossible to estimate what proportion of Ghana's GDP has gone to education in recent years. In 1983 the total public expenditure on education was $80.9 million, i.e., 15.2 percent of total government expenditure. In the 1988-90 public investment program, worth $1.9 billion, only 2 percent was devoted to education and 3 percent to health (World Bank 1991).

The primary beneficiaries of SAPs in Ghana, as in other parts of West Africa, have been those individuals and groups with strong external connections—local entrepreneurs, big traders and exporters, as well as a few wealthy farming households producing cash crops for export (Dei 1992). The big losers have been teachers, bureaucrats, technicians, small-scale farmers and the rural poor majority, particularly, women and children (Elabor-Idemudia 1992, 1993). It is important that this is borne in mind in any attempt to analyse and articulate the impact of SAPs on education in Ghana.[8]

The reliance on external donor agencies for the implementation of various aspects of educational reforms has led critics to question whether these reforms, in the final analysis, are not promoting dependency on the international financial community. Like other critics, I see a contradiction and a contrast between the state's professed aim to develop self-reliance and the nation's continued dependence on foreign financial institutions for survival. In an address to the participants of a national seminar on "The Senior Secondary School Programme and Second Phase of the Educational Reform Program," the Deputy Minister of Education, Mrs. Vida Yeboah (Ministry of Education 1990), expressed the hope of the Ghanaian government that it could count on the mobilization of external assistance and funds to support the various phases of the national educational reforms. Such assistance was sought for the rehabilitation or upgrading of school facilities, provision of office stationery and other school supplies and in the preparation, printing and publishing of school textbooks. Furthermore, the state was counting on the international financial community to provide funding for the purchase of equipment and tools for the teaching of science, agriculture, technical and vocational courses, as well as the provision of workshop facilities for both junior and senior secondary school levels.

As a result of the SAPs recommendation that the state "get the prices right" and align domestic prices with international price structures, inflation rates have soared. The cost of textbooks and stationery for students, teachers and researchers are beyond the reach of the average Ghanaian salaried worker or farmer. Throughout the 1980s, wages and incomes had fallen, which led to a decrease in an individuals' actual purchasing power. For example, in June 1991, a basic science textbook in the senior secondary school could cost between ¢5,000 and ¢10,000 (between $125 and $250 in Canadian funds). At that time the minimum wage was ¢218 (60 cents). It was increased to ¢460 ($1.01) in July 1991.[9]

The goal of improving the quality of education in the country has traditionally been hampered by problems of educational equity. There are problems of accessibility because of high cost, a shortage of qualified teachers with pedagogical training to handle the specialized sections of the educational reforms and a scarcity of resources in general. By making economic conditions unbearable for many people, SAPs have only served to exacerbate educational inequities. Due to the massive retrenchment in the job market, many college arts graduates cannot find jobs. Since 1987, at least 48,000 civil servants have been redeployed. There is an extent to which such developments have dampened the enthusiasm for pursuing a schooling career.

Another SAP recommendation is that the government freeze teachers' salaries to keep costs down and balance budgets. This measure has only served to undermine morale among teachers, who repeatedly threatened to take industrial action. In the early part of 1991, the public elementary school system was shut down when teachers "walked out." During the 1997 data collection phase of this study, poor teacher working conditions continued to be identified as a serious concern by all participants. Although some of the participants felt that teachers in general were very committed to their work, the economic strain placed on them meant that they often needed to take extra jobs. The extra work often was tutoring students/groups of students for a fee. The additional work took away from the time needed to prepare the classes for which they were employed and to assist the students in those classes.

Students who could not pay to attend extra classes offered by teachers to assist them with their school work often complained of the disadvantaged position they found themselves compared to their classmates who attended these extra classes. The reduction in educational spending also contributed to significantly larger class sizes. One participant spoke of having a language class with fifty-six students and a literature class with eighty-two. According to this teacher, it was very difficult to encourage student participation. The pedagogical practice in these situations was, as she said, just "lecture, lecture, lecture." Attracting teachers to poor rural communities that could not entice teachers through additional supports provided by the community, was difficult and a constant concern. To address this ongoing critical concern "a suggestion was made to the government that a service scheme be instituted that would make obligatory for all newly trained teachers to be posted to serve in rural areas for at least three years before they can be transferred to the urban centres" (*Daily Graphic*, Accra, July 17, 2000).

In addition to the underfinancing of education, the freeze in teacher wages, the downloading of costs to local communities and parents, a 1991 SAP recommendation suggested that graduates roaming the streets should be recruited as teachers. This was proposed as a measure to deal with the high rate of graduate unemployment. The teaching profession criticized this recommendation because it failed to take into account that to teach required specialized training. They saw the move as the government's blatant refusal to recognize teaching as a profession in its own right.

In the 1997 interviews with teachers, parents and students, there was a systematic pattern of critique across all the participants that teachers and schools were expected to implement major changes in the school programs, the syllabus, and the curriculum without the accompanying necessary supports in terms of training, texts, and other resources needed.

Educational Reforms at the Village School Level

Nowhere has the impact of SAPs on education been felt greater than in the rural areas. In rural communities, internal structural factors have exacerbated many of the problems associated with the implementation of the SAP educational reforms and probably vitiated the program's success to some extent. For example, local values and traditions have favoured large family sizes. This has increased the pressure on parents to decide which children to educate during harsh economic times. Many trained teachers have been reluctant to work in rural areas because of poor conditions. The state has continually appropriated rural wealth with no sustained program to provide basic social service infrastructures for the people (e.g., piped water supply, health care, electricity). Most farmers have seen their household incomes decrease as a result of unstable market conditions and internal price structures that provide no incentives for higher agricultural productivity. In many areas both customary practises and the trend toward agricultural commercialization have intensified the differential access to and control over land among social groups and between genders.

The imposition of SAPs led to both the questioning and a hardening of locally held views about the relevance and irrelevance of formal education. Parents continually lament their lack of input in the decision-making processes about educational reforms. Some parents question the practical relevance of formal education when jobs for which students have been trained are neither available nor perceived to have immediate bearing on increasing household productivity. On the other hand, some youths have been eager to migrate to the urban centres in search of non-existent, wage-earning jobs without acquiring the requisite skills necessary for many of the vocations to which they aspire. Repeated calls for these youths "to return to the land" have fallen on deaf ears.

To expand on some of these issues, let me briefly highlight schooling and education issues in the rural communities in the mid-

1980s and early 1990s. In the 1980s, a common problem rural communities faced was maintaining basic livelihoods. During this time, the national economy was experiencing a serious downturn, triggered by the global economic crisis and aggravated by the ecological problems of drought and bush fires and by the return of local residents from Nigeria, who had been deported by that state's military government (see Dei 1996, 1992). Adding to these hardships were the structural adjustment policies and the export-led development strategy pursued by the state, which removed state subsidies on most social services and failed to address issues of social justice (see Dei 1986, 1988). It was in such a general climate that educational reforms were implemented at the primary and middle school levels.

By September 1987, the government had received a total of $34.5 million from the World Bank, the Overseas Development Agency (ODA), the OPEC fund, the United Nations Development Programme (UNDP) and the Norwegian Government to initiate the first phase of reforms at the basic level of formal education. This phase involved replacing the existing four-year middle schools with a three-year Junior Secondary school (JSS) education. The new system was oriented towards vocational training and the acquisition of practical skills in handicrafts, agriculture, science and technology, instead of limiting the focus of the program to a more traditional academic orientation.

One of the consequences of carrying out such educational reforms, at a time of extreme economic hardships in many rural communities, has been the decline of educational opportunities for the poor, particularly girls and young women. To begin with, the education of girls and young women has traditionally not been a top priority in the rural communities because parents and guardians tended to discriminate against educating the girl child. Historically, during harsh economic times, parents chose to send boys to schools. Trading has always been seen as a vocation with immediate and direct benefits to women in the community. Within rural households, girls and young women were encouraged to leave school early and learn to trade. In the current national economic climate, trading is generally perceived as a lucrative business because of the increased trade liberalization brought about by SAPs. Some parents argue it makes more sense to let their daughters engage in trading practices, given the lack of jobs available for educated youth.

As Apusigah (2002) also notes in relatively recent times, and particularly since the national reconstruction efforts of the 1980s, gender inequities in the Ghanaian educational system has become a national concern even if mostly in official rhetoric (see Nikoi 1998; Joe 1997; Dolphynne 1991, 1997; Tsikata 2000; and Tete-Enyo 1997). The State has shown some desire to respond to the question of gender education in Ghana. Unfortunately, much of the state's rhetorical responses on improving the quality of gender education in the country have been just that, more words and little concrete action. Apusigah's (2002) review of some of the policy initiatives under the national reconstruction efforts to address the gender disparities in education is telling. The established networks and institutional frameworks such as The Science, Technology and Mathematics Education Program, The Girls Education Unit, The Female Teacher Recruitment and Training Initiative, The Enhanced Community Involvement Initiative, The Girls' Education Scholarship Scheme, and the Food Assistance Initiative, although well intentioned to promote female education in the country are nonetheless far from successful. The approach to gender education has not been systematic enough to directly respond to and integrate broader questions of educational delivery, namely the structures for teaching, learning and administration of education. At the grassroots levels, the performance of gender reforms in education has been minuscule at best (see also Atapka 1995; Ewusi 1987; Apusigah 2002).

The implementation of SAPs in rural communities also exacerbated the existing discrepancies in educational access for urban and rural populations, between the genders and between different ethnic groups. Colonial education was highly selective and, while the post-independent state attempted to remedy the situation through public policies and discourses that espouse the goals of free and compulsory education for all, these goals have not become a material reality for a significant number of Ghana's school-age population. Recent governments have not vigorously pursued such policies. Given the scarcity of national resources with which to implement educational reforms, the state had to make choices in allocating its scarce resources. Such decisions worked against rural dwellers, women and the ethnic groups not in power.

Another consequence of introducing educational reforms during economic hardships was an increase in the dropout rate at the elementary level. Even before the reforms were introduced, it was widely acknowledged that about 30 percent of school age children were not in school. Since the implementation of the JSS programme, many village schools have reported a dropout rate of over 40 percent.[10] Parents are unable to pay user and PTA fees and to provide school uniforms, textbooks and exercise books for their children because of falling farm revenues and off-farm incomes. The continued appropriation of rural wealth by the state over the years has increasingly affected the ability of households to bear the cost of their children's education.

During times of severe economic hardships, rural farming households see competition among the school, the household farm and trading ventures for labour supply. As parents hear about massive retrenchment of public and private sector workers and the high rate of unemployment for school leavers, they are not altogether displeased with children who take up rural activities like farming, basket weaving, pushing of trucks and charcoal production. The pursuit of these activities can lead to frequent absenteeism of children from school and to their eventually dropping out. In some Ghanaian villages, teachers have been chased out of homes when they went to advise parents to send their children to school.[11]

Since the 1980s, educators and community leaders have experienced a lack of community participation and willingness on the part of parents to contribute toward school facilities required under the JSS program. Many parents had come to understand that the state was to bear the responsibility for formal primary education. They were not easily convinced otherwise. Many parents felt it was inappropriate to change their thinking about the state's responsibilities at a time of severe economic downturn in their household economy and income. Parents were critical of the fact that they were not consulted as to the time frame for implementing the reforms and felt that the JSS program was introduced at the wrong time. They had understood the state was going to foot the major expenses associated with educational reform when it was first proposed and opened up for public discussions in the early 1970s. There was a perception that the government did not do its homework properly in terms of trying to understand the long-term impact of its policies on the poor before it imposed educational reform measures that called for further sacrifices. Generally, parents felt that the JSS and the educational reforms were rushed. They pointed to the lack of specialist teachers, resources for workshops, and textbooks for the JSS schools to support their contention. Throughout the narratives of the participants of the 1997 interviews (teacher educators, student teachers, teachers, parents and students) there was a consistency in the views supporting the goals of providing free compulsory Universal Basic Education to all of Ghana's children, of complementing the acquisition of academic learning with that of applied practical skills and of ensuring that the curriculum reflect the histories, cultures, perspectives and interests of Ghanaians. But the narratives also reflected a consistency in the critiques of the way in which the reforms have been implemented, which in their opinions often contradicted the stated objectives or placed the objectives at risk of failure. Systematically highlighted as particular problems was a sense of rushing the reforms through with insufficient preparation, consultation and resources.

Parents also felt that there was insufficient public education about the implications and consequences of the reforms for the household, the village social structure and the domestic economy. One parent felt the schools would be better served if the government had made a conscious effort to tap the wealth of indigenous knowledge and expertise on traditional handicrafts from local craftsmen and women rather than relying solely on "trained" teachers from the technical and vocational schools. In fact some hostility could be detected between the teachers handling the vocational subjects and the "partially literate" local craftsmen and women, who themselves complained that the teachers had not been properly instructed in the rules and requirements of the trade and its apprenticeship. Some parents and teachers also questioned why the idea of teaching vocational and technical skills, science and agriculture was not first introduced at the primary school level rather than at the JSS level.

The impact of SAPs and the educational reforms on the morale of rural teachers cannot be underestimated. Rural teachers have serious concerns about the impact of SAPs and the educational reforms on their profession, individual self-development and basic livelihoods in the community. In the early 1980s, many teachers lamented the fact that the general administration of the new school system itself failed to restore education to its past glory as an admirable occupation for teachers and worthy of pursuit by students. In the current atmosphere of stringent economic hardships, teachers' salaries cannot provide for basic needs. Some teachers have sought to be "creative" by devising means to extract money from parents for admission fees and dubious school activities. It is common to hear parents castigating teachers for lying and embezzling funds. Such accusations were unheard of in the past. The fact that teachers occupy leadership roles in local political action groups in many villages and towns, such as the Committees for the Defence of the Revolution (CDR) and the District Assemblies, has not helped the image of teachers in the communities either.[12] Recently the problems of poor teacher practices had become such a national concern that the Ghana Education Service (GES) Council sent a directive to all regional directors to enlist the support of all stakeholders in the community to deal with the problem by keeping track of teachers who repeatedly demonstrated various forms of bad conduct. The directive was also accompanied with an advisory that the GES would soon include the implementation of an incentive package for teachers who excel in the performance of their duties *(Daily Graphic,* Accra, May 5, 2000 p. 16).

Throughout my various research trips to Ghana in the 1980s and the 1990s, I found that teachers were the ones who were most affected by the national economic downturn. At the same time, the government was asking these teachers to take on additional responsibilities to ensure the involvement of rural peoples in national political affairs and economic reconstruction. Rural teachers, in particular, were overwhelmed by their increased workloads. Many teachers had abandoned their traditional responsibilities of teaching and were engaged in many non-teaching activities (e.g., business and commercial activities, farming and trading).

We cannot underestimate the threat of academic bankruptcy that may result from the lack of research, skills training and improvement for those in the teaching profession. It is a threat that holds unpleasant possibilities for the national education system in the not too distant future. For example, in the newly introduced JSS program, not all the teachers who handle the vocational and technical courses possess the required specialist qualifications. Many have not been sufficiently trained. Some honest teachers openly admit that they received training in the shortest possible time (sometimes two weeks) before being asked to assume their responsibilities.[13]

An integral part of the JSS program is the regular transfer of teachers from their home communities to assume responsibilities in other communities. The state usually paid the transportation and housing expenses, as well as vacation and meals allowances for teachers working away from home. But in January 1991, the government announced in its annual national budget that it was going to consolidate these allowances into the basic wage structure of all employees. The Ghanaian Educational Teachers Union opposed the government's decision. It pointed out that even rural teachers, who were said to enjoy relatively cheap lodging expenses compared to their counterparts in the urban centres, needed such allowances. It was argued that the "traditional" village hospitality of providing cheap accommodation and occasional gifts of food and services to teachers had been abandoned by most rural peoples because of the severe economic constraints. This added to the problem of enticing teachers to go into the villages and towns to handle the requirements of the new reforms. Continuous budgetary constraints and lack of supports to disadvantaged regions and communities have created a crisis requiring concerted intervention strategies. Recent statistics at "the Ministry of Education indicate that only 2.6 percent out of 86.6 percent of children who enrol in the primary schools find their way into higher institutions" (*Daily Graphic*, Accra, May 26, 2000). It is further noted that a wide gap exists between the urban-based senior secondary schools and their counterparts in rural areas in terms of academic performance at the senior secondary school certificate examination for entry into universities and other tertiary institutions. To address this gap, at least one university is considering a quota system for the admission of disadvantage students. Professor J.S.K. Ayim, then Vice-Chancellor of Kwame Nkrumah University of Science and Technology (KNUST), announced that the University was considering making 80 percent of the admissions to be based on merit and reserving 20 percent of admissions for students of less endowed Senior Secondary Schools (*Daily Graphic*, Accra, May 26, 2000, p. 1). The professor went on to describe that schools commonly referred to as "well endowed" became top schools through the contributions of old students, benefactors and Parent Teacher Associations. It has become obvious that the educational fiscal policies of privatization, dependence on user fees, and downloading onto communities has reproduced overtime outcomes that have increased inequities between regions, communities and families with less material resources to contribute to civil institutions (i.e. the school) entrusted with transmitting and facilitating the acquisition and creation of cultural knowledge/capital.

Since the 1980s, both the World Bank and the IMF have been deciding the fate of millions of African peoples through the imposition of SAPs. The educational reforms introduced under SAPs are part of the World Bank's comprehensive policy package to "improve" educational systems in sub-Saharan Africa as a whole. The policy reforms draw on the knowledge that overhauling and revitalizing the educational sector is central to human capacity building and social development.

The World Bank Policy Report (1989) suggested a number of strategies for "improving" education, including adjusting education to current demographic and fiscal realities, with an objective of diversifying the sources of educational finance and containment costs in national budgets. A more recent World Bank report (Lockheed & Verspoor 1990) expressed a commitment on paper to provide assistance for the revitalization of the existing educational structure in Africa by making textbooks and instructional materials available, increasing investments in the maintenance of physical plants and equipments and making a 'selective' expansion of national education, beginning from universal primary education to secondary and tertiary education.

The World Bank's reports on education in Africa (and other developing countries) note the necessity of country-specific policies but have yet to offer appropriate and more effective ways of implementing the proposed changes in the national educational system without bringing untold hardships to parents, guardians and communities. Nor do these reports explore the alternatives to implementing reforms in the face of continuing adverse national economic conditions (see Ngomo and Oxenham 1989; Achola 1990; African Association for Literacy and Adult Education 1990; Bray 1986; Galabwa 1990; and Psacharopoulos 1989). The trend toward privatization in the national economy and in the educational system may not be the most appropriate way of recovering the public cost of higher education, given the existing gender, class, regional, rural-urban differences and other sectoral imbalances in many African societies. If anything, the implementation of the JSS educational reforms, at a time of SAPs in Ghana, has exacerbated regional, class and gender differences and inequities in the communities.

Arguably, SAPs may have some potential benefits for the nation if pursued in a manner whereby economic policies are directed towards meeting local needs and concerns rather than being driven primarily by the urge to make the state economy more competitive in the global market. Such measures as public accountability, improved economic efficiency in the public sector, rational allocation of resources and cutting unnecessary government waste and spending are relevant for improving the nation's educational system. But it requires a political will, the setting of worthy examples and the pursuit of appropriate development priorities by those at the helm of national affairs. Unfortunately, local peoples have become skeptical of the state and its efforts to improve rural living conditions. Many are still unconvinced that the sacrifices they are being called upon to make today will eventually pay off in the future. They have not enjoyed the benefits of earlier sacrifices. When someone tells them to "tighten their belts," they aptly reply that to do so one must first have a belt.

Rural peoples also see the immediate objective of SAPs as aimed at improving the nation's creditworthiness so that the state would be able to import the luxurious items and consumer goods for the urban elite and to pay for the huge expenses of the nation's military. The perceptions and views that rural peoples have not benefited from foreign loans secured by the national government and, therefore, should not be responsible for any debt repayments has been enhanced by the cuts in social services, decline in rural infrastructures and the lack of employment.

Despite pretensions to the contrary, the African state has failed to pursue a development strategy that reallocates resources toward basic primary education, where social rates of return are perceived (rightly or wrongly) to be highest (Glewwe 1991). Even when the state professes to provide basic education for all, parents, guardians and communities have been increasingly called upon to bear some fundamental costs as the Ghanaian case shows. Furthermore, while the World Bank's educational policies emphasize universal primary education through the mobilization of resources and people at the grassroots level, many studies draw attention to the fact that teachers in the schools lack the specific guidelines for educational change, and that the appropriate curriculum for making primary education more relevant to societal needs remains largely underdeveloped (Mundy 1992).

The culminating effect of all this is the gradual loss of the credibility and legitimacy of the state in the eyes of the rural populace. Other writers have pointed to additional mitigating contradictions. Barry Riddell (1992), for example, argues there is a crucial paradox whereby the international financial community requires a strong state in order to implement SAPs while at the same time weakening the government with its conditionalities. The acceptance and implementation of the harsh conditionalities has only led to an intensified rural poverty.

I contend that the causes of the difficulties of SAPs in achieving any success at meaningful educational reform in Ghana are rooted in the increasing pauperization of the majority of the local population and the state's failure to address the fundamental issues of social justice. There can be no improvement in the quality of education in Ghana if the goals of educational equity and educational access are hampered or constrained by increasing rural poverty. As I've just pointed out, the most devastating impact of SAPs has been on the average family income, which makes it increasingly difficult for parents to send their children to primary school. Contrary to SAPs objectives, and with few exceptions, rural household incomes in Ghana have been falling (Dei 1986, 1992a).

In Ghana, as elsewhere in the developing world, SAPs and the World Bank have yet to fully address the basic issues of social development and specifically questions of social justice (see Elabor-Idemudia and Dei 1992). Under the period of SAPs, there have been repeated accounts of malnutrition in some villages, rising infant mortality rates, shortages of medicines and closed health clinics, all of which have implications for schooling and education (Anyinam 1989). The increased workload of rural women and other poor farmers, in order to feed the unemployed or retrenched workers in the urban areas, has significant implications for formal education in villages (see Elabor-Idemudia 1992). The diversion of national savings from cutbacks in education expenditure to paying external debts presents a moral question: Is it moral that so much pain and suffering is endured by the poor majority as the state repays foreign debts, debts which the poor had no role in contracting and from which they benefited least?

The Educational Lesson of the 1980s

I conclude this chapter with what I see as the lesson of the 1980s. A most pressing educational question of the time was: Who is and should be responsible for delivering education for the local populace? It is interesting to note that this question has resurfaced in recent debates on Ghana's education, due in part to the effect of the national economic austerity measures on local peoples and the inability of families and guardians to provide education for their children. There is a school of thought that promotes the idea that the state should continue to provide free education for all, which needs to be critically examined. However, the reallocation of educational cost through national economic policies such as SAPs has failed to consider the ability of the purported beneficiaries to pay the costs involved. In other words, if parents and their communities are to be asked to shoulder any additional costs for educational reforms, they must have the resources and the capabilities to do so. Unless this is done, then attempts to reform the educational system by pushing costs onto parents are bound to fail, no matter the good intentions. In the face of national economic hardships, the poor cannot be expected to identify with educational reforms that bring additional economic hardships. The majority of African societies do not have a publicly funded social safety net. Educational reforms which are promoted by The World Bank having a contrary assumption can only further exacerbate the existing socio-economic disparities in society.

Development programs should aim at generating incomes for rural parents to reproduce their households and loosen their external dependence. The state must adopt strategies to diversify the rural economy in a manner that prioritizes meeting local needs first. The only way it can regain its credibility in the eyes of the rural populace is for the state to be seen as their ally and not the "instrument" that siphons off rural resources to meet the needs and demands of their external accomplices (e.g., transnational corporations). The state must ensure the subordination of external relations to the demands of internal development, what has commonly been known in the world and protected in the past within discourses on national sovereignty and national interests.

I agree that the success of the nation's educational reforms would not rest solely on the availability of financial and other material resources for implementing the reforms package. Without question, the financing of educational reforms solely by foreign donors, particularly by transnational corporations, would only ensure that Africa's education becomes surrogate to the current distorted demands for structural changes in the international economic system. Such developments will thwart any attempts at devising genuine educational alternatives for Africa (see Carnoy 1986; Samoff 1990; Raftopoulos 1986). As Karen Mundy (1992) argues, the current economic crisis in Africa has succeeded in shifting attention further away from innovation and the development of viable educational options to an "unprecedented focus on maintaining quality and standards in formal education" and to adjust the supply of labour to the dictates of the world economy.[14] I believe it is crucial that reforms be directed to the immediate concerns and aspirations of the local peoples first. External assistance should be welcomed if it is guided by the needs and aspirations of the local peoples themselves and not intended to compromise indigenous creativity and resourcefulness to find solutions to locally defined problems.

Furthermore, the search for indigenous educational options or alternatives in Africa requires that the cultural resource base of local peoples be analyzed for its contributions to the development of national educational policy. Local communities must have opportunities to express their aspirations, views and wishes as to how they want to see their schools run or restructured. The schools themselves must become accountable to their communities. Local educational planners must find more appropriate ways to integrate formal and informal educational processes in the task of social development.

Concerns about the impact of SAPs on rural peoples encouraged the Economic Commission for Africa (ECA) to propose a structural economic transformation as an African alternative development framework.[15] This alternative framework emphasizes a human-centred strategy for Africa's economic recovery, involving the full mobilization and participation of all sectors of the local populace (workers, students, trade unions, peasants, women, professionals) in the formulation, implementation and monitoring of adjustment programs. The relevance of the African alternative for national education policy is that it calls on the state to maintain its subsidies on major social services (e.g., health care and education) and to prioritize meeting basic human needs over creditors' demands to implement policies aimed at extracting debt repayments (Wisner 1992).

Partly as a response to demands from the ECA, the Organization of African Unity (OAU) and from other critics of SAPs, the World Bank (in the late 1980s) began a series of policy reforms aimed at empowering the rural poor majority, especially women, through emphasis on local democratization processes. National development is no doubt linked to democracy and respect for fundamental human rights—but democracy as understood by African peoples and not as dictated by transnational corporations and foreign governments. For example, there are basic contradictions in the pursuit of SAPs on the one hand and the initiatives toward political democracy on the other.

Democracy and human rights are not simply one-person-one-vote and free speech. They must include that women, children and the poor have rights and opportunities to satisfy their basic human needs. Cuts in social spending deny fundamental human rights to the poor. Privatization of social services and its impact on the poor's access to fundamental needs (e.g., water, electricity, education, health) may prove in the long run to be a test of morality of World Bank policies in developing countries.

Notes

1.   For many African scholars and other Africanists there is little doubt that one of the primary reasons for the introduction of SAPs was to ensure Africa's creditworthiness through prompt debt repayments. Unfortunately, Africa's debt crisis has yet to improve for the better. The continuing fall in world commodity prices, increasing interest rates, fluctuations in the value of the U.S. dollar and debt rescheduling throughout the 1980s have all compounded the debt crisis. See Tim Shaw, "Africa in the 1990's: From Economic Crisis to Structural Readjustment," *Dalhousie Review* 68 (1988): 37-69; T. Shaw, "Dicing with Debt: The Third World Dilemma," *New Internationalist* 189 (1988): 4-20. African countries continue to be locked in a vicious cycle of debt and since 1983 no country has been able to meet the terms of even debt rescheduling. Africa's debt stood at $218 billion by 1987, three times the continent's annual export earnings. See *West Africa* (December 9-15, 1991): 2060; Paul Zeleza, "The Global Dimensions of Africa's Crisis: Debts, Structural Adjustment and Workers," *Transafrican Journal of History* 18 (1989): 1-53.

2   See *West Africa* (December 16-22, 1991): 2109.

3   Sub-Saharan Africa has the youngest population of any region in the world and the demand for places in the schools is bound to rise with its attendant financial burdens. In fact, it is estimated that one in three children in sub-Saharan Africa (compared to one in five in Latin America and Asia and one in six in the industrialized world) is of primary or secondary school age. By the year 2000, Africa's primary school-age children had increased to about 220 million from 130 million in 1984. Whereas primary school places in 1983 were only 51.3 million, a figure which in the year 2000 can only reach 90.7 million. See Obinna Anyadike, "The Education Crisis," *West Africa* (September 5-11 1988).

4   Ministry of Education, Ghana, citing a keynote address by Mrs. Vida Yeboah, Deputy Secretary for Education at National Seminars on the Education Reform Program, Accra, January 1990.

5   Ministry of Education, Ghana, citing keynote address by Mrs. Vida Ybeoah, p.2.

6   There was an official stipulation that at least 70 percent of the writing panels for manuscripts for use in schools must be Ghanaians.

7   In the mid-1980s, during the days of Reaganism and Reaganomics, the World Bank and the IMF were particularly insensitive to the social consequences of structural adjustment in developing countries. The current situation in many

countries shows that short-term economic gains under SAPs were obtained at the expense of the quality of life for most peoples.

8   See also "Matters of Principle," *West Africa* (1989): 2437.

9   See "JSS Drop Out," *West Africa* (July 17, 1991): 1095.

10   See "JSS Drop Out," *West Africa* (July 17, 1991): 1095.

11   The CDR is a political action group operating at the local community level and in official work places to monitor and/or oversee the activities of community's and work group's leadership, and also to help mobilize local peoples into the process of national political and economic reconstruction. It was established first as a People's Defence Committee (PDC) in 1982, when the ruling PNDC government assumed power. See also M. Owusu, "Rebellion, Revolution and Tradition: Reinterpreting Coups in Ghana," *Comparative Studies in Society and History* 38, no. 2 (1989): 372-397. For a discussion of the relationship between the PNDC government, revolutionary organs, District Assembly members, traditional bodies and local interests in the context of rural development in Ghana, see M. Owusu, "Cadres, and Chiefs: People's Power and Rural Development in Ghana" (Paper presented at the 89th Annual Meeting of the American Anthropological Association, New Orleans, Louisiana, November 28 - December 2, 1990).

12   Mundy, Karen. 1992. "The Case for Universal Primary Education Revisited," 21.

13   The reader is referred to the UN Economic Commission for Africa, African Alternative Framework to Structural Adjustment Programmes for Socio-Economic recovery and Transformation (Addis Ababa, 1989), E/ECA/CM.15/6/Rev.3.

Chapter 2

Ongoing Reforms and the Struggle to Redirect the Outcomes

The Later Reforms of the 1990s

The overall economic and political objective of the reforms was to increase cost-effectiveness and cost recovery. This was to be done through the "effective" use of allocations and the involvement of parents, communities and private business groups in funding education (e.g., provision of school infrastructure such as buildings, furniture, tools and equipment for workshops). User fees for school services, equipment and laboratories, parent-teacher association fees, and room and board charges for institutions of higher learning were introduced. The state reduced recurrent expenditures on staff, staff training and textbooks.

Later reforms have sought to encourage the idea and development of "community-based" schools. Primary and secondary schools and technical and vocational institutes built during the reform period have become locally based community institutions. They have large day-student populations and have made second-cycle education accessible to many more students than was the case in the past when a significant proportion of the secondary schools were boarding institutions. To some educational practitioners, the idea of community-based schooling is also an attempt to deal with the problem of regional, sectoral and socio-economic disparities (north-south, rural-urban and poor-rich) in education. However, the transition from traditional boarding school structure to community schooling has been neither smooth nor clear cut.

In 1994, the first graduates of the 1987 educational reforms emerged from the Senior Secondary School level, and their dismal academic results raised a huge public outcry. For example, Nsiah-Peprah (1998) notes that out of the figure of 149,038 students who took the Basic Education Certificate Examination/BECE in 1991, only 121,255 passed. Under the 1980s reform initiatives, the old Common Entrance Examination was abolished. Entrance into Senior Secondary School/SSS was now based on performance in the final examination of the Junior Secondary School/JSS, which is the BECE. Nsiah-Peprah (1998) points out that the BECE is not a selection examination: "under normal circumstances, children enter SSS at age 15. As a result, senior school students are younger, and more students are of lower ability than those [who] attended traditional secondary schools [i.e., before the reforms]" (8).

Before the 1980s educational reforms, students in the previous secondary school system would take what is called a General Certificate Examination (GCE) at the Ordinary level (O level) after five years of secondary education. Depending on their results, students would proceed to do two years of advanced secondary education (that is, lower and upper sixth form education). After the two years, students would write the GCE Advanced level (A level) examination for admission into the university. The GCE was a selection examination taken by students in the West African region, which is being phased out.

Due to limited space, only 49,078 (33 percent) of the successful students gained admission into Senior Secondary School/SSS; 99,960 (67 percent) "terminal students had to find apprenticeship and other non-formal programmes" (Nsiah-Peprah 1998, 8). Furthermore, of the 49,078 candidates who entered Senior Secondary School/SSS, 42,121 wrote the SSS Certificate Examination/SSSCE in 1994. This means that between 1991 and 1994, 6,957 or 14.2 percent of the JSS students who enrolled in the SSS in 1991 dropped out of school. Of the 42,121 students who took the SSSCE in 1994, only 1,354 or 3.2 percent qualified for admission into the country's universities. As Nsiah-Peprah (1998) rightly observes, this last figure "represents 0.91% of the first batch of students that took BECE in 1991" (8). Disturbingly, 99 percent of the first batch of JSS students could not qualify for admission to university! No preparation was made in the educational system to deal with the students who failed their examinations thereby, jeopardising further education. The 147,684 "terminal" students from the 1991 BECE batch could not be absorbed into non-formal programs even though the reform was supposed to be vocation-oriented. Similarly, there was inadequate preparation to absorb those continuing students who took the route of tertiary institutions. Unfortunately, information that was available to me during my research does not provide a gender breakdown of these figures. (See chapter endnote for a more recent breakdown on student enrolment in the different levels obtained from the Internet Ghana Homepage.)

Ghanaians openly questioned the ability of the reforms to meet their stated goals and objectives and to educate the youth to serve the needs of national development. Public furore over the students' academic performance led to ongoing changes under an "improved educational reform" package of the 1990s. In July 1994, the Ministry of Education appointed the Education Reform Review Committee (ERRC) to undertake a critical examination of the whole reform programme and to suggest changes. The ERRC argued that the crowding of the curriculum at all levels of pre-tertiary education was one of the factors contributing to the students' poor academic performance. Based on the ERRC's recommendations, the Ministry of Education has sought to implement a:

> reduction in the number of subjects at all the levels of basic and secondary education. The nine subjects taught at the primary school ... [have been] ... now reduced to five in the lower primary

and six in the upper primary. At the JSS level, the externally examined subjects are now 10 instead of 14, and at the SSS level four core subjects and three or four electives ... [are now] ... examined externally instead of the total of 10 subjects previously. (Nyalemegbe 1997, 7)

Other significant changes under the "improved reform" package are the inclusion of religious/moral education emphasizing religious and cultural values at both the basic and senior secondary levels and the additional teaching of the different Ghanaian languages, life skills and culture.

Statistical data are notoriously unreliable and do not always provide a complete picture of events in local contexts. Nevertheless, it is important to note that "primary enrolments have grown by 31 per cent between 1987/1988 and 1993/94. Gross enrolment in primary education and Junior Secondary presently stands at 78 per cent and 61 per cent respectively" (Nyalemegbe 1997, 7). Nyalemegbe further points to additional government budgetary expenditures on education since the introduction of the reform programme, in large part owing to assistance from international donors. For example, the national educational budget has "increased from one per cent in 1987 to 38 per cent in 1990. The 1995/96 budget increased by over 700 per cent. Within that total, the proportion allocated to basic education rose from 44 per cent to 65 per cent in the last decade"(7). Also as part of the educational reform initiatives, the government has designed specific schools in districts and regions of the country as Science Resource Centres. The goal is to equip the schools with the logistical, material and physical support and resources required to enable them to function as centres for science education. The idea is that students from other schools taking science as core subjects can use the laboratory and science equipment available in these centres for their training.

To provide a more complete picture of the reforms it is important to include the observations, under-standings and interpretations of local peoples using their words. After all, it is they who have first hand experiences of the outcomes of the reforms in their lives and in the life of their communities. The voices enact stories and provide a rendition of how local people understand what is happening to them, what they see as the problems and their solutions and how they intend to approach any desired change. The voices become the power of knowledge with which to evaluate, assess, interpret and pursue educational reform.

Narratives from the Grassroots: Parents, Teachers and Students Reactions to Reforms

The interviews I conducted in the summer and fall of 1997 highlight the problems of educational reforms as perceived and understood by teachers, students and parents. It is contended that the assessment and evaluation of educational reforms must take into account these voices which reveal subjective understandings of wide-ranging problems afflicting educational reforms in the Ghanaian contexts (see Dei 2000a). In the interviews, these individuals discussed some of the contradictions, ambiguities and contentions of educational reforms. All names used are pseudonyms.

Dankwah teaches mathematics at the senior secondary level. He acknowledges that there are indeed some positive aspects to the new reforms, at least with respect to their theoretical intent. Nevertheless, he is very critical of the implementation process which has, thus far, inhibited the achievement of the reforms' lofty goals and objectives:

> You see, let's take the educational reforms. When they started in 1987, the aim of the government was that the academic year, the number of years that was spent by students should be reduced. That was done. But the government went ahead and said it was going to provide ... you name it, everything for the students. So that by the time the students come out of SSS [senior secondary school] ... at least if you are unable to continue to university you will have something to do, I mean something manual to do. But [then] you go to a school and there is only one workshop for carpentry, for technical drawing ... So those things that government [was to] provide ... [and] secondly, the teachers who are supposed to teach those subjects are not there. Then they said they were training teachers specifically for the JSS and SSS. [But] ... those teachers ... [who] ... were supposed to teach were not ... available. So someone who went to [teach] let's say science is asked to go teach in primary school. I mean what is he going to teach there? This is a problem. And then because of this educational reforms ... so many subjects are being included. And that aside, the number of students in schools now have increased. The student/ratio has ... gone up ... From the research I did ... [the student/teacher ratio] ... is too high. Because of this, most teachers are finding their way out. The work is such that it is not attractive.

So those who were trained are leaving. They are finding places elsewhere, where they can at least enjoy their freedom .... (08/28/97)

Dankwah lauds reforms directed toward shortening the educational cycle and providing students with hands-on practical skills for employment upon graduation. But he is disturbed by the absence of workshops/laboratories and by inadequate physical and material supports for the training required in technical and vocational training. He also points to the lack of professional teachers for vocational subjects. For him, there is the deplorable sight of teachers trained in different subject areas now teaching vocational and technical subjects. Many teachers are frustrated. Dankwah attributes the problem to an increased workload, particularly the rising student-teacher ratio that does not allow educators to give their best.

In fact, the workload issue cannot be underestimated. Teacher shortages, an increase in student enrolments, coupled with the lack of sufficient physical spaces or adequate school infrastructure have contributed to the high pupil-teacher ratio in some schools. In Ghana, class size varies from forty-five to seventy students in both JSS and SSS, depending on the school. The average for SSS was sixty in the research area. A JSS teacher, depending on her/his speciality, would be expected to teach between three and four classes a day, in addition to an administrative workload. In some schools, English and mathematics teachers could be assigned to between four and six classes a day. Like the SSS, JSS teachers are also subject teachers. Hence they teach specific subjects. This is unlike the primary (and old middle school) system where teachers assigned to a particular class taught all the subjects. As far as teaching is concerned, the JSS's are functioning like SSS's.

Osei, who heads the science resource centre in a college, articulated similar concerns with the reforms:

From the beginning I thought it was a laudable idea. First, it cuts down on the number of years that students spend in schooling. Secondly, at every stage students will have some vocation. They will not just be lost. They will have something ... when they leave [school]. It starts from JSS to SSS ... a student must be able to do something with his hands and mind. And then after SSS too, the student should have something to do. But it looks like it hasn't been true in many of the schools. There are few schools that do the technical and the vocational [subjects] ... But it looks like most of the schools don't have [the] facilities. So students finish school and then they cannot do anything as a vocation. (08/21/97)

Osei's primary concern is that there are too few schools properly equipped to offer science, vocational and technical education. Compounding the problem is a lack of an effective apprenticeship program for youth in these subject areas. Such an apprenticeship program could, if developed, serve as a workplace-based training program for students or young adults. The youth could spend time learning skills on the job, with additional time devoted to in-school training. Certainly, it is clear that more than formal schooling is needed for a student to be engaged productively in a technical vocation. In the absence of facilities and a formal apprenticeship program to help train youth so that they have a chance in accessing good jobs, the reforms' objective of promoting social and economic development is undercut.

Kofi, who teaches chemistry and science, also expounds on the problems and weaknesses of the reforms. He too commends the theoretical shift to a practical-oriented, locally inspired education. However, the shortcomings in implementation are not lost on this astute observer:

Hmm ... the reform on paper ... I think is very correct. Okay, the idea is to provide the type of education that Ghana needs, which will solve problems for Ghana and not the Western type of education, which we don't need. That is the main idea for their reforms. But the way the reform was implemented ... is what I am not very happy about. They implement[ed] the whole thing at a go. Meanwhile the teachers are not involved. The equipment [and] a lot of things are not there even now. So personally, I would have thought that the change would have been gradual, from stage to stage. But they've implemented the whole at a go. That is [creating headaches] ... But I hope with time these problems will be solved. (08/13/97)

Kofi is a parent with children in the school system. He is hopeful that the "teething problems" in implementing the reforms can be solved with time. But he admits that it is not going to be easy. Prevailing harsh economic conditions have taken a toll on schools, communities and parents. On the social and economic costs of the reforms and the implications of these costs for parents, he concretely observes:

Well ... hey, they are saying from the onset of the program these reforms will cost ... They said parents will pay less and all those things. But I tell you the fees parents are paying now are too exorbitant. So I don't know whether it is the reform which is causing the fees to go higher or the economy of Ghana which is causing it to go high. So, I can't say much about that side ... I can't draw what is actually costing what. Because if you look at the bills of students, food alone takes about two-thirds of the bill. That we attribute to the economy and not to the reform because even if it were before the reforms students would still be eating. But ... can't say much about parents paying fees. [Whether] the government [is] pumping more money to support the reform is my problem now ... I don't think enough money has been pumped. (08/13/97)

Understandably, Kofi is worried about the high cost of education today. The questions of affordability and accessibility should be on the minds of all who genuinely seek viable educational options. Governments have a responsibility to deliver on their promises; otherwise the leadership loses credibility in the eyes of ordinary citizens. Indeed, Kofi is unsure, to use a popular refrain, whether the government has really put its money where its mouth is. Yet he agrees with the state when it says that the nation has no money.

Payment of fees for school services is a thorny issue for many Ghanaian parents. In 1997 fees for JSS were 3,500 cedis; by 1999 JSS fees had gone up to 5,700 cedis. These are fees for basic services such as admissions, library, entertainment, and exams. Usually there are additional costs to pay for materials, depending on whether the student is taking technical, home science, agriculture or core science subjects. JSS fees are paid annually and cover non-food costs associated with the administration and the incidentals of educational delivery. With additional costs such as sports and PTA, and depending on whether the school is a technical or vocational and in which district it's in, school fees could range between 11,000 cedis and 30,000 cedis. On the other hand, pupils in poorly established schools in not-so-well-off districts pay more than 15,000 cedis. But this is largely an urban phenomenon since in the rural areas JSS fees today are still about 5,700 cedis. These fees are not classified as tuition which parents pay in private schools. Students in publicly funded institutions such as the JSS and SSS do not pay tuition fees. Teachers' salaries were paid through government funding. A constant critique within the public education sector was/is the poor working conditions of teachers (i.e. low salaries, large classroom sizes).

Research conducted for the study showed that fees for the SSS could range from 20,000 to 30,000 cedis. These fees were paid each term and applied to day students. It included cost for incidentals such as sports and entertainment charges. Students in boarding institutions paid between 70,000 and 100,000 cedis. Some boarders paid over 100,000 cedis. These figures should be contrasted with the daily minimum wage of 500 cedis at the time of the research. Average monthly incomes for general staff (including a number of middle level personnel) hovered between 60,000 and 80,000 cedis. All through the transcripts there were comments on the difficulties families of some secondary school students have in paying school fees. Yet, this has continued. The Ghana Homepage on the internet includes a summary on Education in Ghana which lists six items that senior secondary and technical schools have been directed to charge all students (day and boarders) admitted for the 2001/2002 year. The Government directive includes admission, entertainment, science resource centre, library, examination stationary fees and student representative council dues for a total of ¢49,000. Those admitted as boarders have additional boarding fees of over 392,000 per term.

With her bachelor's degree in Social Science and a Diploma in Education, Amina has had many years of teaching experience enough to know what can cripple well-intended school reforms. Her poignant critique of the haste and the politics in implementing the reform initiatives is punctuated with a suggestion:

> Well, I would say they are in the right direction, except that in my view I think we are rushing some of the issues. I would have wanted to have some sort of pilot schools. Then we could study these for some time. But the way they are starting [all at once is confusing], because right now those going into the second year are saying they are going to do environmental studies ... But we don't have a working syllabus. We the teachers don't know how we are affecting the [students]. So, we are confused and the students too are confused. Yeh, that's a problem. I would have liked ... that some things would be well laid out before we started. Because we realize that ... we tend to waste the students' time in the three years that they are supposed to use for the program. You realize eventually that they have wasted half of it ... which I think is not good. (08/20/97)

For Amina, educating all concerned about the reforms and the sacrifices they entail is the key to successful implementation. As matters currently stand, many teachers are puzzled. It is little wonder that students too are confused. Teachers are being asked to teach without textbooks and resources. Educational reforms need effective planning and execution. A pilot study could have brought attention to unresolved issues for the planners. In light of the current problems, Amina maintains that policy-makers, school administrators and teachers need to work in concert with other educational stakeholders.

Making Reforms Work

Mathematics teacher, Dankwah, provides some poignant ideas on how to make the educational reforms more effective:

> ...Now, for every program to be successful, those who are implementing it should have some sort of incentive; if they have the incentive they will definitely work well. We have seen that one of the problems that is counterproductive [and] is hindering the smooth running of this [reform] is that the teachers who are implementing it are not motivated ... The workload of the teachers has increased. Now ... the teacher has no time after school to rest. He comes home, he has to mark exercises [test papers], and with this continuing assessment, he must complete everything. By the time he finishes it will be around 12 midnight... The following day he goes to school. He has a class of maybe even over sixty in the class. And then they expect this person to do [every]thing ... So all these things have to be taken into account. (08/28/97)

Dankwah is alluding to the lack of incentives that motivate teachers. Unfortunately, a "casualty" of the current state of affairs in national education and social development is the erosion of the respect traditionally accorded to educators. A story narrated by Ohemaa, an English and history teacher with eight years of service, clearly portrays the respect for teachers in the community today. When asked how she thinks the nobility of the teaching profession can be restored, she responds:

> Not in Ghana [now]. Because I remember a certain brother of mine once said to our nephew if he cannot make up the [General Certificate Examination] A levels very well, then he will send him to the post-secondary to be one of those teachers. I said what do you mean by saying one of those teachers! Meanwhile, the mother of that nephew was also a teacher and she's living now in the US with a doctorate in philosophy. So it's ... the same teacher. So to tell the child that "to be one of those teachers" was not nice. I don't know we [teachers] have some stigma around the whole profession, yeh. (08/20/97)

There is general agreement that if educators are motivated, they can produce amazing results from deplorable educational conditions. Without a doubt, teachers need encouragement to do their best. Improved service conditions are vital to regaining the confidence of teachers and the teaching profession. The state and local governments must appreciate the increased workload, hardships and pressures many educators face today. There is a perception in local communities that students in private schools do well on national examinations perhaps because their teachers are more motivated than teachers in public/government-funded schools. This despite the fact that, at least in the basic education level, public school teachers are better qualified as professionally trained educators than the teachers in most private schools. The motivation of private teachers may come from higher salaries and better conditions of service. But it is also the case that currently in Ghana there is more accountability and supervision by proprietors and principals in private schools than in public institutions. Reduced government expenditures with increase enrolment has meant less oversight.

For effective implementation of reforms to attain desirable outcomes, administrators and policy makers should listen to students, who are the immediate recipients of any of the reforms' purported benefits. For their part, students shed additional insights on the reforms, their strengths and weaknesses. They are particularly worried about the duration of both junior and secondary school education. It is generally felt that an extension of each (i.e., basic and pre-tertiary education) to a minimum of four years will be helpful. Lati is in the second year of the senior secondary level (SSS) in reading, accounting, business and management. He wants to pursue university education, after which his preference is to seek employment with the Bank of Ghana. Asked about the changes he would like to see with respect to the reforms, he emphatically declares, "I would like to change the time of completing [SS] school ... to at least four years" (10/20/97).

He is not alone. In fact, Nana, an assistant female school prefect, also critiques the new reforms in terms of the duration of course programs:

> Because we don't normally finish completing our syllabus before taking the exams we are supposed to, we end up going to classes with our parents spending a whole lot of money on us but if we are [not] doing [well] ... it simply means whatever they spend on us is wasted. (10/20/97)

Now in the final year of her SSS program, Nana is worried that her parents have sacrificed a lot for her education, but that her school preparation may not have been rigorous enough to allow her to do well in the examinations. She desperately wants to move on to undergraduate studies in university. She does not want to waste her parents' meager financial resources and savings. She feels some guilt and is apprehensive. Similarly, Taba, who is also in SSS taking business, reveals some frustration over her education. She refers to the pressures put on students who study without adequate texts and curricular guidelines. From her vantage point, she articulates the problems of the reforms:

> The problem that I face in this school [is] especially the textbook. We don't have textbooks to look through. If a certain teacher comes in, I'll be able to just read it [textbook] through while [the teacher] is listening, then after that you give to the student, maybe … a mark. If there is a mistake … if you look through the textbook you can see. But if you don't have it you can't … I want them to give us textbooks so that we can learn and understand it. And if we pass to next year, we can give the textbooks to the other [student]. (10/08/97)

Implicitly, she wonders how students can be expected to learn without textbooks and pleads for more texts. However, Taba is not thinking of herself alone. She feels that students who are given textbooks can, upon graduation, pass these resources and their knowledge on to other students. The availability of textbooks is indeed central to students' concerns.

Challenges to Implementing Reforms

Educational reform in Ghana has come with many attendant problems that mitigate against school success (see also Nsiah-Peprah 1998). Educators express concerns about low funding, the weakening morale of teachers, absence of textbooks and other curricular materials, poor and inadequate infrastructure, and inefficiencies in administrative procedures and structures. The narratives in this chapter show that students have legitimate concerns about the pace of educational reform. They have not fully understood the magnitude of change and they generally find both the JSS and SSS curricula to be overloaded. For example, they critique the "short" duration of both junior and secondary schooling. Students feel that an extension of basic and pre-tertiary education to a minimum of four years each will be helpful. Parents complain about the high cost of education and feel the government should do more to shoulder the educational responsibility. The state and the leadership argue there is more local communities can do to shoulder the responsibilities, costs and burden of youth education.

Students and parents also have concerns about school curriculum and instruction and their relevance to Ghanaian society. It is generally acknowledged that emphasizing the teaching and learning of Ghanaian languages at all levels in the school system is a good approach to addressing the question of local educational relevance. It is, therefore, argued that learning a second Ghanaian language other than one's native regional language could be a core subject required of all students. However, the success of this initiative will depend on the availability of trained teachers. Similarly, the goal (central to the reforms) of providing students with hands-on, practical skills for maintenance work remains to be met because vocational and technical institutes still lack the teachers, workshops, tools and equipment for teaching technical and life skills to students.

The problem of the lack of qualified, professionally trained educators to effect the changes initiated under the reforms is acute. In the absence of adequate teaching personnel, the provision of decentralized in-service training and professional development for teachers may be appropriate (see Nyalemegbe 1997). School administrators can work with education officials to institute incentives and compensation for teachers. Otherwise, the problem of educators looking for off-school employment to supplement their incomes can only have long-term deleterious effects on teacher performance, productivity and morale, and on students' respect for authority. The weakening of morale among many educators, coupled with the perceived lack of accountability and transparency among school administrators, could spell disaster for schools if not addressed. Perhaps appointing qualified, well-trained supervisors for school-based supervision is necessary. As Nyalemegbe (1997) further argues, "[E]ach school must be inspected at least once a year and the results published for discussion at annual meetings of parents, school management committees and teachers" (7).

The state has committed itself to implementing a Free Compulsory and Universal Basic Education (FCUBE) programme. But there are no funds to implement such a programme successfully. One idea is to shift the additional costs of tertiary (and particularly university) education onto students and their parents. This idea, supported by the international financial community, is not without opposition and resistance from university students and administrators as well as many parents. Clearly, the unhealthy competition between "tertiary" and "primary" education to secure national priority in funding and resource allocation needs to be addressed.

Historically, financing of education in Africa has been skewed in favour of post-secondary education. English (1994) notes that in the early 1980s, 96.7 per cent of donor aid to education was allocated to secondary and tertiary levels and that "donors were investing 500 times more per student in higher education than they were in primary education" (106; c.f. Jesperson 1992). Funding to the post-secondary sector has contributed to a steady rise in enrolments (see also Salmi 1992). Herman (1995) attests that "between 1970 and 1988, the number of tertiary students [had] multiplied eightfold in Sub-Saharan Africa" (263). Besides sectorial imbalance in funding, there is also the question of gender inequity. In fact, the gendered dimensions of education, particularly of female students' low participation in higher education, is something not lost on some educational researchers (see Bouya 1994; Otunga 1997; as well as the many excellent pieces in Bloch, Beoku-Betts, and Tabachnick 1998; Heward and Bunwaree 1999).

In Ghana (as with much of tropical Africa) the policy of free, compulsory universal basic education is supported with funds from international donors. There is a recognition of the continuing harm to national development posed by the historic regional, gender and ethnic differences in education (access and outcomes). It is widely acknowledged by donors and state officials that girls are under represented in the educational system, especially when one moves to the northern area of the country. Thus programs are being put in place to address the gender and sectoral imbalance. For example, recently the Canadian International Development Agency (CIDA) in a joint initiative with the World University Service of Canada (WUSC) and UNICEF announced plans to assist the Ghanaian Ministry of Education to develop and implement action plans to promote girl-child education in selected districts, local communities and schools in the northern and upper regions of the country. There have been some successes with the girl-child education as it pertains to raising awareness about the importance of female education and addressing questions of gender in education. But much more needs to be done to match the rhetoric with concrete action and results. Unfortunately, good intentions and well-meaning initiatives usually come up against profound structural, material and physical barriers that derail the effective implementation of reforms.

It may be asked: How does this Ghanaian case study implicate African education as a whole? Africa is not an undifferentiated category. The complexity and heterogeneity of African society requires that intellectual caution be exercised in generalizing from one case study. However, it can be argued that the discussion so far provides useful ideas to comparative educational researchers in their efforts to provide a more extensive or global understanding of educational opportunity and reform. The reform problems discussed are not unique to Ghana. As others have shown, many African countries have historically had difficulties in implementing reforms (see, for example, Banya 1993; Banya and Elu 1997; English 1994; Maclure 1994; Obanya 1995; Psacharapoulos 1989, 1990; Sifuna 1992).

Admittedly, there may be different responses toward reform efforts from different African governments and citizenry. By and large many countries are dealing with a myriad of social, economic and political problems of implementing reforms under periods of inadequate funding, dwindling physical and material resources and a lack of highly skilled trained personnel (see also Hough 1989; Salmi 1992). These have compounded the problems of declining primary school enrolment rates (English 1994), low retention rates and low educational achievements (Jespersen 1994), and rising dropout rates (Motala 1995). English (1994) further points out that the myriad of educational problems has forced African governments to define the role of the state vis-à-vis other actors in the budgeting and delivery of educational services and to determine the "current mix of resources going to education in order to obtain better educational results," as well as strive to build" managerial and budgeting capacity in the educational sector" (98).

These challenges of educational reform are not necessarily unique to anyone one country. Under severe budgetary constraints, African countries are implementing reforms heavily dependant on donor support. Governments, schools, colleges and universities have to contend with a shortage of professionally trained personnel and an inadequate physical infrastructure that threaten to cripple educational systems (see also Passi 1990). One response is to push costs onto parents and local communities. For example, parents are being asked to take on additional funding responsibilities for primary and secondary education.

Since the late 1980s, a number of African countries have introduced user fees (see English 1994). Under harsh economic conditions, educational problems are magnified with the inefficiencies in educational administration and management. Using the case of school curriculum reform, Sifuna (1992) offers a good summary of the common problems faced by African countries in implementing school reforms. The diversification of secondary education "is taken to mean curriculum change in a practical or vocational direction"(5). The basic problems faced by African countries in implementing such curriculum diversification include "high unit costs, an absence of clarity in aims and objectives, shortage of qualified teachers to teach vocational subjects and the low status as viewed by the students and the community" (Sifuna 1992, 12). As Jones (1997a) also observes, for most African countries the context for reforms is severe economic "austerity, adjustment measures favouring privatization, reduced government expenditures, user charges, and difficult choices between sub-sectors in education"(373).

The foregoing discussion reveals some of the challenges of implementing educational reforms at the local level. Ghanaian students, teachers and parents in the selected school sites speak about the rising cost of education and the pressures on families. They lament over the absence of school textbooks and vocational equipment, the shortage of well-trained teachers in the vocational and technical subjects. Students decry the shortening of the educational cycle and their being ill prepared for future advanced study. Some educators want to see more efforts placed on in-service training for professionals, alongside the provision of material incentives to make teaching more financially rewarding. Parents show concern over the lack of adequate voice and input into schooling and education of their children. Even as they understand and support the spirit of the reforms, in general students, teachers and parents attribute a great deal of the problems of delivering education to youth to the politics of the reform in terms of the rush by the state to implement reforms before putting in place an effective implementation and delivery strategy. These general problems of educational reforms will be revisited in the context of rethinking schooling and education in the broader African context.

Notes

1. Internet Ghana Home Page (2002): Summary of Education in Ghana includes statistics on school enrolment as follows:

    Overall total almost 2 million breaking down into 1.3 million in primary schools; 107,600 in secondary, 489,000 in middle, 21, 280 in technical, 11,300 in teacher training and 5,600 in University. Obtaining accurate statistics is often difficult in Ghana and there are discrepancies in the overall information provided on Ghana on the NET, which must be kept in mind when examining these statistics. Nonetheless the pattern of students dropping out of school as they move up the levels of schooling (from primary to middle to secondary to post secondary) clearly continues to be very high.

Chapter 3

Recreating Knowledge to Teach and Learn about Africa

The preceding chapters raise the question of how we come to know, learn and teach about Africa as part of the discursive project of educational reforms. The discourse of reforms on the continent is informed by a particular reading of 'global development' and what it means to engage in educational practice for change. In the Ghanaian case study, we are seeing local subjects (teachers, students, parents and community workers) lauding the intent and objective of the reforms, but also expressing serious misgivings about the implementation process and the politics behind reforms. In this chapter I want to further such critical interrogation by placing the discussion in the context of some broad philosophical and theoretical issues regarding teaching and learning about Africa.

One runs the risk of intellectual presumption and arrogance when discussing how most effectively to teach about Africa and African Studies. But sometimes we must take risks, especially when the academic stakes are so high. I believe it is necessary to highlight some ontological and epistemological questions that form the basis of our teaching methods and methodologies. In order to identify particular teaching strategies that contribute to creating relevant, resisting and transformative knowledges about Africa and African Studies, we must first address the pedagogic, instructional and communicative need and urgency to shift away from innocence and toward our collective responsibilities and engagement.

My discussion in this chapter focuses on some general theoretical questions and philosophical positions about teaching African Studies, but not because the practice of teaching is unimportant to me. I plead guilty to not offering any "specifics of teaching tools." My strategic discursive position is that we must first understand the philosophical basis of what we do if our educational/teaching practice is to be effective at all. I also agree that theory cannot stand in opposition to what is pragmatic, and that we cannot reify, neither privileging theory over practice nor the other way around. In fact, I believe the worth of any social theory must be measured in terms of both its (theory) philosophical grounding and the theory's ability to offer social, political correctives.

I am informed by/in my position as a faculty member teaching in the Graduate Department of Education of one of Canada's premier universities (University of Toronto). For nearly two decades I have researched and worked with graduate students who have shared interests in indigenous knowledges, anti-colonial thought, anti-racism education and African development. In my graduate teaching, I have repeatedly witnessed at least three major concerns that emanate from students interested in African Studies. The first is around the processes of (in)validation and (de)-legitimation of knowledges—how knowledges are produced and disseminated nationally and globally. Students have often queried why and how it is that certain knowledges are more important than others. These students realize that knowledge is operationalized differently, given local histories, environments and contexts. Unfortunately, the processes of validating knowledges fail to take into account this multiplicity of knowings that together can speak comprehensively to the diversity of the histories of ideas and events that have shaped and continue to shape human growth and development. In questioning the hierarchy of knowledges, students allude to the problematic position of neutral, apolitical knowledge. It is important, then, that in our teaching of African Studies we lay bare the processes through which, for example, knowledges within the disciplines of Western science are positioned as neutral and universal ways of learning. These become assumed ways of coming to know that contribute to the creation of a hegemony both in process and outcomes and which is often unnamed.

The second concern is for ensuring the role of Indigenous knowledge in understanding Africa and in rupturing the dominance of certain forms of knowledges. Indigenous knowledge is understood here as knowledge "accumulated by a group of people, not necessarily indigenous, who by centuries of unbroken residence develop an in-depth understanding of their particular place in their particular world" (Roberts 1998, 58). As will be argued in a subsequent chapter, Indigenous knowledge is the common sense ideas and cultural resources of local peoples that concern everyday realities. It is knowledge that refers to those whose authority resides in origin, place, history and ancestry. Through the named inclusion of Indigenous knowledges in the academy (schools, colleges and universities), educators and students can rupture the dominance of certain forms of knowledges. For students, the role of Indigenous knowledges in a Western academy is to serve in a project of decolonization (see Dei 2000, 2000c; Dei, Hall, Goldin Rosenberg 2000).

The third major concern raised by students of African Studies is the call to "amputate" pasts, cultures and communities, knowing full well, as Andrew Lattas (1993) says, "that the present is itself constitutive of what it is not. This posture of amputating the self, identity and history contrasts sharply with the Fanonnian idea of 'resistance to amputation.'" The "Africa" that is present today is very much constitutive of the past. For students of Africa, it is unsettling to speak of a "post-colonial view," as if we have obliterated or simplistically done away with that past and history.

Asking Critical Questions

These concerns raise other key questions. For example, What is African Studies? What does it mean to teach African Studies? What knowledges and paradigms do we employ? Who is producing such knowledges, how and why?

These questions have significant implications for teaching African Studies, which I see in terms of the particular academic and political projects that we have in mind when we speak of "teaching African Studies." I do not take the position that everyone must subscribe to these positions. I, however, reiterate that these implications cannot be ignored. So allow me to reframe them in the following propositions. I use "we" to implicate all who read this text and who share in the academic politics being pursued.

- That we teach how to interrogate the role and (mis)uses of past, current and ongoing research knowledge beyond the claim to innocence.
- That we teach Africa and African Studies (as Kankwenda 1994 says) to challenge how the word "crisis" is used to describe Africa, for it has become a powerful conception that everyone believes.
- That we teach how to interrogate the extent of "intellectual aggression" on the continent (see also Ragwanja 1997). I must quickly add that we are all guilty of this and it is not to be understood as a simplistic Black/White duality, African/non-African, good/bad educator split. In the academy we live by this "intellectual aggression." It is part of the political economy of knowledge and credentialism.
- That we teach critically and collaboratively to aid the project of decolonization; to challenge the colonial, pastoral and supervisory gaze on Africa; to undermine the frequent recourse to "static traditionalism"; to make problematic the constant stereotyping and casting of "Africa"; and to offer a corrective to the negativity and the eroticisation of the African presence and human condition.
- That we teach that "politically and personally" is to situate our bodies and ourselves in pedagogic practice, as we interrogate our discursive practices. In other words, we need to understand that the spaces we occupy are as important as what we do politically in those spaces.
- That we teach an awareness that the last millennium was not kind to Africa, not just politically and economically, but we need to recognize that much harm was also done through our academic discourses and discursive practices.

Discursive Strategies

The question then is: What should our teaching strategies be? Let me reiterate that my interest is not in the specifics of teaching methods. I am more interested in the philosophical grounding for the approaches behind these methods.

(Re)Conceptualizing Africa

(Re)conceptualizing Africa calls for understanding Africa based on local subjects' knowledge of themselves. It also requires a sincere acknowledgement that Africa is in many ways an artificial construct and that there is power in the knowledge of theorizing and teaching "Africa" beyond its artificial boundaries. This construct is not meant to give the sense that Africa is no person's land, where as researchers we feel we have the right "to enter." In my pedagogic practice I see it as a strategy that helps students reinvent their Africanness, no matter where they are living. My interest is in the power of self-knowing and the interrogation that can come with this approach to knowledge.

We must also see that Africa is not "homogeneous." We must candidly explore all the emerging contestations, contradictions and ambiguities in peoples' lives. Africa is a community of differences. The politics of claiming universal sameness served well the interests of those who did not want to see Africa challenge their "stable knowledge." Difference can rupture that stability and community of sameness. There is power in knowing difference; in seeing Africa as powerfully demarcated by ethnicity, gender, class, language, region, culture and religion; in seeing Africa as complex and nuanced, not as an undifferentiated, homogeneous blob. This power allows us to challenge the teleological perspectives of those who traditionally have seen Africa simply as a counterpoint in their own histories (see also Chabal 1996). It challenges the image of Africa that simplistically conforms to assumptions that the continent is "backward," "primitive" and fixed in time and space. It presents alternative views/understandings of Africa as self-governing regions that are reasserting their local and continental roots and seeking to overcome the ravages of colonization. They are doing so by renegotiating local, national and continental governing structures to represent their diverse views and interests internally and globally. And, they are doing so fully cognizant of internal and external struggles and difficulties that are part of all peoples' strengths and weaknesses.

Beyond Particularities

The diversity and contextual variations and differences within Africa and among her peoples must always be visible in our pedagogic practice. But that in itself is not enough. We must challenge the essentializing of difference. I say this because there is only so much we can know from the entry point of an unitary fragmentation around difference. Our world today is all about difference. Yet difference when essentialised can mean very little. We must connect the particularities and the historical specificities to their broader, macro-political contexts and forces. For example, we must see Africa within a globalized context and show how the globalized context itself can and is being resisted, just as the "global encounter" still shapes and influences the specificities and the particular. It is always important for us to view Africa in the broader context of North-South, East-West relations.

Creating Relevant Knowledge

The power and efficacy of teaching relevant knowledge about Africa is anchored in local people's aspirations, concerns and needs. It is knowledge that local peoples can identify with and is based on the philosophical position that we must understand Africa on its own terms. Richard Sklar (1993) has noted that those who seek to interpret Africa must develop a sympathetic understanding of African thoughts and values as well as of her history and culture. Africa's history cannot be unproblematically periodized. It is a history of the totality of lived African experiences.

Teaching Africa as a method and a means to create relevant knowledge is crucial if we are to succeed in constructing identities outside the identity that has and continues to be constructed in Euro-American ideology and hegemonic knowings. It calls for developing a particular prism, one that frames issues and questions within a particular lens: Is this in the best interests of African peoples? We cannot take a comforting escape route which says "no one knows what is in the best interests of the people." We can begin our teaching practice by posing the relevant questions. Creating relevant knowledge begins with identifying, generating and articulating a pedagogic theory and practice that uses lived and actual experiences of local peoples.

Collaborative Teaching

I am aware of the desires and perils of collaboration at all times. Yet I can make a case for collaborative teaching in many situations. For example, scholars sharing academic knowledge and pursuing research from different and multiple disciplines or educators engaging students and local communities in the production of knowledge. Collaborative teaching must see experience (and practice) as the contextual basis of knowledge. Such collaboration challenges the split between "the sources of raw data" and the "place of academic theorizing." It must present Africans as active subjects, resistors and creators, not just victims of their own histories and experiences. Such collaborative teaching can attest to the power of identity and its linkage to knowledge production. Thus, who is teaching about Africa is equally important. In our teaching academies, physical representation of different African bodies is significant to rupturing genuine "academic" knowledge about Africa.

Telling Success Stories

Teaching should tell the success stories as well as the failures and disasters. We must challenge the academic attraction and fetish of focussing on "failures" of the continent. We must ask: What can we learn from the success cases; the sites and sources of local peoples resisting and empowering themselves through their own creativity and resourcefulness? Can we devote our research focus to the African success stories (no matter the extent) as another educational strategy?

The Dangers, Perils and Seduction of Romanticism, Overmythicization and the Claim to Authenticity

It is easy to romanticize Africa, given the extensive negativity and selective miscapturings about the continent. But critical pedagogues must eschew this practice. As we speak and write Africa, it is important to be aware of the dangers of using romanticization and over mythicization to counter the negativity and untruths. It serves us well to frequently ask ourselves "Why Write Back" the same way? On a related point, I see all knowledges as contested. There is always a selective representation of the past (and knowledge) (see also Briggs 1996; Clifford 1983; Keesing 1989; Makang 1997; Linnekin 1991, 1992). Teaching is a contested educational practice. I view with deep suspicion any claim to an "authenticity" that possesses authority or an authoritative voice that is not open to challenge or critique (Handler 1988). As many others have argued, there is the impurity of any claim to an untainted past. The past is itself subject to colonial and imperial contamination. But in taking this critical stance to "authenticity" I do not dismiss the power of imaginary mythologies as part of the decolonizing project. As an anti-colonial pedagogue I share Lattas' (1993) view that the past must be recreated "as a way of formulating an uncolonized space to inhabit" (254).

The Socio-Political Contexts of Knowledge Production

For those of us who teach, research, write and in fact "produce knowledge" about Africa, it is important to know and remember that the sources and uses of data are not apolitical. There are always profound social and political contexts and consequences for our constructions of knowledge. All knowledges are contingent on particular social and political contexts. Therefore, in our teaching practices we must always be conscious of the socio-environmental and political contexts of data gathering (knowledge production). In Africa, and in most parts of our world, peoples' freedoms have been taken away when they have taught critically and politically.

I admit that the issues raised in this discussion are by no means exhaustive nor are they the last (un)spoken words on the topic. There is room for further debate. In my discursive practice I prefer to work with a philosophy of hope. I refuse to think that each of our agendas is so powerful that there is not room to hear another's. So perhaps I could conclude with the question: Where am I going with this (what some may see as problematic) fusion of the political and academic? What I am calling for is for teaching African Studies within two specific spheres.

First is the sphere of teaching within the prism of African-centred knowledge and educational practice. That is, the creation and use of African epistemologies and perspectives in our teaching practice based on the idea that there are significant culturally distinctive ways of knowing. Within the myriad African epistemologies, there is a powerful conception that all elements of the universe derive from a similar substance—the spiritual. Hence emotions and intuitions are effective ways of gaining knowledge (Agyakwa 1998). Western scienticism cannot be dismissive of this body of knowledge. Africa must be understood not simply within a so-called western rational thought but instead within an African genesis, or what some may term Afro-synopsis. It is also about putting Africa at the centre of our discursive and teaching practices and our academic engagements. When Africa speaks, we must hear and understand her in terms of the past, present and future. Africa cannot simply be imagined.

Second, we must reclaim an anti-colonial discursive pedagogy. That is, a theorization of colonial and recolonial relations and the implications of imperial structures on knowledge production and use; the understanding of indigeneity; and the pursuit of agency, resistance and subjective politics (Smith 1999; Dei 2000). In this context I use "colonial" not in the conventional sense of "foreign and alien," but more importantly as "imposed and dominating." This view of "colonial" allows us to see how colonialism is domesticated and how those who have been oppressed by dominant/hegemonic discourses may find it difficult to step out of it or even challenge and resist it. Teaching decolonization must not simply deconstruct, interrogate and challenge imperial, colonial and oppressive knowledges but also subvert the hegemonizing of particular cultural, symbolic and political practices and significations (see also Wilson-Tagoe 1997). If anything, I see my project as one conceived in the political and academic practice of imagining and creating shifting representations of knowledge that counter static and fixed definitions and interpretations of Africa.

Critical Teaching

As I have pointed out elsewhere (Dei 1999, 2000), the literature abounds with discussions of the many problems afflicting African schooling and education. Without a doubt there are genuine concerns, ranging from the shortage of trained teachers, lack of basic materials, decaying physical infrastructure, fiscal, administrative, bureaucratic mismanagement and inefficiencies, curricular irrelevance, school indiscipline, maintaining academic standards as well as ethnic, cultural, linguistic and gender disparities and imbalances. But beyond these difficulties, there are cases of educational achievements and success stories that not many hear about. Schooling is not just about educational delivery. The context of education, the practice of schooling, the social organizational life as well as the cultures and environments of schools affect what is learned and how. Implicit in this reasoning is the power and efficacy of "critical teaching."

Critical teaching seeks to provide students with thinking skills that help them to question the taken-for-granted assumptions about knowledge and society and to work for social justice and equity. My understanding of critical teaching centres the interrogation of power relations in the structures for delivering education—structures for teaching, learning and administration of education. Critical education interrogates how schools are addressing questions of equity, particularly how educational approaches deal with social difference and diversity in the school population. Critical teaching also seeks to promote local/indigenous knowledges for decolonization purposes. It also means teaching students to develop a "sense of entitlement" to participate in their education as well as a "sense of responsibility" to create and use knowledge to transform society.

In other words, rethinking schooling and education in African contexts requires (re)conceptualizing issues, which calls for employing alternative discursive frameworks that would help pose new questions for research inquiry. As noted, an anti-colonial discursive framework critically interrogates the structures of teaching, learning and administrating education; it helps us understand questions of cultural power and cultural politics, difference, identity and representation in schooling. Within this framework, as already noted, "colonial" is not simply "foreign and alien," but "imposed and dominating." It interrogates the configurations of power embedded in ideas, cultures and histories of knowledge production and validation in schools and off-school sites. The framework also recognizes the importance of locally produced knowledge emanating from cultural histories, social identities, traditions, daily human experiences and social interactions. As a discursive approach, it sees marginalized groups as subjects of their own experiences, histories and actions and highlights the understanding that any politics of representation and identity needs to continually reassert the presence of those marginalized as knowing subjects (see also Memmi 1969; wa Thiong'o 1986). Using this framework, educational research would be able to generate new knowledge about learning and resistant practices of marginalized/colonized groups that could help transform educational processes.

Local subject[ive] knowings about what constitutes critical [and good] teaching is relevant to the lessons and insights such knowledges shed about how Ghanaian educators can engage local culture, history, language, tolerance and respect for different understandings and also create positive learning environments to assist in change and transformation.

Narratives

Teaching Respect: The Centrality of Culture and History

Critical teaching helps students to apply knowledge to their daily lives. Teaching must integrate social values and the cultural resource base of local peoples. The critical educator interrogates and teaches African social values and mores, such as community traditions of mutuality, mutual interdependence and social responsibility. By integrating into teaching an appreciation of the past, history and culture of the students, they can better identify with the subject. Adwoo, an eighteen-year old female student at the Senior Secondary School (SSS) level, decries the disrespect that can be shown toward the poor and uneducated. To her, critical teaching works with the cultural politics of schooling. Effective pedagogy works with teaching both respect for authority and challenging it, depending on the values in which the authority is based. Adwoo argues that "it's not normal that everyone will be rich or everyone will be educated. So no matter who that person is, that person ... [must be] ... respected." It is respect for authority that comes from membership in a community of people which she values and not respect for authority that is based primarily/solely on status and money. She connects learning with respect and developing a knowledge base about one's culture, history and shared sense of belonging to a place. To her learning about one's history, past and culture is key to developing a responsible citizenry:

> I personally have no other interest. But as a citizen of the country ... I think it is somehow good to know something about the past ... and our ancestors and other things ... It also helps ... [to] be a good citizen ... [and] ... to know the culture is also very advisable, as you know, ... to fit into society. (07/09/97)

A knowledge of history allows Adwoo to appreciate the past and draw on its implications. An educational and communicative project affirming the "past" cannot be interpreted unproblematically as a call to regress to "primitivity" (see Amadiume 1997, 12-13 for a framework that begins to (re)conceptualize African histories beyond the racism of anthropological and sociological paradigms positioning African ancestries as "primitive" or uncivilized). Education grounded in the African "past" should be read as a politicized discourse to interrogate the African history, culture and tradition in order to learn from their sources of empowerment as well as to understand the sources of disempowerment for African peoples. For the critical teacher, education cannot ignore the cultural realities of a people. It means appreciating local culture and generating information that resonates with daily experience.

Meaningful and Relevant Teaching

Adwoo's friend, Adoma, a sixteen-year old student in SS1, identified her favourite subject as Government Studies "because of the way the teacher teaches: [T]he teacher teaches in the sense that ... makes the class so lively that everybody takes part in it and it is not boring" (07/09/97). But she adds that it is not simply the instructional style of a teacher that counts. She connects pedagogy with the issue of educational relevance and wonders why some schools do not offer Government Studies:

> Government is a subject that is everywhere, in our homes, in the schools ... everywhere. And in fact, those who are not offering government I don't know what is wrong with them ... If you study government you learn to appreciate what a government in your time is doing. Like if people just don't quite [like] something ... they just start insulting the government or something. They don't actually know what is happening. So if you learn government you will know the situation and what events have occurred. You learn to appreciate, either [something] is good or bad, you just don't get up and talk. (07/09/97)

From within this desire to understand the workings of governance, a critical learning environment might seek to position this dialogue within the context of the pressures that many local governments are facing to adopt fiscally conservative policies. With an understanding of the local and broader context, students and communities can work out strategies and positions, cognizant of what is in the interest of the people of Ghana and its many local communities and economies. Adoma speaks to this when narrating the specific pedagogical strategy of her teacher, by pointing to how learning from past history and the known present should provide a context for validating knowledge about the self: "You can't start without a past. You can never start without a past. You came from the past, you should always start from the past and build on for the future. Like the Europeans came and when they took countries, we have to learn it in order to know how to behave and assess ourselves and things like that" (07/09/97). The student comes to this understanding of Government Studies in part because of the exposure to the relevance of the subject as conveyed by the teacher and class participants. She sees the subject as meaningful in her daily-lived experience. The knowledge which she is provided is something she can work with to explain contemporary events. Understandably, she wishes the same for other students. In many ways her narrative speaks to the interface of knowledge for decolonizing purposes. Critical teaching emphasizes inquiry and process skills in the application and utilization of texts and curriculum. Classroom teaching must provide knowledge as "life skills" and make knowledge relevant to the learner's lived experience. Thus, a critical teacher would see education as meaningful if it leads in some portion to human understanding and problem-solving. For any teaching to be critical, it must encourage students to think creatively and act self-reflectively about themselves and their place in society.

Kube is a business student in the first year of his secondary education. He echoes the sentiments that students in general share about education and its social relevance. He links education and social development and believes it is through the acquisition of knowledge that students can make valuable contributions to society. Asked about what he sees as the importance of getting an education, he responds: "Yes, you will help a lot to develop our economy in our countries. You acquire more knowledge than those people who don't have any education. You help them in this society to be aware of the importance of the economy" (21/09/97). To this student the acquisition of education comes with some responsibilities to a larger collective not simply the self. The presentation of teaching as active, dialogical and experiential learning in order to think critically about the problem of "development" can help students "develop a sense of their own potential for making a difference to their societies" (Hickling-Hudson 1994, 31).

What is significant in the interview with Kube is his linking of "relevant teaching" to the teaching of history and culture. For example, he articulates the importance of teaching and learning Ghanaian culture as a way to understand ourselves. Culture, he reasons, is a shared attribute, the possession and understanding of which strengthens how as a group we come to live collectively and appreciate one another:

> Culture is the way, the way for people to live in the economy or in society. It is good to learn culture, ... You learn about your historical background ... of the country and then the religious and

the different religions in the country. And so we know how to move about or move with other people. And then you know other people from other religions and other [ethnic groups] and it will help you to develop morally ... (09/27/97)

But for the critical educator it is not simply how culture is lived and experienced but also how it is evoked and what interests it can serve. Therefore, teaching within the context of a politicized understanding of culture is to raise new questions about the construct and the power issues of legitimation and validation of knowledge. The relations of power in the different examples brought forth would also be analyzed.

Positive Learning Environment

Every learner is an embodied spirit/soul. Education must therefore be presented as an emotionally felt experience. Rather than being estranged from one's surrounding environment, the student must instead be engrossed in it. Fela, a student in SS3, identified his favourite teachers. He explained that they were his favourites because they not only knew their subjects but they were also caring and approachable. And above all, they offered useful advice and guidance to students. To the student these attributes of a good teacher enhance learning. The student brings to his or her understanding of critical teaching an appreciation of what the teacher does in the classroom and what she or he stands for, as well as the socio-environmental contexts in which learning proceeds. Fela enthuses:

> Your surroundings ... also give us pleasure ... There are a lot of activities ... that normally go on in our campus ... [and] ... people from different schools will come ... [When] we have activities ... [our teachers] ... allow us to go and participate or take part in certain things ... Our entertainment program ... [has] ... a lot of academic work and it is something like the [academic] ... quiz and then drama which help us to learn something. (09/21/97)

It seems that one way for an educator to popularize "school/academic knowledge" is through the use of local popular culture. For example, community talks, folk drama/theatre and songs and other forms of folkloric production (Thisen, 1993) as forms of "entertainment." The pedagogic effect is that learning becomes an activity with pleasure, combining the "academic" and the "social." Furthermore, the collective engagement of students in these activities helps to cultivate a sense of identification with the school and the educational process.

Dealing with Change and Transition

Omari, a father of six, received his postgraduate training outside Ghana. He agonizes over the changes currently taking place in the educational system, particularly the competing forces of modernity and traditional values. He sees the roles of teachers and parents as helping youth deal with the challenges as they straddle between two or multiple cultures. He argues that education the past and the present that connects schooling and teaching must help equip the youth to deal with the problems, constraints and opportunities of society under transition. Omari's narrative is worth reproducing at length since it captures some of the dilemmas, tensions, ambiguities and contradictions that students, educators, and parents experience when they confront change and look for ways to create a sense of responsible citizenry among learners. In many ways, Omari presents an understanding of the tension between two parents' roles and responsibilities. In fact, he offers a critical reading of school-community relations that move beyond the traditional approach of pathologizing families, parents and communities for the educational problems of youth. Asked to put his own interpretations on current tensions in schooling, he offers this view:

> Because of certain tendencies, it is [now] a whole system, Western civilization and the students are taking on certain airs, certain attitudes toward things, even toward their parents. But things were not like that in the olden days. So it is the influence of western culture which is now very easily acquired through the present communication system For the kids they are now torn between these two cultures. Is it the European culture which is good for them or the African culture, the African way of thinking? I'll give you an instance: A kid [would] return from school in the olden days [and be] expected to help with the family chores. [But today] he would come maybe the mother has finished preparing everything [and] he just needs to go to table. He won't bother about the chores. He will expect the mother to go and clean everything, why? Instead of sitting down to study, they come and go. There are so many of these outside influences which are really having very bad influences on our kids. But now, it is very difficult to sort of reverse the trend things are progressing and it is no fault of the kids because it is rather the form of the interdependence in this world.

> So nobody can do anything about it now. But the only thing is a
> question of tolerance and a very big responsibility of parents, too,
> to visualize the sort of problems these kids are now [facing] in the
> twentieth or twenty-first century Their problems are quite different
> from what we were used to. So we have to learn to adapt to the
> present system so that the kids will also adapt to the system. So the
> two, the parents and the kids, there is need for them to
> interchange, to adapt. Because the kids can't go back to the old
> days. Theirs is just to move ahead. But it is our responsibility, the
> responsibility of parents to sort of adapt ourselves because our way
> of thinking needs to be changed. And this is what we have to do in
> order to sort of be at par with our kids. (09/16/97)

It is important to note his reference to the influence of Western
culture, which is now easily acquired through the present
communication system. Understanding the power and influence of
this tool to colonize local cultures, particularly in the next generation
of youth, is an important message to both parents and educators.
Awareness of and engagement with this challenge facing the youth
starts the process of seeking to find learning and teaching strategies
that enable students and communities to understand and use
communication technology for their needs and interests and not to be
passive recipients of the new outside colonizing culture. As he says,
educators and parents need to adapt thought and action to meet
current realities. Such critical teaching can help to deal with these
changes.

Defining a "Good" Teacher

Ferdio teaches life skills at the secondary school level. At the time of
the interview, he had made a decision to leave teaching temporarily to
pursue postgraduate studies at a local university. His future plan is to
obtain a doctorate in education in a North American university. He is
very clear as to the qualities of a "good teacher": patience, humility, a
readiness to learn from students, and the ability to allow experience to
shape personal thoughts and ideas:

> A good teacher is someone who accepts his students as they are in
> the first place. Then he has the patience to know [their] problems,
> and always tries to teach from the known to the unknown, where
> he bases his teaching on known experiences, or [using] the
> environment [for] examples, before he shifts to the abstract. The
> good teacher should always be ready to listen to his students. He
> should be authoritative in the class. And, at certain times he should

participate in the class activities by giving them examples. Then when he is observing it must be participant observation, where at certain times he will bring himself into teaching, becoming a role model for [students], before they shift on to what he wants [them] to know. Then also in the classroom, he should be prepared to listen to the problems of the children [and] help solve them. (08/11/97)

Ferdio sees the teacher as a listener, an initiator, a participant in the classroom and a role model for students. Above everything, a good teacher is one who makes knowledge relevant to the students. As already alluded to, this is a theme many students share and identify with.

Strategies in Critical Teaching

The good teacher as a critical educator must know what specific instructional strategies to follow with her or his students in the classroom. Ohemaa is an English and History teacher with eight years professional service at the local teacher training college. In her work with student teachers, she shares her thoughts about preparing students for practical assignments in schools. She powerfully alludes to how local context, history and subject of inquiry are crucial to the pursuit of critical teaching. Besides the challenge of ensuring that teaching and learning happens simultaneously, Ohemaa speaks of the need to address the relevance of what is taught. To her, this is important so that students can establish some form of identification and connectedness to the knowledge production process. Practice and experience become the contextual basis of classroom knowledge and teaching. In responding to how specifically she generates discussions in the classroom with her students, she affirms:

Well, okay, that depends on the topic. But then I try as much as possible to use current issues. I tell them [students] that they should consider the [local] environment. For instance, if you are teaching in maybe in [mentions subject matter and place] ...try to use those examples you know which is within the children's experience so that you build on that. So I tell them that the way you handle a topic ...will be different from the way you handle ... Let's say for instance you are teaching the history of the school, the history of [this school] is different from [that] of the Catholic school ... So that you give them the guidelines ...You know what I do is I make them do some research on the school itself ... And, I tell them that it is not that I don't know but I want you to do it so

> that when you go, … wherever you are posted … you will be able
> to teach those people the history of their school. (08/20/97)

Asked to expand on how and from where she draws her classroom
examples she enthuses:

> I would say it depends on the occasion. But basically I try to build
> on what they know, I say we start from the known to the unknown
> …[for example if] you're handling [a subject] like "division of
> labour." You can start right from the home where the household
> chores are divided or you can even use the school environment
> because the school depending on the level …[has] people
> performing different functions. We have the blackboard monitors,
> etc., and other things so I always tell [students] that you should use
> what you think is within the child's experience and that one I really
> emphasize. [When] you do [that] the more they know. (08/20/97)

It is clear from Ohemaa that critical teaching must be situated in
appropriate contexts and must draw on powerful analogies to register
ideas with learners. She agrees emphatically that students can teach
the teacher as well. Her narrative clearly shows the humility that is
required of a good and effective teacher. Such humility provides a
sense of comfort and security for the learner to know that she/he can
also lay some claim on the knowledge production process. In effect,
critical teaching works with the idea that students do not come to
school as empty vessels to be filled with knowledge. Students can
educate the teacher because they come as embodied spirits and
empowered subjects with some knowledge to impart and share: "Sure
they can because I always tell them they shouldn't see the teacher as
the one giving them the knowledge. It is give and take and [if] there
was a discussion I tell them they should feel free and … if [what is
said] is right we all accept it" (08/20/97). The teacher's humility and
desire to learn allow students to intellectually and politically empower
themselves. Similarly, no knowledge is innocent. All knowledge has a
politics, whether or not it is explicitly acknowledged and engaged. The
shift away from mere theorizing and intellectualizing academic issues
to concrete and political engagement is another important aspect of
critical teaching. In Ghanaian schooling, some educators present
teaching as learning for self and collective emancipation and eventual
human survival. Such critical teaching assists students to examine the
school curriculum for hidden messages that infantilize all students,
but particularly cultural, ethnic, religious and linguistic minorities.

Additionally, a few educators have come to see critical teaching as "eco-political education," that is, education for political action in order to confront structures of exploitation and to challenge unsustainable development (Hickling-Hudson 1994). Such recognition gives an explicit political dimension to teaching so that education is not viewed uniquely in terms of its overtly observable phenomena but rather in terms of the consistencies and tensions between policy and practice at a systemic level. When anchored in social politics and activism, critical teaching can assist learners in challenging the techno-fix and techno-centrist approach to education. It allows teachers and students to see themselves as creators and subjects of change. Critical teaching helps students understand the structural roots and causes of human poverty; that poverty is not an independent variable but the result of exploitative social, economic and political structures that create social and material wealth for a few by disadvantaging many. There are many ways the critical educator can pursue such transformative education. As Hickling-Hudson (1994) pointed out, an "ecologically-activist teacher" can use popular culture, drama/theatre, local media, folktales, songs and myths to teach students to understand the nature of the environmental crises in local, regional, national and global contexts. This is working with available local knowledge and cultural resources.

Indigenous Knowledge and Teaching/Learning "Science and Technologies" as Praxis

In critical teaching, teachers can use indigenous knowledge principles and epistemologies as an important basis of instruction (Jegede 1997, 16). To exercise intellectual agency, teachers and students should engage in a process of recuperation, revitalization and reclamation of African knowledge as a necessary exercise in empowerment. Kofi, a highly respected community worker and science teacher, complains that not enough money "has been pumped into science education in Ghana," whether at the primary, secondary or university level. He teaches chemistry and core science at the secondary school level and utilizes experiential knowledge to argue that science is a practical subject and students must be taught to work with materials and apply knowledge to everyday practice. He criticizes the early education he received at school with its emphasis on rote learning, memorization and regurgitation of facts. Critical teaching is helping students create, act and interact with knowledge rather than merely reading about and regurgitating knowledge. Kofi forcefully articulates the problem of the legacy of colonial/western education:

> It was in the university that I had a feel of the science proper. At the O-level and the A-level we were taught to pass. We memorized everything. We were bored. But when we got to the university, we were made to do all our practicals on our own, every time. So until that time (university) I saw science as Western. But now science seems more indigenous to me than [it was] previously. (08/13/97)

In the conversation, Kofi points out that rote learning, promoted in his early education, was not critical education. It never challenged him or the social order of things. Critical teaching must allow the learner to know that instruction cannot be detached from learning. Furthermore, critical teaching means working with the idea of the compatibility of multiple knowledge systems and the learner's ability to grasp different ways of knowing through "collateral learning" (Jegede 1997, 13). Through critical teaching, students can move from the mere regurgitation of facts to critical analyses of the social and political constructions of knowledge. In classroom teaching practices, educators help students choose from "technologies" that contribute most to the solution of daily human problems. Critical educators must resolve the conflict of conceptual and instructional models between the school and the home by making knowledge relevant and applicable (see also Jegede 1997). In other words, educators must use critical teaching as a way to subvert didactic, authoritarian learning based on rote memorisation and regurgitation.

In fact it is in defining indigenous education that Kofi brings issues of relevance and the practical application of science as something worth starting from the known to unknown:

> What I mean by indigenous. What I mean is all things that are pertaining to Ghana, or to the peasant, or maybe a child from the village and it is done in science. How he can go back to the village and apply the science. So in teaching how to make soap we deal now with the indigenous raw materials like coconut, the plantain peels ... and the ash to get the paste which is essential ... [What] western science would have used in making their soap, we use our own palm oil and other raw material to use for the soap rather than buying the imported oil or whatever type of oil they use. So presently science means more indigenous than western. (08/13/97)

The critical educator strengthens links between the "school curriculum" and social environments, relating the teaching of science and technology to local situations (see also Thisen 1993). More importantly, Kofi's narrative attests to the power of indigenous knowledge to not only subvert cultural domination by western culture and technology but also the potential of developing alternative local economies through the application of indigenous science and adaptation of other sciences to local needs. Critical teaching will affirm rather than devalue local knowledges. Itwaru (1999) argues that part of the imperial and colonial ideology is to see the colonized as the "inferiorized other. The "other" becomes the disauthenticated person/personhood, one devoid of an indigenous knowledge, identity, ancestry and history. Yet, the "othered" subject brings a knowledge that can be oppositional or rupturing to conventional/standard/stable/imposed knowledge. Hence, the imposed knowledge is always insecure of its own existence. Threatened by oppositional knowledge, imposed knowledge will move to destroy or devalue any critical thought and action. In other words, the imposed order anticipates resistance and moves to destroy it (Itwaru 1999). In fact, one way of destroying such oppositional knowledge is to deny authenticity and an Indigenous identity to the self that seeks to create such critical knowledge. Thus, the authority of the Indigenous self is questioned.

To Kofi, there is something to be learned in the Africanization of the student and her or his knowledge base: anything Indigenous, local or African is not inferior. Africanizing the teaching process helps the learner develop an awareness and a deeper consciousness of one's own identity, culture and history. It is, therefore, the task of the critical teacher to equip students to draw on local environments as important sources of knowledge. Critical teaching must pay attention to traditional knowledge as well as the values embedded in local cultures as important sources of cultural resource knowledge. In the specific area of science, it means teaching "science" as a way of life for local peoples, teaching from first-hand experience and by practical example. It is helping students develop a local scientific culture so crucial to human survival. In other words, a certain degree of local science knowledge is essential in becoming an informed and responsible citizen.

Ecology of Educational Change in Ghana

This chapter has focussed on how critical teaching allows students to make connections between local and other knowledges. For example, as Toh (1993), observes teaching critically about the concerns and sufferings of others outside one's local world, "can be helpful in reorienting learners towards parallel problems in their own society (Toh 1993, 11). This is not simply learning but applying knowledge. Speaking more directly to collaborative research, Day (1981) [cited in Troyna and Forster 1988] provides important insights into the pursuit of critical education. It is argued that effective learning can occur when a learner is allowed to confront problems which are central to her or his own practice. This "self-confrontation" can be a process of learning which leads to change "through internalization rather than compliance or identification" (Troyna and Forster 1988, 293-294). Also, when teaching proceeds from a process of reflection on actions, intentions and a review of personal, social and institutional factors, the learner can claim "ownership" and "control" in the knowledge production process to define issues of relevance and application. For critical teaching to succeed it is important for educators to "move away from knowledge transmission teaching by using resource-based learning" (Troyna and Forster 1988, 295).

In critical teaching practice, the high intellectual pursuit for "universal culture" is problematized as it conflicts with the search for knowledge that resonates with local peoples and their conditionalities. Critical teaching allows the student to use her or his own creativity and resourcefulness in producing relevant and meaningful knowledge. By providing students with the intellectual tools to resist colonizing and imposed knowledge, they are able to destabilize dominant cultural, social and political forms.

A very simple and concrete example from this study of the power of knowledge creation when it is generated from within the context of the local is illustrated by the quality of responses to different types of questions. The questions that were more effective in tapping into the rich source of student knowledge about learning were not the more general and universal types of questions about what makes a good teacher or a good lesson. Rather, the best questions were those that asked the students whether they thought it important to learn about local history, the local culture and local languages and how they understood the value of Western science and Indigenous science. The questions that tapped into specific local realities, values, and student life were those that brought forth a dialogue with a greater depth of understanding, insight, and discussion to the interviews. This contrast was particularly salient in the interviews with high school students.

Conceptually, critical teaching cannot be separated from the understanding of power issues in education. Critical teaching allows for the examination of the dynamics of power around classroom instruction, curriculum politics, social organization of knowledge and the effects and implications in terms of differential schooling outcomes for learners. More important critical teaching allows us to rethink the processes of producing, validating, interrogating and disseminating oppositional/counter knowledge that can destabilize status quo knowledge. Hence, it is a question of the re-conceptualization of schooling and education.

In the Ghanaian contexts, a critical teacher can make use of African knowledge principles as a "cultural frame of reference" to rethink schooling and education. Scheurich and Young (1997) highlight the ontological, epistemological and axiological positions that may characterize different knowledge systems. The ontological position speaks to the primary assumptions that people have or make about the nature of reality. In African systems of thought, the ontological viewpoint stresses that to understand reality is to have a complete or holistic view of society. The view stresses the need for a harmonious co-existence between nature, culture and society. There is the idea of mutual interdependence among all peoples so that the existence of the individual/subject is only meaningful in relation to the community that she or he is part of. On the other hand, the epistemological position enthuses that there are different ways of knowing about reality. There is no one reality. Thus, in African systems of thought, knowledge is seen as cumulative and as emerging from experiencing the social world. Practice and experience are seen as the contextual basis of knowledge. Knowledge is for survival. Both go hand in hand. While membership in community accords rights, there are important matching responsibilities. The axiological position maintains that there are "disputational contours of right and wrong or morality and values ... [that is] ... presumptions about the real, the true and the good" (Scheurich and Young 1997, 6). In African systems of thought, therefore, cultural, spiritual beliefs, values and practices are evaluated in the history and contexts of communities as societies strive to set their own moral tone. While these ideas may be shared by other indigenous peoples, it is the privileging of certain core social values for "reward" (e.g., responsibilities over rights; community over individual; peaceful co-existence with nature over control or domination of nature) that sets different knowledge systems apart.

The question is, What is the relevance in rethinking schooling and education in African contexts? This study helps to interrogate the four characteristics of "valid knowledge" as promoted in schools (see Hatcher 1998). Through the combination of four characteristics of *abstract universalism* (that downplays the specificities of local school situations), *decontextualization* (that gives no recourse to the importance of students' experiences, histories, cultures and identities in the learning process), *consensualism* (that avoids dealing with conflict and controversy) and *managerialism* (that privileges a top-down approach to schooling administration), schooling reforms have failed to address the structural, political and historical dimensions of change.

There are broader implications for educational change in the African contexts. An examination of the ways critical teaching and learning are understood and pursued in some Ghanaian contexts suggests some viable educational initiatives for educational change in Africa. There is an imperative need to focus on the innovative educational practices of some teachers (e.g., communicative, and instructional practices) that point to the importance of local creativity and resourcefulness to deliver education in a very comprehensive way. Briefly, I will mention six areas as important lessons (see also Dei, James, Karumanchery, James-Wilson, and Zine 2000; Dei, James-Wilson and Zine 2002).

The first is the place of the individual learner and the use of personalized and intuitive learning. Local school teachers work with the idea that learning begins with the self and that every way of knowing is subjective and based in part on experiential knowledge. To be effective, learning must be personalized in order to develop the intuitive and analytical aspects of the human mind. Individual attention permits the educator and the learner to start with the self and project onto the group. Therefore, specific attention to individual students goes beyond child-centred learning.

The second is spirituality and spiritual learning. I am using "spirituality" in terms of the understanding of the self and not simply the ascription to any high moral or religious order. It is the ability to understand the self, relate to others and to act for collective interests. Promotion of the self-concept and personhood can be a site of individual agency and resistance. By working with a broader definition of education that encompasses emotional and spiritual dimensions, local teachers aim at youth empowerment for social change. Local teachers' understanding of education is that learning must be an emotionally felt experience. Therefore, specific educational strategies address the learning needs of students by integrating spirituality with school curriculum, instruction and pedagogical practices. Teaching practices reconcile the "secular" and the "sacred." Rather than shying away from spiritual dimensions of education, school and classroom practices integrate secularity with individual and community notions of religion and spirituality. Education is not pursued as the pursuit of a secularized, fragmented knowledge, but as a process to understand the workings of the body, mind and soul, and the interconnections among society, culture and the physical and metaphysical realms (I further discuss this in chapter 4).

Third is the use of local knowledge as a powerful cultural resource and instructional base. Critical teachers tap indigenous, traditional and culturally-based knowledges as important educational resources for the learner. Specific instructional practices ask learners to situate knowledge in the everyday practices and interactions of society and to relate common sense knowledge to schooling and education. Classroom teachings draw from the ecological contexts of students' homes, communities, social and cultural frames of reference.

Fourth is co-operative education and the broader concept of "educational success." Critical teachers have high expectations of their students' academic performance. For students, parents and teachers, education is valued as key to economic success and social mobility. Critical teachers, parents and students stress the connection between "academic" and "social," arguing that academic success is only meaningful if it leads to integration into the local community as active contributing citizens. This is a broader definition of what it means to be "successful." Success is defined to recognize the learner's strengths, limitations and extent of community involvement, as well as her or his non-academic proficiency in areas such as psycho-social development and the ability to utilize cultural knowledge and capital. This educational approach helps to improve and sustain the learner's self-esteem, pride and sense of identity. The rights of success are accompanied by reciprocal obligations and mutual interdependence between the individual learner and the community. School and classroom teachings privilege self and collective empowerment, voluntarism, group participation, collaboration and solidarity.

Fifth is the centrality and importance of culture in critical education. Local schoolteachers allow learners to participate fully in school life and culture while continuing to develop and practise their home cultures and personal and collective identities. Local educators work with the notion of "culture" as shared, dynamic and expressive of collective values and aspirations. Students, parents and guardians are seen as educators by embodying knowledge about local culture (norms, social values, traditions and histories) that they can impact on the youth. Cultural teachings emphasize strict discipline of the learner. In [traditional] schooling, discipline is understood and enforced as showing respect for authority and tolerance for each other. Generally respect is defined as something which is "given," "received" and "expected" depending on one's social position as well as one's interactions with others. So students will be expected to show respect to their teachers because of their position as educators and as adults. But students' response to educators is also matched with a reciprocal acknowledgment of the importance of adults and educators acting responsibly and responsively towards youth. This knowledge was a base of cultural knowing and a resource that was taught to learners. Local culture teaches that respect for elders and gerontocracy is positive and should be valued by all learners. But there is mutuality of respect and concern for potential abuses of adult authorities that must also be guarded against. Teachings of culture address these problematic and ensuing contestations. The teachings of reciprocal obligations among multiple parties permeate all aspects of local culture. Those whose authority resides in age and social status have obligations to be socially responsible. Punishment at school and elsewhere is intended to seek reconciliation and to transform the individual. It is not merely for the sake of retribution. Alternative strategies of conflict resolution focus on the learning process of culture and privilege negotiation and reconciliation, rather than simply punishment and retribution. Within the post-colonial and the current global context, the importance of learning about local culture and its relevance for critical teaching, rather than being enhanced has been eroded (and to some extent subverted) by a focus on market-driven forces with its rigidity of rules of 'law and order' in schools.

Sixth is the recognition of the necessity of creating working partnerships between schools and diverse local communities. Critical teaching stresses that education is a process within a larger continuum and broader context such that schooling issues cannot be understood outside the macro social, cultural, economic and political forces that impinge on society as a whole. Providing education to youth is a task involving several stakeholders: teachers, students, parents, families, governments and local communities.

The Ghanaian case study also shows that to transform education to meet contemporary needs and aspirations of a diverse population there are other areas that need some attention. These concerns reflect the struggle of Ghanaian schools to deal with minority education in the context of prevailing discourses of nationhood and citizenship. One of these concerns is the idea of uncontested culture, place and identity. The approach to accentuate similarities by denying difference can be problematic to the extent that the silencing and negation of difference is an abuse of control or strength. Within local schools, not only is culture assumed to be homogenizing, but there is also the tendency to privilege dominant groups' cultures (see also Fine 1991). Furthermore, the power differences and contestations around culture, tradition, class, ethnicity, and gender remain unresolved. This is particularly evident when students' and educators' narratives affirm the discourse of the dominant by suggesting that schools treat all students equally and that the issues of socio-economic family background, gender, ethnicity and religion, and what these mean in terms of social difference, are not really salient in the context of schooling and education in Ghana.

Finally, there is the issue of representation. To rethink schooling and education in the African context, viable approaches must be grounded in a philosophical understanding of the powerful linkage between identity and knowledge production and the need to validate difference for learners. School and classroom practices need to address issues of representation (see also Dei et al., 1997). Concerns of "visual representation" (i.e., the inclusion of class, ethnic, religious, and linguistic minorities, and of women and their cultures within the visual/physical landscape of the school and the classroom) and "staff equity" (i.e., the representation of teachers from a variety of ethnic, religious, cultural and gender backgrounds in staffing positions) barely arise as "problem areas" in the context of existing hegemonic discourses on Ghana's education. Local schools have an ethnically diverse teaching staff without a conscious political practice to do so. Gender representation in staff is still a problem as can be evidenced by the low number of female teachers in top administrative positions and in post secondary teaching positions. The area of knowledge representation (i.e., the centering of African cultural knowledges and discourse within the school system) also needs addressing. Knowledge representation is a commitment to valuing different cultural knowledges as well as a concrete validation for difference and multiple identities. Admittedly, local schools are not all to blame, given that the national emphasis on promoting indigenous scholarly works is a powerful rhetoric that is not matched by a genuine and sincere attempt to promote materials and texts written by indigenous Ghanaian and African authors from an African-centred perspective. However, there are useful lessons from some schools as educators strive to include texts and other materials from indigenous backgrounds to allow students to make linkages between their local reality and broader transnational issues.

Chapter 4

The School-Community Interface: Parents, Local Community, Culture and Language and Schooling

This chapter looks at the relationships of schools with parents/guardians, local communities, cultures and languages and how these can enhance the learning experiences of the young and of students of all ages. Context is very important if educational systems and strategies are to be truly inclusive of and for all students in a locality. History and context requires that educators modify/adapt their practices to suit specific needs and concerns of students as identified by the citizens/ residents of a local community and the culture(s) in/through which they live their individual and collective lives. Engaging family and community cultures in schools has implications for many aspects of education. But what knowledges do parents and local communities carry that schools may find relevant and useful? For example having an elder participate at the school site by sharing the knowledge of her/his religious/spiritual faith or cultural traditions can make the curriculum more inclusive by introducing other non-hegemonic, non-dominant, non-Western ways/ideas to students. The practice can also promote social and educational change, by displacing what has been a Eurocentric worldview in the structures and culture of schooling. It also disrupts the teacher centred/directed practices of the more traditional classroom. Furthermore, taking the time to listen to different points of view cultivates/enacts a respect for difference. Also, by letting youth speak and inviting in ideas from the students' communities of origin, they and their communities are empowered (see Dei, James-Wilson and Zine 2002, Cummins 1986, 1996).

In recent decades "Western" educational policies, literature and everyday discussions on the notion of community school and community participation in different aspects of schooling has had a focus or has been appropriated by research on and a discourse of parental involvement. The move to increase parental involvement within the classroom and in the decision making processes within other schooling structures may have begun with the good intentions of bettering home/school communication, and of seeking to claw back to the local school some of the power for decision making from large bureaucratic institutions responsible for education oversight and policy directions. However over time, the outcome in some Western English speaking countries (England, the US and Canada) the narrow and limited focus on parental involvement has become problematic. It has increasingly run the risk of placing children of different home backgrounds, particularly those of lower socio-economic backgrounds, at even greater disadvantage than their middle-class counterparts. It has also significantly increased the expectations of additional unpaid work for women. In recent years more and more is being expected from women in both the paid and unpaid sector of the economy and with increasingly less public sector supports. "Parents" are not just being asked but are increasingly being expected to teach their children at home, to assist in the class and to help run and fund raise at the school. (In Canada and the US, parent as used here can generally be referred to as mothers' work.) In this context, the parent involvement movement is receiving greater and greater support from the Right of the political spectrum. And it is increasingly being criticized by many on the Left for failing to take into account questions of gender, class, ethnicity and race. Failure to name the different realities and needs of diverse populations of children and "parents" places public education at risk of being less and less of an institution that seeks to further democratic participation. [For critiques of "Western parent involvement" discourses that are in ways both different and similar see Aguiar 2001; Brown 1988, 1990; David 1993; de Carvalho 2001 and others].

We should be mindful of the risk of decontextualization. It is also important that the recent parent involvement discourses from the Right in the West not be adopted for schooling in the African context. Supporting and seeking to involve all parents in some form is part of the equation. But community schools in a local geographic community need to seek participation and support from all members of the community in a variety of ways that are appropriate for those participating (students and adults), in the environment/setting, the subject area, the field and the structure. In different locales discussions on critical issues/areas such the education are laced with different viewpoints, and contentions. The discussions from the participants in this study were no exception. Parent involvement, community participation, educational partnerships and funding elicited strong feelings from all of the participants in this study. Many offered strong classed critiques of an educational system that strongly disadvantages students with less material capital to access educational resources ranging from the problem of a strongly fees based education, to access to texts and other necessary supplementary resources. Classed and gendered critiques came through in the interviews with the majority of participants, but more so from students and parents (particularly girl students and mothers) with less material resources. The afore-mentioned literatures of critique from the West can contribute to informing the dialogue. But the strength of the forthcoming discussions in this chapter lie in their ability to bring to the fore the dialogues and tensions present in Ghanaian communities which can in turn contribute to further discussions that can propose local solutions to the very real concerns of students, parents (mothers, fathers, other guardians) and community members at large. The chapter opens up a broad dialogue on very critical issues in the participation, delivery and financing of educational programs in local Ghanaian communities.

The study confirms that for inclusive educational change to take place, it is important to acknowledge the shared and defined roles and responsibilities of all stakeholders in the system. Parents/elders and other community members are to be seen as knowledge creators; school guidance counsellors, advisors, educators and students can be the prime change agents in collaboration with the local community networks such as parent groups (i.e. Parent Teacher Associations/ PTAs, parent councils) business and professional groups, spiritual leaders, artists, craftspeople, farmers etc. providing supports. Within a locality, schools need to be linked to the social and cultural life of the communities. Recognizing the boundaries that define different roles does not mean a false/artificially-imposed separation between the "academy" and the "local community." There must be processes of accountability—beyond the question of governance—in order that local communities develop a sense of collective responsibility, establish priorities and objectives. For example, strong partnerships between schools and the local community can be forged by reporting on the progress of programs to locally elected bodies, advisory working groups and through workshops and symposiums. Educational strategies developed within the community can enhance learning for those considered to hold the position/s of elder, for adults (guardians and parents) and other community members. Ways of involving them in the areas of pedagogy, instruction and curricular development need to be further explored. Strategies for greater participation in the school activities and programs would be developed under the direction of school administrators and educators but in close consultation with an advisory or elected community body. School-community strategies must challenge the traditional practice of merely inserting parents/ guardians/community members at large into already existing structures of schooling; rather, they need to become active makers of new cultural, community-responsive meanings.

Community participation is essential for ensuring that local cultures are reclaimed and used as knowledge resources in the processes of education. Some practical approaches for community involvement include community leaders participating in discussions on their understandings of the challenges, responsibilities and duties of adults in the processes of schooling. Forums for participating in this type of knowledge generation would take place at local meeting sites, of which the school would be one. Parent/guardian participation in school activities would include putting forth ideas and organizing ways for them and other parents to participate beyond conventional interactions (i.e., parent—teacher night). For example, ways in which individual teachers, parents/guardians could meet more regularly (formally and informally) could be established. These would have to be facilitated in ways that recognize the time obligations each has to their families, their work and the community. Educational administrators need to consult with stakeholders on strategies that can facilitate teacher learning from community educators/resources (i.e. parent/teacher tutorial exchanges, time and resources to facilitate informal adult learning as professionals, parents, citizens on issues of local public education). There is a substantial amount of knowledge to be gleaned from how parents/guardians/community members at large define their roles in and responsibilities to the schooling process. Educating the young is a responsibility that falls on the adults (individually and collectively) in a community.

The Ghanaian case study illustrates how parents speak of their roles and responsibilities in the education of their children and of their responsibilities as community members to all children. I highlight some of these voices in this chapter not simply to address the challenges of education through schooling to date, but to bring home the necessity of developing strong school-community relations and to point out the possibilities and difficulties that can result from meaningful partnerships between parents/guardians/community members at large and students.

Individual Parental Roles and Responsibilities

The first part of this chapter focuses on parental responsibility and how it relates to the education of their children individually. This covers the everyday physical, emotional and educational care of children and includes parental involvement in the social structures of education at the school and community level. I have found it informative to draw on the voices of parents who are also teachers and those who are not, as well as on the voices of students and other guardians. Both mothers and fathers spoke of parental duties and responsibilities primarily as providing for the daily physical care of their children, ensuring their attendance at school, monitoring their homework and maintaining regular contact with teachers. In describing their responsibilities parents tended to stress their duties in priority. First and foremost, they saw themselves as responsible for their children's physical needs and for monitoring the schedule of their daily activities; that is, ensuring that the children are fed and clothed, that they attend school regularly, and can account for their after-school activities. Mensa is a parent-teacher who strongly articulates his understanding of parent-teacher relations and of parental responsibility:

> Yes. It is very important. It is very important that parents get involved in their children's education. It is their responsibility to find out what their children are doing in school. First of all, it is the parents' responsibility to provide for the needs of their children. For example, a child should eat before he or she goes to school so that the child will have the energy to study. The clothes that the child wears to school—the parents should make sure that every thing is in order. The parent must also make sure that the school fees are paid and all other needs of school are met. If the parent is able to do this for the child, the child will not need anything so far as school is concerned. At times, the parent should be able to go to the child's teacher and find out how the child is doing at school. The teacher may advise the parent. And when the child is not doing well the parent can look for extra tutoring for the child, so that whatever problem the child has can be improved. (08/28/97)

Mensa understands parental responsibility as providing for the basic needs of the child, which include providing material and social supports. But there is also social accountability. Parents must be seen as performing their roles and duties and to be there for their children. The parents are expected to address problems they see or perceive in their children's life and the "good" parent cannot shirk these responsibilities. Along with ensuring that their children's basic needs are met, Mensa points out that parents are responsible for ensuring that children do their homework, and for monitoring their academic progress and behavioural development by maintaining regular contact with teachers. He stresses that contact with teachers helps parents follow their children's development and collaborate with teachers in guiding their development.

A common description of basic parental responsibilities is conveyed in the following extract with Mama, a mother of seven children. She identifies giving "help" to children as a parent's cardinal responsibility:

> [As a parent, how do you help your children with their schoolwork?] When they come home I see to it that they review what they have learned in school. [What other things do you think parents can do to encourage or help their children to be successful

learners?]Parents must visit the school regularly to know about the performance of their children and what are the issues. If a parent sees that his child falls short he must hammer that area at home, help the child to learn and [give her/him] all necessary help. (10/05/97)

Neither Mensa nor Mama identified any limitations or structural conditions that could inhibit their performance or cause them to shirk their parental responsibility. Their narratives are laced with words like "duty," "help" and "must." Similarly, Memmi, an elderly mother speaks of her responsibilities:

> *[What are your responsibilities that ensure your children are successful in school?]* I see to it that they prepare at home and they go to school. I also see that their needs are always met in good time and they become responsible. *[What do you mean by a student being responsible?]* That the student must be ready to take on any duty given to him [or her] to perform. *[Do you think that the parent has a role in making sure that this happens?]* Oh yes, very much so. For example, one of my children likes sleeping and waking up late in the morning, so I know the time [when I have to] force him to get up. (10/05/97)

Understanding, knowing and responding to your child is part of being a "responsible parent." But responsibility is a multi-way affair. Parents have a responsibility to themselves, their children and their communities. Children also have responsibilities to themselves, their parents and their schools. The ability to delineate parental roles and responsibilities is itself significant as a starting point to fulfilling what is required of an adult. In these narratives, parents identify the connecting link between schools and homes. Parents/guardians need to meet their obligations if schools are to succeed in their role of teaching children. Parents and teachers must maintain regular contact to see how each can help the other. The task of educating children is not to be relegated to the school as an isolated institution.

There was consistency among these parents on what they considered to be their basic responsibilities. But they were also very clear in articulating how financial ability (class), gender, region (rural/urban) and their own educational background affected their ability to meet those needs.

The Challenge of Navigating Different[ial] Responsibilities

Financial Capital

There are cases of parents who struggle to financially provide for the family. In some families, mothers and fathers take on extra work to earn enough money to send their children to school. When questioned as to how he finances his children's education (e.g., paying their school fees) Momoh, an educator with five sons and three daughters, makes this observation:

> You know we have few cedis to be collected at the end of every month from the government because he is our employer. That is the number one source. I also run extra classes as a business and I must tell you, I must confess that it pays me even more than what I collect at the end of the month. My wife is also a teacher by profession and she has been very supportive. We have other small businesses that we run, like selling at this small grocery. They all help a lot to finance my wards' education. (08/11/97)

Parents take on multiple work assignments and duties as additional sources of income in order to cover the costs of schooling. Momoh notes that he earns more from his "outside" work than his professional work with the government. He links the issues of fees and the provision of students' daily care to the ongoing reforms:

> Now I said that the Free Compulsory Universal Basic Education has "a" at the beginning but the "a" is written very small. Our inspectors who come round explain to us that the smallness of that "a" indicates to us that it is not yet free so as parents we should contribute our quota in terms of money ... I even mentioned the recent increase in boarding fees. And, we have so much debt to pay. We are still making up for that. We will have to provide clothing, and sometimes, we supplement the food that our children eat at the boarding house. Those who live with us at home, we cater for them day in and out. Transportation in and out, textbooks. I even have got a teacher who has charged me four hundred and fifty thousand cedis to teach my ward economics and geography. You see that I still want to provide for the child the extra help, to keep him busy throughout so as to get the best out of him. We even pay for other extra classes organized by the school. There are some computer lessons they are taking and all those things. So you see that for the funding of children's education; we

bear about sixty percent of the whole thing. I know the government has something going, so we don't pay for tuition and all those things. (08/11/97)

Educational policies propose and state that primary education is supposed to be free. But to Momoh it is not! There is a cost sharing which burdens poor parents. As a parent, he feels that all he can do is complain. But he must still find the means to provide for his children's education. They cannot wait.

Gigi is a father who works as a civil servant for the Ministry of Health. He is a poultry farmer who owns about ten to fifteen pigs and some birds. He says, "I get little [money] from those pigs, birds and the little farming that I am doing." He laments the educational reforms, particularly the huge financial burden it places on parents:

The education is very good. It is a new thing—this reform that the child will [not be in school long] before he [or she] graduates or before entering university. So I appreciate that, but [there are too many] subjects for the children. That is my sole question about it. The reform is good in that for them to enter secondary school it [doesn't take] as long as it did in the olden days. Before you entered university you had to take about fifteen years, and now it takes about twelve ... and if you are successful you go to the university. (09/01/97)

Gigi appreciates the spirit behind the reforms, which may result in some cost savings for parents. To him, shortening the school years may mean poor parents are not unduly burdened. But then at what other costs? His narrative points clearly to the role that social class plays in the parents' ability to fulfil their obligations to their children:

We learned that they gave us some free education but as it is now, we don't see that what they gave us is free. Simply because we have been buying the textbooks. We have been doing everything. And right now, we know the boarding fee we have been paying has increased. So I think the government should come in and subsidize us, so we the poor people can send our children [to school]. Without the subsidy, we the poor people can never send our children to secondary school. So we are appealing to the government to direct a little of what they have done to help us. Because all is not well in our education system. The government is doing a bit but it should step in [more aggressively], otherwise only the rich people can send their children to school. As somebody said, those who are rich will always be richer. (09/01/97)

There are genuine fears of an economically tiered school system. The children of poorer families facing financial hardships may suffer the most. Gigi, therefore, wants help for poor parents. Parents, educators and the children themselves are aware of the problem facing poor families. Many female participants made reference to the extra work mothers take on. For example, Madam, the local Queenmother, points out that some parents do not seem to involve themselves very much in their children's school. When asked if she knows any such parents, she replies in the affirmative:

> Some parents do not involve themselves in their children's schooling. Yes I know some... [and] it is mainly due to financial problems. *[When you say financial problems, what do you mean?]* For some parents they may have money, but it is their habit ... they do not see the value in education. As a result of this, some parents may not involve themselves in their children's schooling. (10/08/97)

Attending to financial needs and worries may give the impression that the parent is less interested in the child's education. When broached further to explain her earlier assertion that some parents do not involve themselves in their children's schooling, she offers this analysis:

> Every human being loves what is beautiful. Every parent would love to do the best for their children. On the other hand if the parents do not have good jobs, it becomes difficult. It may appear as though such parents do not know what is right. It is all due to financial problems. (10/08/97)

Thus, it is financial limitations that may hinder a parent providing the required resources and tools necessary for the child to succeed in school. Other parents were less careful in blaming individual greed as a possible cause of parents' inattention when it comes to their children's education. Mina, another parent-teacher, asserts:

> There are some parents, especially those who are traders, and I don't know whether it is their educational background or their mentality, [but] they just want to make money to look after the children but don't have personal time for their wards. They just want to go and bring the money home, so they leave money in the house for when the child is up. So maybe by the time the child gets up the mother is already gone; both parents are gone and the money will be there. [It doesn't matter] whether [the child] washes

or not, [he or she] just takes the money and comes to school. (08/27/97)

The need to put food on the table presents the parent with a challenge and may give the appearance that she or he does not have the time to teach the children attend PTA meetings or discuss their children's schooling with teachers. But as already noted, many parents insist this is not an excuse for failing to keep up with their children's educational needs. Other parents argue that a child's physical absence from school cannot be translated or accepted to mean that a parent is disinterested in the child's schooling. While acknowledging the issue of class and poverty, Gona, a mother of six, points to other directions for parents facing financial hardships:

> A good parent can go to the class teacher and ask about their children's progress, the things they lack, and so on. A good parent also seeks the private help of a teacher, say for home tuition. *[Have you seen or do you know of any parents that don't help with their children's education?]* Many. *[Why do you think that is so?]* Poverty. You know they have to go to farm in search of something to sell; things like firewood, kolanuts, *kontomire* [cabbages] to get money for food. With kolanuts, you have to go very early in the morning. Many parents leave their children at home. They aren't there to see whether their kids go to school or not. When this continues for a while, a teacher may go to [the home to] inquire, because it's our responsibility. When we find out what the matter is, we advise the parents to do their best to send their kids to school. Sometimes we advise the parents to bathe the kids before they go to bed. When they get up early morning to go kola hunting, they should wake the kids up, brush their teeth and oil them. By all means there should be someone to help them dress for school. When it happens like that we go to the parents to advise them so they'll know what to do. *[So when parents indicate that they don't have time, what do you tell them?]* If you know of a means by which they can obtain the things they don't have, you can show them. For instance, if you know of a shop bar owner who needs "pounder" [assistance] , you can direct the parent to that place so they can make some income with which to look after their kids. (09/03/97)

Embedded in many of the statements are popular refrains about youth and schooling: parents need to make the time to care for their kids; the teacher is there to help the parent and the child; children must fulfil their end of the bargain; and parents need to realize that while money is important there is much more to adult responsibility than providing material needs for children. These themes recur throughout the interviews with parents, especially when they are discussing the role of the parents (the home) in the child's education. There is reference to differences between those who can provide for their children's daily care and additional school supports, and those who work extra in order to provide the basics that will enable the children to stay in school in the hope of having better employment and financial prospects than their parents. Children in the latter case often refer to the hope of pursuing a career that will give them job satisfaction in terms of both enjoying the work and receiving the remuneration that will enable them to provide for themselves, their children and their parents.

Throughout the narratives, there is reference to parents who do not have the resources to adequately provide for their children's daily care and their schooling needs. In some of these cases, the children are seen as a source of family labour and income. Viewing children as part of the family economic unit carries responsibilities (helping with day to day care of the home and contributing financially) which frequently place these children at a disadvantage academically. In cases where students receive scholarships or financial assistance (allowance) to be in school, it is widely accepted that the parents may need this financial assistance to fulfil their responsibilities. It is pointed out in some of the interviews, that some parents come to the post-secondary institution around the time the student receives the school allowance. In such cases, attending school is seen as a source of family income.

Students also discussed and described their understandings of parental involvement and responsibility. They spoke of the differential access to a good education based on parental ability to pay fees and contribute in other ways to their education. Abba, a female high school student in SS3, points to the dilemmas that students face which also create anguish for the parents:

> [*Do you stay with your parents at home?*] Yes, I stay with my mother. [*So your father is not staying with you? Is your mother involved in helping with your education?*] Yes. [*How much is she involved in your education?*] She was educated but not as much as I am. So I'm praying that I manage. She comes and tells me to go and learn so that I can get a good job in the future. [*Apart from the advice what else?*] (Long silence) [*What else apart from the advice?*] By giving me money for school everyday. [*She gives you money for school everyday?*] Yes ... and she buys

MORNING THUNDER CAFE
557 LAURENCE ST
QUINCY, CA. 95971
530-283-1310

MERCHANT ID: 385200000065831
DATE: 09/20/06 9:50:00 AM

* VOID SALE *
RECORD NUMBER: 005
SERVER: 7
ACCOUNT: ************6014
CARD TYPE: VISA
TRAN TYPE: VOID SALE
AUTH CODE: 474202

AMOUNT: 60.14

TIP: _____

TOTAL: _____

THANK YOU.
CUSTOMER COPY

me some attire when I'm in need of it. *[What about your fees and the rest?]* She is not the one who pays the fees. That's why I didn't mention the fees. It's my father who pays the fees for me. *[I see so your mother is … ?]* The one who gives me food … food when going to school, then after school. For fees its my father who pays. *[What about maybe after school—how much is your mother involved in your education? Does she ask you, for example, what you learned, if you have any assignments, and so on?]* No. It's my father who would ask me what I learned today. (09/21/97)

The differential in parents' duties can be read along gender, class and age lines. In fact, the above narrative points to the need to more closely examine a single mother's struggle to provide for the daily care of her daughter. The cost of a child's daily upkeep is not covered by the father's payment of the school fees. There is also the father's expectation of power that comes with paying the fees in contrast to the mother's lack of power for her hard work in providing for her daughter's food, shelter, clothing and daily spending money often required for school. This and other narratives point to the possibility of a power imbalance and the expectations demanded of children by fathers who cover the fees because their income is greater. The issue of parent gender roles is taken up more extensively in the discussion on cultural attitudes and expectations of single- and two-parent families.

Providing basic support, textbooks and paying school fees are seen as critical to supporting students in school. An inability to do so is a clear definer of inequitable access to a good education for children from families whose financial resources are minimal. It is important to note that in the interviews with parents and high school students, there was extensive dialogue on fees, the cost of care, ability to purchase textbooks, transportation and so on. In interviews with teachers and with post secondary students (in teacher training), there was some discussion of these issues, but it wasn't as extensive in comparison to the concerns of high school students and their parents. Students in the teacher-training institute receive a monthly financial allowance from the government to help alleviate some of their financial constraints. However given the financial limitations and concerns of parents and students, the cost of education cannot help but be one of the more critical aspects that needs to be seriously addressed.

Aki is a high school student in SS2 who clearly understands the connection between educational success and having funding needs met:

> Being able to complete [school] successfully depends on your parents. [For] some of us, our parents are poor. Others they are rich. If you want to complete this syllabus before taking the exam, simply you will want to take classes from background masters [teachers] who come to your house teaching here and there. Take extra classes. Get fees from your parents to attend classes. And, stick constantly to your books. (10/07/97)

Aki points to the importance of extra classes, hard work and financial security from parents as successful schooling strategies. He concedes that money is important and that right now the government is not doing enough to bear the cost of youth education. So family income is crucial and has a direct effect on chances of school success. He points out that his parents are heavily involved in his schooling by providing money for extra and remedial classes. In addition, his parents perform other responsibilities:

> They feed us. They buy clothing and all this sort of thing for us. They pay our school fees, [and buy] our textbooks. The government only takes on a ... [supplementary amount] ... [Parents] pay over seventy per cent where the government pays only thirty per cent ... [But] we also have the Parent Teacher Association. Parents come here to discuss things with the administration and think about how [to help]. (10/07/97)

When asked to clarify what parents do, apart from paying the fees and being involved in the Parent Teacher Association, to show that they care about their children's education, he retorts:

> That's really going to depend upon me [i.e., the individual]. At times if I have good behavior, anything that I ask of them they will do for me. If they ask me [to do something] or they send me someplace, I have to be willing to go. I have to accept their demands at anytime. I have to be respectful, obey instructions and take constant instructions, [and] I take part in household chores. (10/07/97)

He acknowledges the role of the student in meeting her or his obligations and responsibilities. Thus, it is a question of matching rights with responsibilities. Aki also notes that his parents "do come to school, not only for PTA meetings but they come to school to see how [I am] doing ... [and I am] ... very glad about that" (10/07/97). His narrative points to the support poor students need from their parents in order to do well in comparison to economically privileged students. The huge financial burden that parents carry to ensure that their children have the educational opportunity to succeed places added expectations on students to do well. Throughout the narratives there are references to students of privilege not having to work as hard as those from less affluent homes.

> If we say one is rich, it simply means he is given a lot of money—a huge amount of money that he brings to school and then spends nonsensically. What I'm saying is because the person knows he is given a great deal of money he is not going to focus on his books. Instead, [he'll spend] the money, pick a friend and do whole lot of bad things. I can give an example: —In school, those who have money try to influence other good friends [to win] their company and then they do bad things. They never study. They know they have a better future. (10/7/97)

Throughout the interviews, less affluent students make references to the need to do well, to respect, obey, contribute and to give back. This ties back to the issue noted earlier regarding the power and expectations that come with paying fees and other costs of education. There is this implicit and explicit sense that parents who sacrifice such a financial investment have certain expectations. Often the one who is seen to foot the school bill is the male parent. The costs and contributions of the female parent are often less visible.

Cultural Capital

Educational Background of Parents

Thus far, the discussion has examined individual parental responsibilities from the perspective of class in terms of financial capital. There is also extensive discussion on class that would fit into Bourdieu's (1996) analysis of cultural capital. Taking this perspective, parental ability to help is also dependent on their educational background. In this, the tasks of educationally involved parents are made easier if parents recognize the importance of being well informed about the issues affecting the schooling of their children and they understand the processes of schooling (i.e., curriculum, student evaluation, teacher training, school governing structures, educational policies and practices). Usually, if parents have moved through the various stages of schooling themselves, it is easier for them to have a deeper, broader and more detailed understanding of the educational processes and politics of schooling. It is important, then, to tie the discussion into the role of the parents as guides and how they understand success within the context of their own educational training and upbringing. The question of cultural capital in terms of educational background enables some parents to help their children with the subject matter. The role of guide is, in many ways, tied to their ability to understand the value of education, to understand how the system works, what is expected of them in terms of helping with homework, paying fees for extra tutoring, purchasing textbooks and how to effectively advocate on behalf of their children. Furthermore, the issue of cultural capital questions the value of education and the differential definition of success based on values in the family and the community.

Momoh, an educator with eight children in the Ghanaian public school system, has an interesting reading on the value of parental education. When speaking about how parents can and do help their children with homework, he exemplifies particular constraints that parents may face in meeting their obligations and responsibilities to their children. He discusses the privilege of being an educator himself and how this better enables him to monitor, guide and teach his children, compared with other parents:

> *[I would like to know some of the strategies that you use at home to help your ward "become something in the future"? I remember you made mention of giving your child extra tutoring at home.]* (laughter) If I should say so! I have learned about six subjects at the advanced level. At the O level I learned about ten subjects. So, in fact I have access to information. I have so much. So I teach him myself. When he comes back from school, the one at secondary school, I go through his notes. In fact, I made him choose the same subjects I did. I've got all the materials I used, and I've been borrowing them from the library and they are there. I also have those that I bought. So he has access to these things and I have been asking him questions, teaching him and he's been writing back. So I've been monitoring [his school work]. You know, from time to time, when I visit him at school, I'm able to deduce the progress of [his] work and then [I] advise him to redirect his learning and to make the best out of the time. As for the younger one, the one in the primary school, my wife has

been taking care of her. So in fact more or less we are doing our best. (08/11/97)

Momoh admits his own educational background has been helpful and since he knows the subjects his child is taking at school he is able to assist him with his homework. As an educator, he also values constant monitoring, supervision and guidance of the student. Not all parents have the skills to carry out their role in the way Momoh does, but it is important for a parent to be, as he says, "there for the child at all times."

The role of parent as guide is critical to helping children develop responsible study habits and selecting good subjects. It is also critical in encouraging them to find career directions that fit well with their vocation and desires, and also have a practical focus that will help them find employment so they can support their families when they become adults. This is where the parents' knowledge of schools comes into play and why it is important for schools to work with the local knowledges of parents, guardians and elders. Schools must bring adults into the school to actively collaborate as partners interested in the development of educational programs. The possibilities for involvement can cover a wide range of activities, among them assisting with the teaching of local culture. Seeing parents as teachers and guides also breaks down the walls separating schools from their local communities.

In speaking about their roles as guides, parents often navigate between their children's desires, interests and choices and what they as parents perceive to be in their children's best interest. In responding to how parents balance different expectations of children and adults, Tano, another parent-teacher, reasons:

> [Do you discuss with your children the type of jobs they will want to do in future?] The older one will be entering training college this academic year. The next one indicated he's not interested in teaching, so he chose art. But my concern is that after studying art he has to go [and] teach and if he is not interested in teaching, then I don't know. We have to wait for him to finish and decide what he wants to do. The eldest intends entering training college this year. [So when your child chooses a particular program and you are not happy with it, how do you approach it?] You see, when you try to interfere with what your child is interested in you may end up getting them to drop out of school. So when my child declares his intention in some job area, I have to support him ... because our eldest child, for instance, he

was going to technical and his father asked him to go into business. But just after the first year he was thinking of coming back home because he was not doing well. (09/15/97)

Parents have the critical role of serving as sounding boards for youth. It is only as a listener that the parent can effectively play the role of an advisor and counsellor for the learner. When it comes to schooling and educational matters, Nsaawa, a mother, speaks on the importance of resolving tensions, conflicts and differences between parents and their children:

> *[Assuming you had had a disagreement with any of your children about their choice of work, what would you have done? Let's take your son, who you said was a very good student. Let's say you wanted him to do medicine and he insisted on being a teacher. What would you have done?]* I wished one of my children would become an engineer. But you don't put so much pressure on people. Especially with the eldest, I was happy with his choice because I believed he was setting the pace for the others. And, I hoped that one of them would end up being an engineer. I didn't reach his level of education, so when he said he liked teaching it helped because the others emulated his example. One of the young ones got a scholarship to go to SSS. Now, he's preparing to go to university.

Nsaawa admits her limitations in terms of not having the educational background to assist her son at the advanced levels. But she insists that by not putting pressure on her child yet offering support and guidance she has been effective in helping him achieve his aspirations. It is better that a parent helps the child make the right decisions rather than forcing a certain interest upon the child. Sometimes it helps when children have some useful examples to emulate. Older siblings who find their way through the school system also play a significant role within the family unit, as may aunts, uncles, cousins, neighbours and friends who have educational experience. When asked if family members encouraged or discouraged her from going to school, Gina, a female student in the Teacher Training College, replied:

> Yes, my family members encourage me to stay in school because all my cousins ... are well educated. So, when they come to our house they tell me how school is and that how when you educate yourself you gain from it. So they influence me, encourage me to learn and sometimes advise me, too. (07/09/97)

However, it is important not to limit the involvement and influence of parents who haven't gone to school. Antwiwaa, a mother, says she recognizes the importance of education because she never went to school herself. She insists she has always been a source of guidance and counselling to her children. Asked to give some specific and concrete examples, she responded:

> The ways in which I help them is that I help them with my strength ... I advise my female children to work hard at school so that in future when I am not around they will be able to take care of themselves. I do not do government work. I do petty trading to help them. Even when their father lost his job, I took over and helped through petty trading. When I run out of money, I go to ask someone to help me by loaning me some money, until such time that God will give me some so that I can use it to help the children with their schooling. So I am also helping. *[Why do you think parents should involve themselves in their children's schooling?]* The children have come to the world through us, so in every way it is the parents' responsibility to help the child. If you send the child to school and you are not able to help the child, it creates problems. If it is a female she ends up leading a wayward life. She ends up following boys. If it is a male, he ends up a truant or maybe a thief. As such the children cannot achieve their goals. This is why parents should involve themselves in their children's education. *[If you have a friend who has children and says she does not have time with her children's education, what advice will you give her?]* I will advise her to try and help the children. Even if she is not working I will show her how I go about my trading. There are times when I buy the items on credit. I can even go with her so that she can also buy some of the items on credit and sell. I will show her how I manage the petty trading so that she can use it also to help her children in their schooling. (09/08/97)

When this mother talks of "strength," she is referring to material, physical and emotional strength as social supports for her children. She needs to be strong for her children's sake. She will sacrifice for the children and do all what she can to assist with their schooling. She worries about what will happen to her children if they do not pursue their education. As a woman trader with mothering responsibilities, she notes the advice she gives to her female children regarding the connection between schooling and employment. But she also speaks of her concern and responsibility as an adult in monitoring the emotional and moral development of her adolescent children. She notes risky behaviours for all youth but separates her overall general concerns along gender lines. With different responsibilities, concerns and difficulties she has as a mother and a trader, she highlights the importance of parents socially supporting each other. She is willing to take time to help other parents find ways to support and enhance their children's education.

On the Notion of "Success": Value of Education and Future Security

For many parents, educators and students, education can provide the tools and the means by which they may become successful in society. But education is not simply viewed as a means to individual accomplishment. In fact, the Ghanaian participants brought a very nuanced understanding to school and social success. Some see a linear progression, while others challenge such thinking. Mina, a parent-teacher we met earlier, sees success in this way:

> The society as a whole has got its standard by which they assess someone. Therefore, if you are able to achieve that end it is assumed that you are a successful person. *[So what does that mean?]* In Ghana, if you say academically you are successful that means maybe you attended university or you had your education outside. Being able to get to the university or to go outside depends on the individual not the parents alone—it's the effort the parents put in and the effort the child too puts in ... We have SSS [and] if you are able to successfully go through the JSS, the SSS and [then] enter the university, polytechnic or the training college; well, in that sense, you've made your mark and you are going to be gainfully employed. So your success has been crowned now. You will be able to attain the qualifications to make it. *[So your definition then is still focussing on academic success. What about the social?]* That also counts. *[In what ways?]* If you are able to attain academic success it helps socially, because you are going to be gainfully employed and you are going to contribute your quota to society. So in both ways you are successful but if you are not able to attain an educational qualification, it will be difficult. If there is no money or capital coming home to help you, you will not be able to make it. (08/27/97)

In defining her idea of success, Mina alludes to the intellectual ranking and the ritual of going through hierarchical stages of the academy.

Reaching the top (a university education) is crowned with good employment. It is this intellectual passage that also grants the social recognition of success. Without the educational qualification, it is more difficult to be seen as socially successful. Okolie has been teaching accounting in the school for a number of years. He is aware of what it means to be successful and what is required of parents who assist their children:

> Most parents consider success [in school] to be coming out successfully in examinations. But, I think it is more than that. After coming out successfully, you must expect that your children ... will lead very good lives, will be able to cope, will be a good mixer and will be tolerant. All these things are provided by both the school and the home. So after your child comes out with flying colours [academically], you should also expect that he is morally good and that [he does] all that I have mentioned. (09/12/97)

The school may grant the credentials of academic success based on the ability of the individual and the existence of home/family support to achieve academic excellence. But to Okolie, social success is heavily (not solely) dependent on the home and the community, on the morals and values adults impart to children. Teaching youth to be responsible citizens may start at home within families but such an education needs to be formally reinforced by the school. Some parents distinguished between schooling and education, claiming that much of what may be taught in schools today is not necessarily education but simply academic learning that did not include the knowledge/s of what it takes to be a citizen, a community person with understandings of local culture, history/heritage and language. They see education as all encompassing in terms of material, physical, intellectual, social, spiritual, emotional and psychological development of the learner. In this vein, parents and educators speak of the high premium and value of education.

The issue of future security comes up repeatedly as an important justification for children to take schooling seriously. Bonse has taught in the school system for over twenty years. As a teacher-parent, she had this to say on the value of education and students' future success:

> Unlike long ago, when the early people had forests [and] they farmed and they gave their farm to their children, these days there are no farms. Land is difficult to acquire and for that matter the child's land is his brain. So he has to make sure that he learns hard when it is time for him to learn now. So that in the future he may

make the best use of his knowledge. Because they say "Knowledge is Power." (10/19/97)

Education is seen as the most important legacy a parent can bequeath to the child. Today it is no longer the land but education that is the source of income. To this educator and mother, the question of what constitutes school success for a child is significant. Success, to her, is the development of the skills, character, and talent that will make one enjoy life in the future. In other words, the question of success and future security are linked:

What will help a child to be successful in education is ... [foremost] the child's willingness to practice what has been taught and his character. You see, somebody may get aggregate twelve but ... his bad character will not help him in the future. So if you do well and you have a good character and you actually practice what you are taught, no matter what your area of specialization ... you will be successful in life. *[So being successful in life, having good morals and intellect would be your identification mark for a successful student?]* Yes. The intellect; not necessarily meaning somebody who is academically inclined, but somebody who has developed in his area of specialization, a good character. Somebody may not be good academically but he may be good in doing something with his hands. If the person is able to develop that area and practice that with good morals or conduct that will earn him something, somewhere in the future. But [having many] degrees and [being] morally unsound, you see, that will not earn him anything and he will be a problem to himself and even to society. (10/19/97)

The talk of good/bad and unsound morals and character is all in direct and indirect reference to the local discourses around what it takes to become not only an academic scholar but also a responsible citizen. This is what education should be about. It is to develop the individual into a social and responsible person who uses her or his knowledge not simply for individual advancement but to enhance the community. In other words, it is not just what one acquires through schooling and education for oneself, but how the knowledge helps one meet her or his obligations, duties, and responsibilities as a member of a community. How one matches rights with social responsibility is what can be termed a more nuanced interpretation of the relationship between education and success.

To summarize, the basic parental responsibilities are seen to be helping the child meet her or his obligations to self and society while at the same time, achieving educational credentials. The educator Momoh expresses this emphatically:

> We are not talking about anything [difficult] ... In fact, if you want to involve yourself in your child's education you should first, be ready to take on the onus and responsibility of funding your child's education, making things available for the smooth running of the learning process. Second is effective control—you will have to control his [or her] learning. Third—supervise. Fourth—liaise with the teachers to actually [monitor] the child's performance. Although you will get the terminal report and read it so that you know the performance, you will have to go down to the teachers. In fact, all the teachers of my ward know me very well, because I always go to them and get first-hand information from them. So, you will have to keep in touch with the teachers who are monitoring [your child] so that if there are other deviations, [or] if there are any bad [behaviour] that the child is trying to adopt, you can effectively correct it. I have also mentioned that if you are not disciplined you cannot learn. [It is important to team up] so that the child gets the best out of that. So you find, you monitor, you also control and you supervise. You have to be there to see how your child is progressing. I mean, ask [about] his [or her] problems. You know, [the child] has to participate so much in it. He [or she] comes out with problems and you find solutions to them. You go to the teachers and ... you sit down [with them], so you know the stakeholders. The government has played its part and you as a parent, you have to put in your best. The teachers are putting in their best so you have to be there too. You control the child, supervise the child with the teacher so that you can make the best out of the whole thing. (08/11/97)

Momoh lays out a course of action that parents and guardian can follow in order to understand their roles and responsibilities in supporting the child as well as building connections between the families, the community and the school. By doing so, it is possible to strike meaningful working partnerships among teachers, educators, parents, students and local governmental structures and authorities. In order to understand these structures and how they can work together effectively to enhance learning, we must also understand the challenges associated with the economics of schooling.

The Economics of Schooling: Resourcing Education

The theme "economics of schooling" elicited many strong responses from study participants. Throughout the interviews with parents, educators, teachers and students on the broader issue of educational responsibility, there is extensive discussion on educational funding and the role of the reforms, government, communities, the PTA, and parents in the joint funding of education. Based on the interviews, it can be safely said that Ghanaian parents worry daily about the problem of rising educational cost and educational accessibility. Bonse, a long-standing educationist and mother notes that socio-economic class differences have implications for schooling:

> Yes, the differences have influence on the students. For example, somebody from a rich family may be able to pay his fees at once. He can buy books recommended by the teachers and can even go to some bookshops to buy books on his own for the child. Because the child has tools for learning, he learns easily. On the contrary, somebody from a poor home may even come to school without food. Psychologically he is debased and in the long run you find him at the bottom. So children from rich homes do better than children from the poorer homes. *[Having said that, is there anything that the school is doing to help bring up people from the low-income group so that they can improve on their performance?]* We organize extra classes for the students and the fee we charge is low so that the poor people can participate. Apart from that, we invite students from poor homes here and advise the parents to do their best to help them supply their children's needs. *[Do the teachers specifically pay a little bit more attention to these [disadvantaged] students?]* Definitely and not just schools, [so do] parents and local communities. (10/19/97)

Bonse shows that educators are aware of the problem of access and particularly the emotional and psychological results of economic hardships for families. Teachers help out in many ways. But, families and communities also have important roles to play. When asked to speak directly to how her school deals with the different needs of students, she retorts: "Well they do, but not often because of the large number of the children in classes. In a class you may have fifty-eight to fifty-nine students to one teacher. Individual attention is relatively low. Because of the large number of classes, the teachers don't have enough time for such work. However, they are trying to cope with the problem" (10/19/97).

Akua, a female high school student, reinforces the hardships students face. She notes how the issue of providing resources for education presents additional challenges for poorer families. She argues that it is tough coming to school if you are from a poor home: "…because if you are from a rich home there are textbooks that you can buy, but if you don't have money and your parents cannot afford it, it is very difficult to buy textbooks. *[Do you know some students whose parents cannot afford to buy textbooks?]* I [have] a friend Ruby [who] always learns from other friends' books" (08/14/97). Clearly, there is another layer of parents' involvement in their children's education that goes beyond basic responsibilities for daily care, ensuring school attendance and the monitoring of homework. It is that of providing textbooks and tutoring. How do parents, students and educators define this parental responsibility? Parents with the resources provide their children with extra classes and assistance in areas in which they need help. In many cases, the teachers themselves provide the extra classes for a fee. Students who do not have access to these classes speak of their disadvantage in relationship to other children. They speak of the importance of having peers (as friends) who are diligent in their schooling. In that way, students who receive extra classes because their parents can afford to pay for them often help out their less-affluent friends by working with them on homework assignments, sharing textbooks and sharing the knowledge learned in the classes. Some of the parents who could provide academic assistance by purchasing textbooks and paying for extra classes spoke of welcoming their children's friends into their homes and sharing these resources with them as a way of contributing to the education of all children. But they also spoke of the need to correct this inequity, pointing out that all children should have access to textbooks, science resource centres, equipment, and other materials whether or not their parents can afford to pay for them.

Students of less affluent homes spoke of the unfairness of classroom teachers being the ones who provide the extra tutoring in the evenings or on weekends. The problem they identified was critical. Often, the classroom lesson that is directed to the entire class is filled with references to the tutorial of the previous evening. Some students even complained that teachers would not teach as they should in order to recruit students to their tutorials. The solution proposed by the study participants was for teachers to have adequate training, resources and remuneration so they can teach all students.

All were adamant that teachers should not have to depend on providing extra classes to supplement their income. It is interesting to note that teachers critiqued their teaching conditions during their interviews, yet the practice of tutoring some but not all students, which was a recurring theme in students' narratives, was not discussed by the teachers in their narratives.

Students frequently spoke of bringing problems at school to the attention of their parents so that the parents could then take up the issues at school. If it was specific to a teacher-student relationship, the expectation was that the parent would take it up individually with the teacher, school principal or both. If it was a practice that was common and seen to be problematic and unfair, the student would bring it to the attention of the parents who were involved in the Parent Teacher Association (PTA) so it could be addressed at that level. As noted above, some students complained of teachers who taught to the tutored students rather than to the whole class. Other students whose parents made the financial sacrifice of paying for the extra lessons sometimes took on the role of consumers evaluating whether or not the class was worth the cost. If it wasn't, the students would inform their parents. The parents would then take it up with the teacher. In general, the financial sacrifice made by parents was not lost on the students and teachers. Gina, a female high school student, was clear about how financial worries affect academic progress: "Concerning my home, the only thing that affects me in my school is paying the school fees ...There are times [during school sessions] that my father would get the money to pay. At times they delay [payment] because the money is not there. And, that affects my studies" (07/09/97).

Students are active agents in assessing how the policies and practices of schooling affect them, but also how they affect their fellow students. Interestingly, the comments of Ampene, a female high school student whose parents can afford to pay for her schooling, is aware of how schooling practices can be unfair towards students from lower incomes. She uses the payment of school fees and its impact on poorer families to make a point about educational inequity. In one of the exchanges, Ampene expressed the following:

> It's very difficult because now the school fees are very high. So if you are not able to pay that money you will be sent home and that's making education for the poor a problem. *[How would you suggest that we change that?]* Maybe the school fees should be reduced a little so

that those who are poor can send their children to school. *[If someone can not pay his or her fees what happens?]* The person is sent home to either go and bring the school fees or to go and call the parents to explain why he or she didn't pay the fees. *[So if a parent comes and says I cannot pay because I do not have money, what happens?]* They will ask [that] when you have the money to come and pay, [and] when that time comes and you don't come and pay then it means you didn't ... *[keep your promise?]* Yes. *[So a student can be sent home or expelled from school if they cannot pay their fees!]* Yes. (08/15/97)

Ampene expressed strong concern that such practices can lead to the possibility that an otherwise bright student may have her or his academic dreams cut short if parents cannot pay the soaring school fees.

Resourcing Education: The Challenge and Possibilities of Gender and Single Parent Families

Schooling and financial worries play out differently depending on how families are constituted. Issues and questions relating to gender that emerged in the interviews include parental involvement, how students perceive the strengths of two-parent households, the particular struggles of single mothers and the question of whether or not fathers separated or divorced from the mother of the children should continue to provide for their education. Mensa, a parent-teacher, reasons that it helps when both parents live together:

> To be frank, when both parents live together it is very good ... [and] it helps in the upbringing of the child. It means [both parents can help] the child with [his or her] studies as compared to when the child lives with just one parent. Sometimes the child may not be living with the parents but with a guardian. I notice that guardians are not able to help the children because the children are made to help at home by trading. What happens is that the child's mind goes off education. And [then, he or she] may end up not finishing school. If both parents live together, you are aware of how much you are investing in your child's education. (08/28/97)

The metaphoric interpretation is that both parents constitute four eyes and four hands that watch, guide, and assist the child. With this the child is less likely to go astray. It takes both parents who are committed to their child's welfare to push the child through school and not away from it. When asked to explain why it is that some parents cannot help their children in school, she adds:

> First of all, when the parents are not financially secure it makes it a
> bit difficult. The money is something that is very important.
> Sometimes too, the parents get divorced and when this happens
> the parents' fight over who should look after the children. When
> this happens some of the children drop out of school. [If] the child
> goes to school, sometimes it is a mess—The child is in school
> today. Tomorrow he is not. This affects the child's education and
> the child may end up a truant. A truant is a child whose parents
> assume that the child is at school but before they know [it] the
> child is hanging out with children who do not go to school. They
> may stop going to school altogether. Some may even end up as
> thieves. So, divorce is a big problem for the education of children.
> (08/28/97)

Mensa does not problematize the traditional view of two-parent
families as "fit or ideal" but sees that single-parent homes can be
"unfit" for a child. She sees divorce as having a negative influence on
children, no matter what. And she sees that it places a burden on a
single parent that may be too much to carry. Single parenthood in
those circumstances usually refers to the responsibilities mothers take
on. Gona, a parent-teacher, also agrees that it is necessary to have
both parents around:

> Absolutely, because ... you see, we [the mothers] are always at
> home with the kids, and they [don't] tend to take us seriously. But
> when their father comes and is stern, the children are attentive and
> listen to anything he says. So when the two of us are there to look
> after the kids, it's very good. (09/03/97)

The position she takes is that the father can be a strict disciplinarian,
and that this is something which works to the child's own good. This
reality connects to an earlier discussion on the power the father holds
when he pays the school fees. Here again the comments allude to the
power of the male breadwinner, to the disciplinarian, to the adult.
There is an underlying assumption that an authoritarian relationship
based on the power of gender (male), age (adult) and discipline is
good for the youth. When asked to further explore the perception
that kids in single-parent homes don't do well in school, Gona notes:

> The mother is the one giving primary care. Some guys, when the
> marriage breaks up, push the kids onto the woman and she has to
> do everything. So it happens that when she has to pay something to
> benefit her children's education, she cannot afford it. When
> children are sent home, all she can say is; "Stay home till I get

money." All that while the other children in school are studying. And when it's exam time, such children don't do well. So if both parents will team up to look after the children, it will be ideal. If the mother doesn't get it, the father is there to help and the children progress. (09/03/97)

While this mother does not draw a simple correlation between single parenting and academic failure, she highlights the pressures on single mothers when the marriage breaks down and the fathers abandon their responsibility to their children. The material consequences on the mother who is left to care for the children have implications for her day-to-day family life and for the schooling for her children.

Antwiwaa, who sees herself as a "counsellor" and works as a petty trader, speaks of her struggle to ensure that her daughters do not find themselves in such vulnerable economic positions. She draws on her experience of looking after the family when her husband lost his job as the basis for advising her daughters to get a good education. Her perspective of schooling comes from the experience of a woman whose husband does not get involved. But her position is not a blanket statement on all fathers, for she recognizes that some do get involved. Also, her perspective of life as a trader and a mother contrasts with the views of those who will see trader-mothers as only caring about their business. In her analysis, she recognizes that there are mothers who do not get involved and those who do. But, she also recognizes that financial and work difficulties can make involvement harder. Nonetheless, she agrees that it is important for a child to live in a home with both the mother and father:

> Yes, it is very important. If the parents live together and the child grows up living with them, it is important that the child lives with both parents in the same place. *[While we were talking, you mentioned that when your husband lost his job you helped with your children's education. Do you think it is difficult for a single parent to care for a child, be it the father or the mother?]* It is difficult for one parent to care for a child. Our elders have a saying that one person's hand is not enough to close the eyes of God ... Whatever the situation, it is important that both parents put their heads together to help the child ... [One parent's] efforts will be more than the other but [no matter how] trivial it [is, it] adds up to help the child. (09/08/97)

When questioned to elaborate how divorce can affect a child's schooling, she highlights the question of parental responsibility and how mothers in particular navigate the difficulties:

Most of the time when parents divorce, the men refuse to take care of the children and this affects the children seriously, in so many ways. It could even be that the mother of the children does not have anywhere to live. So when that happens, the children's living situation becomes "half and half" and it is difficult for the children to achieve their goals. On the other hand, if the mother has somewhere to live because she loves her children, she will draw the children to her side and do whatever she can to help her children. *[Do you know any divorced parents whose divorce has affected their children?]* Yes. *[You don't have to mention names.]* I know so many. When such things happen, I always advise the mothers, especially [mothers whose husband] is not helping the children. The Ashanti's have a saying — "you never see a cock with the chicken following it. The chicks always follow the hen". So I advise the mothers that nobody knows why the marriage is broken, so all she has to do is draw the children close to her side because her reward is the children. So I always advise the mothers who are divorced. *[Do you discuss these issues with your husband?]* Yes I discuss it with him. *[What is his take on it?]* As for that man, he has not made up his mind to help the children. All he says is that if the child is prepared to go to school, the child should go and if the child does not want to go to school, he doesn't care. I know that the children are mine and so I am always on their [backs] as compared to their father ... In my case, I am very concerned about the children's schooling as compared to their father. Some men too are more concerned about their children's schooling as compared to the mothers. Some women do not have time. [Often mothers who are traders may] wake up ... in the morning [and be] off. Whether her children will eat or not, does not seem to concern her. A man who is concerned about his children will have time for the children even when their mother is not around to make sure they study hard so that they can achieve their goals. As for me, I am very concerned about my children in order that they can achieve their goals in the future. I continue to encourage them. (09/08/97)

She acknowledges that her husband may have different perspectives on the schooling of their children than she does. But she avoids making sweeping statements. In this same interview, Antwiwaa talks about the importance for girls' education by looking back at history, tradition and culture:

[In the past, the elders did not allow their female children to attend school. These days, things are changing. Why do you think females were not allowed to go to school in the past?] In the past, it was assumed that no matter

how much schooling a female had, she would get married and end up in the kitchen. She would find herself cooking. But we must take note of the fact that as we are developing, women can do the same things as men. As a result of this, where the males are allowed, we should give the females too, a chance. So females should be allowed to school to the same level as men. This is why today we send both males and females to school. I am happy that my male and female children will all be at an equal level in their schooling. *[Currently are there certain jobs that you see as male or female jobs?]* Yes. *[What are some of these?]* Before women could not become soldiers, [or work in] trades like car mechanics, carpentry or masonry. Today some women are masons. I know a woman in Kumasi who has her own shop and is a mechanic. Even driving—formerly only men learnt how to drive. But, I know a woman in Kumasi who has her own bus which she runs from Kumasi to Obuasi. This has been known to be a male job but she is a woman and she is doing it too. Women can be soldiers. Women can work with the police. They can work as wardens and watch over prisoners or help the police force to go on. Before, only men were allowed to do certain things. But today, women can also do them. That is why I am so eager to send my female children to school *[Why is it necessary to send a female to school?]* It is necessary to send the females to school [because] the job that a man can do a female can also do. Previously it was assumed that a woman only cooks and ends up staying in the kitchen. But with the catering in schools these days, females can work to help the government or the society as a whole. This is the reason I want my female children to attend school. (09/08/97)

Antwiwaa sees how times have changed and that traditional views and habits have and can be subverted with powerful knowledge. She sees knowledge as power and believes the education of girls holds the key to female emancipation. Madam, the Queenmother, also presents this view of gender education and echoes Antwiwaa's reading of history, culture and tradition. Madam concedes that boundaries are being crossed and barriers are being broken. The challenge of male education is the same for female education:

In times past, women were not allowed to go to school. The saying was that female education could not be compared to male education. Now you can see that a lot of women attend school …Now, females and males are competing. Some females are even more intelligent than the males. Now every parent seems to see the value of education. No parent in Ghana will forbid a female child from attending school. Educating females has become very important. *[What is the difference between female and male education?]* In my case, my children are all females. I see it this way; they are all the same. I do not see any difference between male or female education. If the female works hard and the male works hard, they will pay the same school fees. If males make it to the secondary school, the females can also make it to the secondary school. If the female is intelligent, she can also make it to the university when the males are entering university. The most important thing is to study. There is no difference between male and female education. (08/9/97)

Ansong is the young daughter of a single mother and is now beginning her teacher-training education. Her mother in the past had the support of her extended family member, specifically, an uncle who at the time had no children of his own. Looking back on her own family experience, Ansong credits her mother for supporting her efforts: "Actually … it is my mother who is [taking care of my schooling]. So I give a lot of credit to her … Sometimes my uncles [help] as well. One of my uncles was helping me but …he also has a child of his own to look after. And [so] now my mother is trying all her best to give me all the necessary things" (09/08/97). Ansong acknowledges that her mother made many sacrifices to help her through school, including turning to the PTA as a place where she could find help. She says her mother regularly attends the PTA meetings, and usually comes back to discuss issues raised at these meeting with her:

Yes, [when she last went] I gave her some things to talk about. I told her that there are certain occasions where we pay for the extra classes but when we go there the teachers don't come. One will come today, but [the next day] the other won't come. And you see, we have many good subjects to study. So if these masters [don't come then in] the end you cannot complete … So I told her to raise the issue that if they are not ready to teach us they should put a stop to it. [And then we'll] know we are not going to have extra classes so that we do not pay anything and [that we can] find some place where you go and the [teachers] are there. When she came back, she said they were trying to discuss this [and resolve that problem. It was agreed that] if they don't come then we should report back to the chairman of the PTA. (09/08/97)

Interrogating Parent Teacher Associations (PTAs): Roles, Duties, Projects and Mandates

Muwanga's (2000) work highlights the extensive literature on the role of PTA's in African education. Much of the debate has centred on the structures and political functioning of these associations and their effectiveness in promoting school change. For some parents, PTAs provide a space and an outlet for dealing with the challenges of schooling (e.g., hardships of educational financing). Some parents see the PTA as a place to voice concerns about the inequities in the school system. Other parents complain that the PTA itself has become an outlet for the rich and most powerful to have their voices heard. The following extensive extract between the interviewer (who was a student leader at his former school) and Okalie (a noted school teacher) is very informative, particularly as the critical voice rings clear:

> [I would like to bring your mind back to an issue concerning the PTAs. At times the executives may decide something for the "moborowas" [the poor/ ordinary people] without their knowledge and just come and dump the decisions on them. For example, they'll decide that students are going to pay a certain amount— maybe these executives are well off and they'll decide that students will pay fifty thousand [cedis], whether these people like it or not.] I think you are right. But you see, it is the complaint of people whenever there is decision making. But we [live] in a democratic world and I don't think the executives will just meet and decide for the rest. Whatever the executive decides, they bring to the members and then they cast a vote. So the majority wins. So personally I disagree with anybody who says that executives, no matter their status, will meet, [make a decision and] then dump it on the "moborowas," as you said. There is always a chance for voting. So if by the way the voting is cast and the majority wins, whichever amount the majority decides to pay is what everybody should pay. But there is one disadvantage; sometimes some parents do not even attend the meetings. And when they do not attend meetings and some decision is taken on their behalf, they think it has been dumped on them, but it isn't so. That majority decision binds everybody who is a member. I remember in our school when they were asked to pay the fifty thousand cedis per child [to help build a jubilee house], the parents who initiated the idea decided to pay that sum. They voted and the majority won. But those people who didn't attend the meeting or who didn't win were still

complaining. If we do that it means we are not pursuing a democratic system. So that is my contribution in connection with that teacher's idea. (09/12/97)

PTA decisions are binding when taken by the majority at a meeting. In his analysis, Okalie makes no attempt to interrogate why some parents fail to show up for such meetings. The concerns over lack of transparency, the growing mistrust of some PTA leadership and the backdoor and arm-twisting tactics that may be adopted only to turn off parents are not seen as major problems. When asked about what happens to a parent who fails to attend a PTA meeting, Okalie responds:

> Well, they have instituted some measures and [one measure is that you] sometimes pay a fee [if you miss a meeting. And, parents are always] encouraged to attend. But …when you charge a fee of say one thousand cedis for your inability to attend a meeting, and the person pays the thousand cedis, he still [won't] get what was really discussed. He was not a party to the decision [that was made in his absence]. So he will grumble, [when] he sees that [the fee for missing the meeting] is high and he cannot afford it. *[I see. The reason I asked my first question concerning the PTA executives making decisions without the knowledge of the "moborowa" is that the floor members [are sometimes given parcels] …At my school the executives met and then they gave us some parcels. For instance, I had a parcel. When I opened the parcel, I saw that it was twenty thousand [cedis]. Others had been given fifteen thousand [cedis] …without the other members knowing. So, when they had the meeting there was a controversy over that issue?][Question of clarification: Are the executives trying to "buy" the members on the floor? Are the executives giving money for certain projects to other members?]* As far as I know, you cannot get everybody to like the executives …Some PTA executives are doing well. They consult their people before they do whatever [they do] because the money is for all of them. So it is very wrong for such things to be done without informing the "moborowas," that is, the floor members. (09/12/97)

In continuing the discussion, Okalie shows how some PTAs have become political tools for hidden agendas that serve parochial interests. He suggests that often times some executives of these associations are more interested in maintaining their legacy than in serving the needs of students and schools:

> I would like to add that the PTA is a good association. And, some executives in the PTA think they have to do something concrete during their tenure. Forgetting that the PTA is an ongoing

[organization, that] it will not end since the school [will continue to] exist. So they are compelled to bring up ideas that will require the payment of heavy, heavy sums of money. For instance when there is a project, some of the executives like to complete the project within their tenure of office so that their name will be put on that project. Somebody will say it was during [so and so's] tenure ... that this was built. Because they want that [so badly], they [may] not care how much parents should pay ... That attitude is not good. So I suggest that ... whenever there is a project, the [executives] should do it gradually, so that people are not [pressured into it]. (09/12/97)

Students also raise the issue of accountability when discussing PTAs. Aki, a high school student shares this concern:

You see, one thing is that the rich people are trying to overreach the poor. They normally decide for us. Rich parents and the poor parents ... don't come together to share ideas. Normally they talk only among themselves. The last time I did research, [I found out that] [to prevent the poor children from coming] to this school [they increased] the fee to 1,005. How are the poor even going to pay 800 cedis let alone 1,005? But now they are being forced to pay [this fee to send their children to this school].

There is a limited amount of spaces and funds to subsidize the children of poor parents. It is easy, therefore, for those with the financial resources to impose an increase in fees so that more spaces are open for students whose parents can pay higher fees and less space is available for students whose parents cannot. The narratives of some of the less affluent students were very vocal about this problem. They highlighted that to gain access to these spaces their parents made great sacrifices in order to pay fees, and the students themselves needed to achieve high grades not only to gain access but also to be granted subsidies that would help them financially. They knew of rich children who did not have the grades but whose parents made financial contributions to the school in order to secure a space for their children. This blatant unequal access does not even take into account the privileges of extra tutoring, the ability to purchase textbooks, parental education and many other extra curricular activities and opportunities.

PTAs have become very powerful organizations and often approve incidental fees that schools charge their students. In the process, the voices of the powerful are heard. Students note that it is the rich parents who are more likely to make decisions without due consultations. Most of these decisions affect the poor and students want to see that changed by the schools. They point out that there must be cordial relationships between the rich and the poor. And if a decision has to be made, it should be made with consultation among all the parents. In fact, there are differing opinions on the role of the PTA, the particular projects it takes up, the assistance it offers in financing education and its mandate and *modus operandi*.

Gina says she regularly attends PTA meetings whenever she is free. She argues that other "parents participate well and the parents have great influence. We meet regularly and then when there is a need for anything, the teachers put it before us especially through the headmaster. We discuss it and if it is necessary then we implement all decisions that we take"(10/05/97). She sees some relevance in the PTA functioning as the meeting ground between teachers and parents and acknowledges that the PTA has some specific roles to play:

> The Parent Teacher Association helps in providing needed articles [publications and reprints of texts] in the school and renovations and so on ... because where the government cannot provide certain amenities in the school the PTA [can help to do so]. (10/05/97)

Gigi, a father who works as a civil servant for the Ministry of Health, heads the local PTA. He is enthusiastic about what PTAs can do to assist local schools and governments meet their obligations to the learners:

> Right now I am the chairman of the LA Primary and JSS PTAs [in name of town] ... Because the government is not able to cope with what you ought to have, we have to help the children. So, I wrote a letter to the district assembly [asking them to give me] that mandate. The teachers have been collecting about a thousand cedis every academic year. With this money I was able to build a KVIP urinal. And, I have made about three hundred dual desks and about forty-six mono desks. We, at the Parent Teacher Association, should help the school and if the government puts a little effort in, we can [both] help the children in their studies. Because I am a parent and my children are attending secondary school, I [have attended] Parent Teacher Association meetings [for some time]. I was with the PTA when we built a library complex for [my children's] school. (09/01/97)

During the interview, there was reference made to a critique that the executives of the PTA sometimes decide for the members and that often these decisions are "dumped on them." Gigi considers this comment:

> Yes it is true. [Often] if you call a PTA meeting, those who are illiterate, who do not know anything about education, won't come. Say if you have about three hundred wards, you are expected to get about two hundred relatives or guardians to attend the meeting. [But when you go to the meeting], you have only thirty people. So these thirty parents will decide for those who did not come. It is not the executives who decide for the parents ... Let's take for instance that we are going to build a library complex for the school. [The parent or guardian has] to come and express [his or her] view. If I tell you we have to pay twenty thousand [cedis], somebody will raise up his hand and tell you twenty thousand is [too much and] we can't pay [that. Let's] pay ten thousand. Then somebody will say fifteen. Then, we will put it [to a vote]. The amount that [the majority chooses is what] we take. So if you don't come and we have only about thirty people ... then the majority have the nod ... This is what is worrying us PTA chair[persons]. You call meetings. They don't come. A parent will tell you, "I don't have time to go. If you go, come and tell me what they say." ... The executives have our own meetings ... Then we [discuss] the agenda before calling the meeting. (09/01/97)

Again, there is little or no attempt to critically interrogate why parents fail to attend meetings. The focus is on a limited reading of "democracy," one where those present at a meeting vote on an issue, and the majority decision is binding! Speaking about the mandate of the PTA, Gigi gladly adds:

> To be a PTA chair[person] you have a lot to do. You have to attend to the children, attend to the teachers, see to it that they actually come to school and do what is necessary for them to do for the children. At times you see a child and ask him, "Why didn't you go to school?" He will tell you, "Our teacher doesn't always come to classes." You will have to find out the reason why the teacher is not attending classes ... You will have to go to the school and have some conversations with the teachers. You will ask them what their needs are, so that you can help them. With this the teacher will have interest in the school and in teaching the children. I have been going there to look at their books ... [observing] how the teachers are teaching the children. If they [need something, they will ask. For example,] if they need jerseys,

> they will come and tell you, "Chairman because we don't have
> jerseys the children can't play." We have the means to buy jerseys
> for them. If a child is going to school barefooted and somebody is
> wearing "kambu" [running shoes], that child may not be happy ...
> If you are able to dress your child well ... he [or she] will tell the
> teacher we are going to school today because the dress is okay.
> These are some of the things we have to do to encourage them to
> study hard. (09/01/97)

By providing certain amenities to schools, acting as counsellors to
teachers, checking on the educational activities of teachers and serving
as watchdogs for parents and local communities local PTAs see
themselves as important links between the local community and the
school. Also, Gigi adds, some of the community responsibilities of
the PTA help in the schooling of all youth:

> My concern is that dropouts may be good at school but because of
> the financial problems ... they can't make it. The question is
> whether the PTA is addressing this problem, so that it will
> recognize that maybe Mr. Donkor's child is doing very well but
> because of financial problems the child is not attending school?
> Can the PTA solicit help from our funds so that we can contribute
> and send the child back to our school? (09/01/97)

When asked about what these associations can do to assist bright and
gifted students from poor homes who may be at risk of dropping out
because of soaring fees? Okalie points to some of limitations in the
work of PTAs.

> Well that has not been the concern for the PTA just because the
> PTA is made up of all parents of all children in the school. I don't
> think it has become our way to think about somebody's child who
> is financially [disadvantaged] ... We think about the general welfare
> of all of our children and our teachers, not just a particular student
> who is financially [disadvantaged]. That hasn't come up at all. And,
> I don't think it is done anywhere. All I know is that probably the
> NGOs and the churches ... come in to help. But ... it isn't on the
> program of the PTA to help financially [disadvantaged] children.
> (09/12/97)

Obviously a major problem is the limited financial resources of PTAs
and the many tasks and responsibilities that these associations are
called upon to perform. But as is also clear from the discussion above,
the nature of a school's PTA is to address the needs of the students
who are in the school not the needs of those who, for whatever

reason, are not attending school. There are many reasons a child may not attend school: parental views on the importance of education; the child may have a learning or physical disability; financial reasons; family problems; transportation and distance; behavioural problems that require special assistance and others. Within the frame of limited educational democracy, as practised within the structure of Parent Teacher Associations, the local community has the responsibility for taking into account the educational needs of all children in the community regardless of their personal abilities (physical and other) and their family situations.

Just as local communities and schools try to assist their own students, discussions on the PTA were in fact laced with what the government should be doing. Gona, a grandmother and retired educator, refers to the "Nkrumah regime" when education was free and "the government spoke of the importance of education being free, without cost of fees or textbooks" (09/03/97). This parent-teacher felt that the current government ought to learn from that regime.

Generally, students, educators, and parents speak positively about the activities of PTAs by providing needed funds to help build school libraries and residences. But there is a sense that local communities and schools need substantial help from the government if education is to be a right for all citizens. Educators lament the working conditions of teachers, pointing to how the local communities, the parents and the government need to work together to adequately deliver the education services that are needed.

Joint Educational Financing: The State, Parents and Local Communities

Mensa, a parent-teacher, uses his professional work as an entry point to discuss the role of the government in education/in schooling. He too laments the poor working conditions of teachers, the absence of incentives and the need to boost morale. He hopes the government will read this study and listen to his concerns:

> As a parent, I am pleading that the government ... provide enough teachers for the children [and do so] quickly. Also, the government should provide the equipment that is needed for teaching the children. To be honest with you, the one who works with the children should eat. So, the teachers should have an increase in salary [so they can] do their work diligently. This is because we all

shop from the same market. We have some people who have been [taught] by teachers and have become successful. You will find these people driving good cars while teachers will be walking to their various destinations. All these things discourage the teacher. So the teachers [salaries] should be raised up too. I am not trying to blow my horn [but I built this] house. And yesterday, a certain woman who teaches at the training college and used to come to our school for teaching practice came looking for me. She did not know my house. So my son-in-law brought her home. She was surprised to know that I lived here and this was my house. She then remarked that I have raised the esteem of teachers. *[I share the same view.]* Do you see what is happening? I have worked for thirty-eight years and why is it that I can't do anything? Putting up this house has not been easy. Considering the fact that I have worked for thirty-eight years. The respect given to teachers is not enough. And, the salary is bad. The government should increase the salary because we do not know where else to get the help we need. (08/28/97)

Mensa wants something to show for his long service to the profession and thinks that unless something is done quickly many people will leave the profession. But the role of the government goes beyond improving the working conditions of teachers to making substantial investment in education. A number of parents, educators and students believe in "cost sharing" in education. But it seems these are the well-to-do families. When asked who should finance education, Nimako, an economist with a well-paying job, responded:

Ah, it's a double-edged sword. It cuts both ways. The government has a responsibility and the parents too have a responsibility. But I would say that the government has the [major] responsibility. The government decides. It is the government that has got to provide the facilities, the buildings, the teachers, and so on. The parents have a responsibility to contribute in the form of physical cash, payment of school fees, and other contributions. It's a two way process. *[Given your background as an economist, what do you think of the days of free education?]* No, I would not ... [call] for free education. I would not want free education because the responsibility on the government would just be unbearable. The parents will have to absorb some of the costs. But then government is becoming too much dependent on the parents now because with this system the parents are expected to pay. School fees put up some of the physical structures and contribute to both the private schools and government schools too. It's too much. (08/16/97)

Another parent-teacher, Mina, agrees that the government has a major responsibility as well as the community:

> Now the community is playing a part. All the same, the government will have to bear most for the running of education. Because everything is community based, the parents contribute in putting up the buildings, furnishing the rooms, and then they pay some money too. I can't say that the government is fully bearing the cost of education. It is now fifty-fifty. (08/27/97)

But she insists that the government cannot shirk its responsibility in the current climate:

> Everybody has got a duty and I think it is the duty of the government to do that. Secondly, you know everybody is paying taxes and we are being told that these taxes are used to provide such facilities for the community ... [As long as we are] paying the taxes, it is the responsibility of the government to provide. And after we have our education, we are coming out to work for the government and the society. So I think the government has a part to play. (08/27/97)

Mensa maintains that the government cannot actually pay for everything and that parents must shoulder part of the burden. When asked where she would draw the line between what the parents should do and what the government should do, she lists the paying of tuition, building the infrastructure, providing school laboratory equipment and textbooks, and paying teachers' salaries as the responsibility of the government.

Nsaawa, a parent, suggests ways for the government to come to the aid of poorer families who cannot afford the cost of schooling for their high-achieving children. When asked what ought to be done for parents who can't pay their children's school fees, she reasons:

> There are some brilliant kids whose parents can't pay their school fees. Sometimes people are compassionate. Say a friend of the parents can take it upon her/himself to look after such children— [giving them] used uniforms [or even buying them new ones]. Most often, this will depend on the child. The [child has] to be good and show promise in [her/his] studies. If that doesn't happen, parents will not pull their weight, let alone outsiders.

She suggests that the same compassion be extended to average students. In fact, she suggest that perhaps some family members would take up the responsibility out of love for their "brother or sister."

Reflecting on the Issues

I have identified four issues related to home (parent/guardian) and community involvement in education: parent-child relations; parent/guardian responsibilities to the child's development/learning; the role of Parent Teacher Associations; family (parents) and local community contributions for funding universally accessible schools. The issues of power, knowledge and discipline emerge within these themes. The question of power in parent-child relations is discussed in terms of parental authority; the schooling of children is also characterized by relationships of power in parent-teacher interactions. As an organization the PTA must also address questions of power in their relationships within group members and in their relationships with the school and other organizations in the community. Which parents exert greater power in the PTA? How does participation in the PTA affect different parents in terms of their acquiring a greater or lesser sense of empowerment? Furthermore, what is the relationship of the PTA to the community in terms of the projects they take up (i.e., building libraries) in comparison to the relationship of the school administration and the government from the perspective of expectations, access to the resources (projects), which projects are identified by whom, why and which are taken up?

Parental Involvement

In the study, many parents engaged in the dialogues with the dual categories of parents and teacher with others just as parents. There is differentiation in parental involvement by class in terms of the cultural and material capital they posses to help with their children's schoolwork. Among the factors strongly differentiating parental abilities to help with schoolwork are the financial abilities of parents to purchase additional resources to help their children (i.e. textbooks and after-school tutorials). The ability to pay the fees and the sacrifices necessary for some parents to pay fees is another strong differentiating class factor. The one responsibility consistently identified as parental involvement by all students is the payment of fees. From extended dialogues, the roles of monitoring and helping with homework, guiding the student's career in terms of advice, relating to teachers and helping with teacher work become important themes. For lower-income students, often the focus of the discussion is on the payment of fees and on providing the essentials of daily care.

The discussion on parental involvement touches on the question of the differential roles of parents and teachers. For many of the study participants, the boundaries are clearly demarcated by parents being responsible for fee payments and daily care, and teachers' responsibility being that of teaching. For others, the separation is not so clear. The importance of ongoing communication between parents and teachers is seen to be critical. But it is teachers who are framing the dialogue on parental involvement. It is significant that in such discussions the term "parent" is not differentiated in terms of mother or father. Yet when the concept is further explored or explored in other contexts there are also references to parents as a unit of two, to mothers, to fathers, to divorced parents or non-two parent families, to single parents, single mothers, guardians and to extended family members. Within Ghanaian communities there are assumed "norms" of what or who a parent is. It is interesting to see how this understanding is being contested in the day-to-day lives of female-headed families, particularly. As noted earlier, discussions about families have tended to separate parent-child relations from parent involvement and parent involvement from PTAs. Yet these separations are not absolute and there are incidences of overlap. But for those for whom the roles of teachers and parents are demarcated, this separation is significant. This is because teachers who are also parents are seen to be continually involved in schooling of the youth and as members of PTAs. For those parents who are not schoolteachers, a discussion of parent-child conflicts often brought to the fore the issue of parental authority and tradition.

Conventionally, the teacher is there to answer any questions the parent/guardian may have about their child's school progress and to inform them of any problems. Critical educational practice can turn this on its head and use the parent/guardian-teacher meeting as an information gathering opportunity for the teacher. The teacher can prepare questions to bring to a parent/guardian-teacher night so as to find out about the views of parents, guardians, students, the community outside the school and the potential for interaction between parents and school. There are questions that teachers, parents, administrators and other community members can ask about the relationship of the school to the community and vice versa.

- What concerns do local communities' have about schooling?
- What are community and parents'/guardians' expectations of teachers and of learners?
- What makes for a good teacher? A good school?
- How does the community and the school administration engender an environment/a culture in the school that supports the learning of all children (individually and as collective group) and the work of teachers?
- What supports do parents/guardians, teachers, students need to carry out their work as students, as teachers, as parents?
- How can parents/guardians and teachers help each other in their work of educating the young?
- In what ways might parents have input into and/or monitor what is taught?
- How can the local community participate in evaluating educational policies, schools, teaching practices and curricula?
- How can the school become a meeting site for advocating for services/programs for children, for youth, for families, for the community?
- How can the community ensure that adequate materials are available, are developed and that these materials are richly diverse in their subject matter and reflect many ways of observing, being in, communicating and acting in the world?

Although there are times and situations when some parents are very involved in their children's lives and with the school in relation to their child, it does not necessarily mean that these parents will be active in the PTA. Nevertheless, the importance of parental involvement with the PTA is noted as one way of knowing how the school influences the child and an important way to understand the potential social problems being dealt with (e.g., peer pressure, teachers not coming to tutorials). There is a general sense that this knowledge can help parents in their role of guiding and monitoring their children's development. There is also the recognition that some parents may not get involved with the school· or with the PTAs for any number of reasons. But just as there is overlap in the way PTAs can help parents' traditional role as guide, involvement in the PTA could bring the needs of lower income children to the fore of school policy and resources if, for example, groups of low-income parents were to become more involved. However, low-income parents often are not or cannot get involved. Consequently, the participants clearly articulated the concern that the needs of low-income students are not always addressed. As in other countries, some low-income parents who do try to get involved frequently find that they do not have the material and cultural power to carry the issues. Very often, parents see the PTA not as venue for addressing issues that affect students as a body or the needs of specific groups of students but as another venue for advocating on behalf of their children individually. This can cause inter-personal problems within the PTA between the executive and the general membership, particularly between those who participate regularly and those who attend meetings more sporadically. This can be further complicated by parents not understanding the mandate, procedures and boundaries of the organization. Study participants who were PTA executive members spoke of these concerns. The voices of other parents, guardians and caregivers pointed to other concerns such as the particular projects the PTA takes up, and the issues of participation and obstacles to participation.

Curriculum and Community

On curricular development, parents, guardians, social activists and community workers have a role to play in terms of formal curricular initiatives that promote the inclusion of the social and economic life of the local community, its history, its culture and the goings on of its everyday and its festive days. On the evaluation of existing curriculum materials/resources and the development of new resources, teachers and identified community members can work together. Collectively, the groups can devise procedures for centering/infusing/integrating/synthesizing the local into various aspects of the syllabus. Old and new texts/materials can be critically analyzed for omissions, bias and exclusions of the local collective experiences and individual group identities (i.e. gender, class, ability, sexual identity, race, religion, rural, urban, region and other differences). Direct participation in the class and at the school by parents/guardian and elders is to be encouraged and facilitated. The types of activities can range from in-class and field trip assistance, presentations, interviews, storytelling, teaching of traditional songs, dances, philosophies, myths, legends, teaching local craftsmanship and other ways of life skills. Also, many parents/guardians spoke of providing tutoring and homework assistance to not only their children but of extending their home and help to their children's friends. The value of these kinds of communal supports and contributions would be acknowledged and encouraged.

Student involvement in local community service is another way of connecting the school to the local community. Schools may identify community groups and organizations where students may volunteer work on weekends. The school administration and the PTA would be involved in the volunteer services that were promoted or put forth by the school. The question is: How, specifically, can a community and its many community organizations be involved in educating and preparing the young to become active adult citizens? To ensure that the volunteer initiatives are for the benefit of the young (social development) and not for groups to promote their businesses and other interests, such co-operative projects must be accountable to the community, the schools and parents, through an advisory or appointed working group/body. To this end the group/s would work to help identify, assess, monitor and evaluate the activities. The school may itself undertake to organize some community involvement/ service initiatives. This would require that schools and communities work together to develop instructional and pedagogic practices that promote collective learning and responsibility by redefining "success" broadly to include within its academic and social success paradigm, the learner's responsibility to her/his community. This shift would include service to the local community as part of the curriculum requirement. For example, schools can require community involvement/service. To complement this work, classroom teaching would examine the organization providing the service, the types of services being offered and how the different contributions (paid and volunteer work) fit into the overall work of the organization and of the community. With the student, the organization and the parents, teachers can develop a learning contract as a basis to evaluate the appropriateness of assigning a volunteer placement to a student and on an ongoing basis assess its learning outcomes. The learning contracts as a collective (not individual) database could be used to tangibly measure the "success" of the initiatives for individual students and for the community. These partnerships may be extended to teachers and administrators. As role models/players and members of the wider school community, their involvement as volunteers offers a powerful model of community-based development, knowledge acquisition, leadership and social justice.

Community Support

There is strong community support for learning local histories, Indigenous knowledges, cultures and languages, because of the widespread recognition that by doing so the resistance to the imposition of colonial education is strengthened. The value of the local is not limited to an examination, valuation or critique of the past but to its place and value in the present. Discussions of the importance of local histories and cultures are framed in terms of the power to know ourselves, to work as teachers in different communities across the nation, to go into communities and understand the cultures and to speak with the members of a community—both the elders and the youth. Within the concept of "community school," the idea of working with parents, building local partnerships and developing educational resources would mean supporting committed teachers who can participate actively in the cultural life of local communities. This is one area in which the reforms are viewed positively and where the framing of the need to value local communities and locally based knowledge has led to a broader community discussion and to an appropriation of the reform agenda by the community to achieve the positive reforms that they need on the ground.

Broader Implications

It is critical to understand the broader theoretical implications and questions evoked by understanding the roles and responsibilities of adults in schooling and the readings adults, students and teachers bring to the challenge of education. Obviously parents and local communities have relevant knowledge about the schooling of youth. So the question I am posing is: In what ways can schools effectively break the barriers separating them from the local communities in which they are located? I answer this question by pointing to areas that can tap local community knowledge in schools to enhance learning for all youth. The narratives suggest that local communities are important sources of knowledges for schools to work with. Not only do parents, community elders and members speak about their concerns of schooling; they also bring relevant knowledge to bear on how their children engage schools. As noted elsewhere (Dei, James-Wilson and Zine, 2002), the process of integrating multiple centres of knowledge in educational practices of schools may begin by diversifying the school curriculum. Parents, guardians, community leaders and elders have knowledge that is not considered to be academic knowledge. They have knowledge about the cultural traditions of their communities. They cannot only teach about culture and the cultural logics of a society; they can also discuss local peoples' conceptions and local attitudes to the earth (e.g., farming, hunting, spiritual connection). Such understanding can span from how and why indigenous communities farm, to the purpose of the land, and its spiritual connections to human beings. Such cultural resource knowledge is the basis of sustaining social existence in communities.

In other words, the home, family and local community itself are an embodiment of knowledge. What parents, students and elders do in their homes, families and communities as they meet the requirements of daily survival have a lot to tell us about ourselves and our relationship with broader society. Schools can use their communities as fertile grounds for producing knowledge. By researching various ways of providing for oneself and one's family in a specific community, students learn of the adult challenges and constraints in performing their roles and duties towards the young. In many Ghanaian local communities, traditional economic (e.g., farming and hunting) practices include the instruments used, the processes and the products (kinds of local vegetation farmed and animals hunted). Students could examine which economic and subsistence methods are still used and which have been modified and why. These projects could include library research as well as speaking to parents and elders. School projects could include verbal descriptors, pictures, actual instruments and drawings done by the students or local artists of those practices. In some cases, where communities may still be using aspects of these methods, students or groups of students might go on a field trip to these communities, bring back stories, descriptors, photographs and perhaps explore the possibility of organizing small local garden plots on their school grounds according to these methods of farming. If a school's local community can successfully raise interest, the actual implementation will likely result in the entire community becoming involved in the project. Teaching about hunting and farming methods and their philosophies such as local attitudes to natural resources, ownership of resources and their views on conservation of natural resources provide important knowledge to prepare youth for responsible adult living in the local society and in the wider world. By engaging in this discussion, a distinction is created between the Western view of land ownership and the Aboriginal view of stewardship of the land, which becomes centred knowledge.

Along with practices of sustenance farming are rituals of planting, harvesting and food preparation. Through carefully archiving these rituals—which may include prayers, chants, dances, celebrations the students could write essays describing the different aspects and they could enact the festivities or plan for celebrations to include these rituals. It is also possible that within families and homes (backyard gardens, local businesses), some rituals of food preparation may be still very much practised, while others may only be spoken about and others only retrieved in discussions with elders. Understanding how ethnographers and others who study traditional cultures retrieve knowledges that seem to have been lost is an important part of the learning process. Placing all cultures within such a historical context is important for students.

The education of culture must not only focus on past practices but also examine how cultures continue to influence our daily lives as members of a particular cultural group but also as peoples whose cultures intersect, connect and influence each other: how we sustain ourselves, the very physical and material aspects which are imbued with ritual, relationships and a sense of an interconnected world (cosmos/spirituality) that help sustain individual and communal life. It is important that students also examine some of the breaks with those relationships of balance and sustainability and what have been some of the advantages of seeking to improve the natural conditions.

Chapter 5

Spirituality[1] and Spiritual Learning in African Schooling

How people have understood, understand and seek to further understand their world necessarily includes in a place and time many aspects, among them the world of ideas, the material, the social, and the spiritual (however the individual or group/s perceive and/or define "the spiritual"). In encounters of persons or groups with different ways of knowing in the same locality or from different localities, unfortunately history has repeatedly demonstrated that what is seen to constitute "valid knowledge" within the context of those encounters of ideas, ways of living and being in the world is often determined by those (individuals or groups) who from their dominant positions can exert more power in the exchange. This does not mean that those with "less power" merely reproduce the dominant view. They may also resist, challenge and transform the view. But within certain contexts there is then the question of the degree to which oppositional knowledges can influence certain circles of power. In encounters between Western and non-Western societies the references of the former about what constitutes culture, valid knowledge and viable languages for communication between and among communities have dominated. Intellectual, political, cultural, spiritual and linguistic advances in our understandings of the complexity and richness of different languages, religions, cultures and ways of organizing social life in diverse communities may be furthered or threatened by technological advancements. The current thrust towards what has been called the revolution towards a knowledge-based economy poses a risk by the commodification of knowledge into information to be disseminated, consumed or disposed.

Western dominance in formal schooling practices and in what constitutes "valid knowledge" is not a new concern. School as a site for education is socially contested. Parents, educators, and communities have always struggled with questions of what knowledges to teach, with which languages, in which cultural contexts and for what purposes. Obviously preparing the next generations with the tools to participate in their time and for their future in a changing and interconnected world can be accepted as one of the purposes of schools. Is this formal learning to take place in isolation from other world views? Is it to take place disconnected from a community of place, its past and its present social and environmental milieu? These are but some of the questions which educational professionals have struggled and contested. In what have been Western dominated schooling structures, the search for viable educational options and alternatives is increasingly complicated by transnationalism with its impact on knowledge "nation," "culture" and local market economies, which in turn impact the understandings of the self, of group identities and of collective politics. From within the academy's position of being located in a community but connected with academies located all over the world/globe, it is important for critical educators to explore ways of rethinking education to reflect the aspirations and desires of diverse peoples. The spiritual development of the learner is an important dimension of learning, of education. The blurring of the specificities of places and its people is counter to the spiritual connection of the individual in community. The way in which knowledge is being produced, disseminated, consumed and disposed of is counter to the time required for individual reflection, collective discussion and integration into the way of thinking, of living and of being of a people. Time, place and human connections are necessary for communication that goes beyond the depositing/marketing of information into people and communities. For many, spirituality is an important dimension of human existence and how we come to know and make sense of our worlds.

A few years ago, I presented a paper at a local community gathering in Toronto. When I was introduced to the audience, the speaker said, "George is a leader in our community." During the refreshments after my presentation, an elderly woman walked up to congratulate me and poignantly asked, "So, I hear you are a leader. Well, who are you leading and where to?" I had no immediate response. After nervously laughing it off, I said, "Oh, he meant a leader in the spiritual sense." This African mother then responded that it was well and good to speak in the spiritual sense since, as she put it, "the Black community has had many people emerge as leaders and yet these leaders have not taken the community anywhere!" She then went on to point out that spirituality was central to the development of our individual and collective identities and sense of purpose, particularly in the Diaspora. Thinking back on this exchange, I realize that it helped me to understand better the importance of spirituality in the liberation of individual and collective minds.

The processes of coming to know are not always determined by the acquisition of what one does not know. Each of us has knowledge that may not easily manifest itself in how we understand our social existence. There is a place for spirituality and spiritual knowledge in the construction of subjectivity and identity. The self (as identity and subjectivity) is itself linked to schooling and knowledge production. It is this awareness that also makes knowledges situational, positional and contextual. The assertion of spirituality as a legitimate aspect of students' learning and knowledge is a contested social terrain. In the context of western education, spirituality in modern schooling also encounters, as Butler (2000) points out, the following danger: in a knowledge economy, spirituality can easily be commodified and rendered as individualistic and solipsistic rather than as emerging out of a community/human struggle for justice and dignity.

Approaches to spirituality need to attend to and be critical and respectful of different religious traditions, including secular thought.

A failure to do so could make the theorization of spirituality in schooling basist, fundamentalist or laissez-faire. There is more potential for students to develop a sense of spirituality and strength from the local communities outside the school. Therefore, in order for spirituality to be fostered in schools, there need to be teachers who understand the value of the spiritual and emotional development of the learner. Our searches to understand questions of spirituality must not shy away from examining issues of power. From past and present historical perspectives spirituality cannot be discussed outside the context of power. For example, we need to explore how certain spiritual values come to dominate others. Educators must eschew a liberal understanding of spirituality that separates the material from the non-material existence. Because of the predominance of western science and dualistic thinking in schools, introducing spiritual discourse into various social imaginaries has been viewed with suspicion. The spiritual discourse has most often been rendered invisible, negated, devalued or at best marginalized by modern Western philosophical traditions and scientific thought. In fact, important intellectual, cultural and political movements that have claimed to resist the violence of Western science and colonizing knowledges have been wary of anchoring their analysis and debates in a spiritual foundation.

I begin this chapter by asking: How can educators organize learning and pedagogy in the context of spiritual education in our schools to motivate and enhance student learning? The strategies for empowering students should make spaces in our schools for spirituality to be discussed and, more specifically, for spiritual knowledge to be taken up as part of a school's curriculum. Spirituality and spiritual discourses broach ideas and ontologies that emphasize connection, belonging, identification, well-being, love, compassion and peaceful co-existence with people and with nature. In this chapter, I highlight how students, educators and parents understand spirituality and how such knowledge is evoked in the context of Ghanaian schooling.

In the tradition of the secular skeptic, spirituality has no place in education. In North American public and academic discourses, the mention of spirituality and education is frequently countered with a reminder of the separation of church and state. As Groome (1999) points out in another context, "an established religion shouldn't mean excluding common spiritual values from our educational system.

Proselytizing on behalf of a particular religion is very different from allowing spiritual values to permeate our approach to education" (1). Hence the evocation of "spirituality," as earlier stated, is not in the context of subscribing to any high moral or religious order. The discussion of spirituality is not necessarily in association with any religious denomination or particular dogma. Religion may be a way to strengthen the spiritual sense of self. But "spiritual' is not necessarily synonymous with religion. My interest is in how spirituality influences education in Ghanaian contexts as part of the schooling processes. That is, how do Ghanaian educators and students work with an understanding of the self and personhood as a basis to engage schooling collectively? How does schooling serve the spiritual development or unfolding of the learner and her or his community? In what ways does spirituality manifest itself in schooling and what are the challenges for promoting genuine educational options for Africa?

The transformation of schooling and education includes diverse knowledges and ways of knowing. I assert that these pedagogical struggles and tensions, which occur on many educational fronts, include spirituality. What many see as the amputation of the self from the community is one of the consequences of the importation of colonial and imperial forms of education (see also Carnoy 1974; Mazrui 1975). This is why many voices call for a renewed spiritual grounding of the African identity and consciousness in opposition to Eurocentric knowledge (see Asante 1987, 1988, Ani 1994; Dove 1998; Asante and Abarry 1996; Mazama 1998).

Theorizing Spirituality

Among cultures, there are varied meanings of spirituality. Some see the individual being as essentially spiritual. Spirituality is also understood as connected to humility, healing, a valuation of wholeness, self and collective empowerment, liberation and "reclaiming the vitality of life" (Palmer 1999, 3). Teaching sacredness, respect, compassion, and connection of the self to the world and to others, in this sense, is spiritual education (Palmer 1999, 3). For the context of this chapter, I borrow Rahnema's (1995) view of spirituality as encompassing a "sensitivity, the art of listening to the world at large and within one, from the hegemony of a conditioned "me" constantly interfering in the process; the ability to relate to others and to act, without any pre-defined plan or ulterior motives; and the perennial qualities of love, compassion and goodness which are under constant assault in economized societies" (130).

Spiritual education is about the survival of the self and the collective spirit. The self is a complex being with multiple layers for interpreting and continuously making meanings from life. The individual as a learner has psychological, emotional, spiritual, and cultural dimensions not often taken up in traditional or conventional processes of schooling. Holistic education that upholds the importance of spirituality would recognize this complexity by speaking to the idea of wholeness (see Miller 1989, 1997, 1999). Context and situation are important in understanding the complex wholeness of the individual self/being. To promote education for social change is to view the self as a resisting subject. It is also to destroy the self/other dichotomy, rendering the self as not autonomous but connecting to a larger collective. The individual has responsibilities to the community and it is through spiritual education that the connection between the person and the community is made. Spiritual education stresses the dominance of individual spirit and the power of self and self-mind for collective empowerment. The subject as the person upholds an inner understanding of oneself and of one's relationship to others.

There are local and contextual variations in the understandings of knowledge, reality, subjectivity/ objectivity. For example, African spiritual knowings are intimately bound up with the affirmation of self and indigenous subjectivity. Spiritual and emotional involvements are inseparable in the production of knowledge. Many African ways of knowing affirm that personal subjectivity and emotionality must be legitimized rather than devalued. Such knowing also asserts that the subjectivity/objectivity and rationality/ irrationality dualities or splits are false. In fact, while spiritual knowledge challenges subject-object dualism, it simultaneously upholds "objectivity" to the subjective experience and, similarly, "subjectivity" to the objective experience. The subjective is capable of comprehending the "objective universe." Subjectivity is a personal interpretation, while objectivity can be simply the material and immaterial reality. It is important to reiterate that this understanding of spirituality (unlike liberal conceptions of spirituality) does not efface questions of power and power relations (self/ other/group relation). Nor does it falsely dichotomize or separate the material and the non-material.

The individual can be both spiritual and non-spiritual; spiritual in the sense of acknowledging the power of the inner will to know and understand the self and to be able to interact with the outer world and the collective. To be non-spiritual is to fail to show individual humility and to fail to work with the knowledge that comes with knowing the self and inner spirit. African spirituality stresses mind, body, soul interactions. Such spirituality is about values, beliefs and ideas of integrity and dignity that shape individual consciousness into a collective and unified existence. Spirituality need not be imposed. The individual develops a spirituality through her/his engagement with society, culture and the natural environment.

The view of emotions as an important source of knowledge is closely connected to spirituality. But emotion and spirituality are not synonymous. Emotion is that body of knowledge gained in and out of both the subjective and objective forms of existence. Emotional knowledge develops alongside intuition. It is knowledge that is embedded in the self and speaks to compassion of the human sense and mind. Read in a broad context, the notion of "emotional intelligence," as espoused by Cooper (1997), is very useful. Cooper (1997) sees emotional intelligence as "the ability to sense, understand and effectively apply the power and acumen of emotions as a source of human energy, information and influence. Human emotions are the domain of core feeling, gut-level instincts and emotional sensations. When trusted and respected, emotional intelligence provides a deeper, more fully formed understanding of oneself and of those around us" (13).

These definitions of the spiritual and the emotional raise an important ontological question: What are the working assumptions about the nature of reality held by educators and students? In Ghanaian systems of thought, the ontological viewpoint stresses that to understand reality is to have a complete or holistic view of society. The view stresses the need for a harmonious co-existence among nature, culture and society. There is the idea of mutual interdependence among all peoples such that the existence of the individual/subject is only meaningful in relation to the community of which she or he is a part. The view also stresses the physical and metaphysical connection and the fact that the subject cannot be understood in its atomistic sense.

These definitions also raise an important epistemological question: What are the ways of knowing about such realities as applied by educators and learners? The epistemological position enthuses that there are different ways of knowing and conceptualizing reality. In Ghanaian systems of thought, knowledge is seen as cumulative and as emerging from one's experiences of the social world. Knowledge emerges from the interplay of body, mind and soul. The existence of a metaphysical realm also means that there is an uncertainty of knowledge and the possibility that intuition and emotions offer sites of knowing for the human senses. Relying on intuition and experiential knowledge allows the self to know and understand the outer world. If practice and experience are seen as the contextual basis of self-generated knowledge, then knowledge and survival go hand in hand. Furthermore, the knowledge that membership in the community accords rights, ties the individual self to the collective.

A further body of knowledge connects epistemology to ethics. The axiological position maintains that within societies there are "disputational contours of right and wrong or morality and values ... [that is,] presumptions about the real, the true and the good" (Scheurich and Young 1997, 6). As already argued, in Ghanaian and African systems of thought the cultural, spiritual and ideational beliefs, values and practices are evaluated in the history and contexts of communities, as societies strive to set their own moral tone (see also Dei 1994a, 2002a, b, & c). While these ideas may be shared by other indigenous peoples, it is the privileging of certain core social values for "reward" (e.g., responsibilities over rights; community over individual; peaceful co-existence with nature over control or domination of nature) that sets different knowledge systems apart. The understanding of the spiritual self allows one to define her or his moral tone within the broad contexts of the individual's society. The individual is a subject. The individual is part of a community. The cultural norms of the groups guide and influence human behaviour and action. And the spiritual existence is central to material existence.

As noted earlier, the Ghanaian concept of spirituality is part of a worldview that is often difficult for a Western-educated person to understand. Western secular educational discourses tend to regard the subject of spirituality with suspicion, thus not seeing a dimension that, many would argue, is of key importance in African education. There is a form of local, spiritual knowing that is connected to the land, to the people, to ancestors, and to community. For example, individuals are traditionally brought up to appreciate the community and to know that they live in a land bestowed unto them by their forebears. Their ancestors still guard over the community. They keep a watchful eye on everyday practice and social activity. There is a belief that the individual living subject could be punished for going against the wishes of the ancestors and/or for not looking out for the interests of the larger group or community. This is an important knowledge base. Unfortunately, with time it has been corrupted.

In connecting knowledge, spirituality and religion, I am not suggesting that all local cultural knowledges are spiritual, or that religion is synonymous with spirituality. Rather, the concept of spirituality that emerges from this study embraces all three realms. Many Ghanaians who grew up in traditional communities view with concern the erosion of the kind of education they received. Their concerns refer to the separation of education from local communities that has left many poor rural communities disenfranchised from schooling, both in access and in content.

The separation of education from local communities in Ghana must be understood in the privileging of schooling over education—a schooling that takes place within formal institutional structures and practices. It is, indeed, the formal schooling tradition that the various reforms have tried to change. As discussed earlier, children from poor rural communities have been excluded from opportunities of formal learning because many of their parents cannot afford to send them to boarding school. Those who do go to school are uprooted from their families, local cultures and communities. Thus, their formal learning is disconnected from the land and its community of people. The narratives of Ghanaian students, educators, parents and community workers point to the importance of reclaiming these grounded understandings in the search for genuine educational options.

Spirituality and spiritual knowing are a valid body of knowledge that can be pursued in schools to enhance learning outcomes. Spirituality encourages the sharing of personal and collective experiences of understanding and dealing with the self. Much of what is "universal" in spirituality is manifested in the particulars of knowing and asserting who we are, what our cultures are, and where we come from. The discussion, in this respect, is an implicit antithesis to the concept that the learning of curriculum is ever solely "universal," where universal means neutral and common to all. Through the narratives of teachers, students, local parents and community workers, I argue that spirituality is a form in which we identify ourselves and the universal and is, therefore, an implicit way of asserting ourselves collectively and individually. Therein lies a powerful tool for resisting mis-education, domination or discriminatory forces. The assault on spirituality can have destructive consequences when spirituality itself is negated in schools and the systems of education. If nurtured and respected, spirituality can be utilized to involve and energize schools and local communities.

Situating the Critique

Critical scholarship cannot continue to pursue a "human capital" approach to educational reform and change, an approach that privileges the cultivation of the intellectual mind and human capacity as outside spiritual and emotional considerations of the learner. Each individual learner is a spirit being and has a spiritual and moral core. This "spirituality of being" motivates and provides meaning and hopefulness for learning. Spirituality is about rebuilding the human spirit to embrace gentleness, humility, and compassion. It is about a powerful force beyond the immediate and observable culture, one beyond human control that directs social action. It is about the individual identifying with the source of the universal meaning of human existence while acknowledging the diversity "that expresses that universality in many different ways" (Miller 1999, 2). It is worth repeating that spirituality in education connects learners "to each other as human beings, to the earth and to the whole cosmos," and the learner shares the experience of "being in community and being in relationship to other people" (Miller 1999, 4). Spiritual education problematizes "rugged individualism" and extreme competition that is propelled by greed and encourages the individual to disassociate from the collective.

Emerging concerns about modern schooling have, to a degree, focussed on the inability of educational systems to serve the spiritual needs of the learner. Instead of moving in the direction of becoming ever more healthy and sustainable communities, schools are at high risk of becoming increasingly less and less regenerative, thereby, less sustainable and healthy places of learning. For some educators and community workers, these criticisms have translated into calls to re-centre spirituality in education. Schooling in a highly individualistic and competitive society has created a social hierarchy of knowing and of knowledge forms. Knowing subjects are separated from each other. Rather than present new and creative ideas, competition

(Palmer 1999, 2) has actually fostered a culture of fear and a complacency that does not deviate radically from the knowledge of the *status quo*. In a competitive and merit- based system of teaching and learning, schools create losers and winners. To rupture the sorting and hierarchical practices of schools, education must bring about a connection between the learner as a whole person and her or his community. Education must affirm personal and communal spirituality.

In fact, spirituality has always been an integral part of the self, personhood and the collective identity. Throughout the years, spirituality has influenced educational change in many indigenous cultures that have developed an "inherent respect for things spiritual" (Palmer 1999, 1). Teaching, learning and the administration of education have not primarily been about seeking information or satisfying the dictates of the job or market economy. Education has been about healing and creating the wholeness of being. Bringing spirituality into education thus challenges modernist projects as well as the excesses and vagaries of the post-modern culture which have served to uproot the learner from a spiritual base. Palmer (1999, 3) also notes that spirituality has always been about liberation, empowerment, compassion, resistance and "reclaiming the vitality of life." Similarly, what is considered sacred is what is spiritual. It is the inner knowing and power that lies at the heart of knowing, teaching and learning. The connection of the sacred and the secular (material, tangible and outer) allows the individual to engage with social reality as both a material reality and a metaphysical realm.

Religion, Spirituality and Colonial Education

The anti-colonial framework allows for a critique of colonial education and the implications of having colonial remnants in the current educational reforms. The framework also allows us to understand how these (colonial remnants) are being challenged, reproduced, appropriated or modified in the current context of post colonial education. To interrogate current educational reforms and change appropriately, it is important to look at the history of education in Ghana from the perspective of colonial education delivery systems: how it was delivered, who taught, who attended which school, where the schools were located and how answers to these questions reveal a strong connection to the historical context in which the reforms are currently taking place (e.g., the defence of the boarding/residential school system, the rising cost of education, the non-use of local languages, and the difficulty of introducing local languages within the old educational structure given the diversity of languages within the nation and the international currency of English). It is also important to see how the issues of spirituality and multi-faiths have been engaged in schooling.

Historically, colonial religious institutions assisted in the delivery of education in Ghana. The spread of Christianity and colonialism went hand in hand in Africa and education was a clear example (see also Quist 1994). The work of the early missionaries in establishing boarding/residential schools/colleges to further the missionary project of Christianity is well known. Missionary schools followed the pattern of other schools set up by colonial authorities, and taught Christian ethics and values as a major component of the school curricula. The English language was the sole medium of instruction. Boarding/residential schools were concentrated in the southern parts of the country, specifically along the coast. This meant students in missionary schools, like their colonial government-funded schools, would study away from their homes. The teachers of the missionary schools were usually members (both lay and clergy) of the affiliated religion as were their students, the latter often prior to coming to the school (parental affiliation to the Church) but also upon entering the school or during their school years through compulsory participation in religious services. Religion was seen as a powerful source for the spiritual development of the learner.

In order to make the administration of education more affordable, governments (colonial and African) entered into partnership with religious educational institutions to provide schooling for a broad sector of the population, separate of any identifiable religious denomination. With time, there have been efforts at including different practices of worship within public schools. Consequently, there have emerged tensions and struggles between the supposedly "sacred" and "secular" institutions. In Ghana, as elsewhere in the African Continent, the partnership with religious institutions has colonized African spiritual traditions in very real ways. Of course, this has not been without resistance and not without African peoples' appropriating these religions and making them their own as well. Also, within different religious structures there are ways in which many people voice a spirituality that goes beyond imposed structures and reaches out to other spiritual expressions across religions. Some of these can be seen in the ways in which a common sense of community and community values are expressed within, outside and around specific religions and faiths.

It is in this vein that ideas about African spirituality must be understood. Even when my research study did not mention the issue of spirituality directly or address the issue in any systemic or concrete way, aspects of spirituality and spiritual education emerged indirectly from interesting entry points (e.g., as students and educators articulated their meanings of schooling and social difference, the importance of self, group, community and cultural and religious identities). That is, discussions on spirituality emerged in a context of how differences of ethnicity, class, gender, religion, language can be and are addressed within a shared local community site.

For many students, spirituality has been understood primarily from the perspective of religion and how students of different religious faiths find a voice of difference in a common school. On the whole, such interpretations are excellent conceptions/understandings of the link between religion and education in Ghana. However, they demonstrate a gap in examining spirituality from a different perspective (that is, not so much differences of religions and/or religious spirituality) but within a broad and more critical view of spirituality outside of religion. This gap can also be explained in the extent to which current and ongoing reforms have failed to tap into the wealth of existing local knowledges (including spiritual knowledge) that may well enhance learning for youths. In the context of educational reforms, how are these spiritual knowings and understandings used to promote learning?

Spirituality as a Personal Knowledge Base

As an academic, I should acknowledge my privileged status and yet be critical of it. To engage in self-critique is to admit one's complicity in the maintenance of dominant and colonizing knowledges. However, one cannot allow self-critique to paralyse or immobilize one's political engagement in the transformation of dominant relations. In this way, I cannot perceive my project as only uncovering the "problem of [my individual] attitude rather than of institutionalized inequities in economic, political, and social power" (Armour 1993, 1). Notwithstanding that the deconstruction of individualized manifestations of colonialisms and imperialisms would not be sufficient to produce systemic shifts in the balance of power, those of us who are working within the academy often position ourselves hierarchically as the only subjects capable of theorizing. In the process, we invalidate other experiences and knowledges. Armour and others have recognized the importance of de-centering the (privileged) individual from analysis to listen to and be informed by the voices of "those deemed our others" (Armour 1993, 1), but also to consider these voices for their political/social implications for systemically organized relations of power/difference. At the same time, because we all bring different meanings to spirituality, an important starting point to transformation is recognizing and naming the knowledge of "self" and of others. From my position of privilege, I want to explore how spirituality is grounded in a solid knowledge base through diverse, local voices in order to challenge and rethink conventional processes of schooling and education.

I recall a particular discussion in one of my graduate classes at the Ontario Institute for Studies in Education of the University of Toronto (OISE/UT). Discussing indigenous knowledges as a decolonization project, I highlighted the need for Africans in the Diaspora to maintain links and ties with the past and present histories of Africa. Speaking from her position as Caribbean-born, one student rightly observed that Africans of the Diaspora have been continually urged to identify with mother Africa, yet not many continental Africans necessarily "reconnect" to the Diaspora. While partially agreeing with this observation, I pointed out that Africa is an artificial socio-political-economic construct and the continent needs to be theorized beyond its geographical boundaries. I questioned how much knowledge North-American students know or possess about Africa. Usually information about Africa is filtered through television images and popular culture. In schools, Black youth have to deal with the constant negation and devaluation of Africa and her peoples. In fact, one needs to revisit colonial education to acknowledge that African youth learn more about other places and peoples than about Africa and her peoples. When Africa is presented, it is as if it were merely a place without a history. Insofar as Africa is devalued, the Black student in North America is taught that she or he has no connection to the continent. Yet the Diasporic experience cannot be understood without its connection to the continent. In response to the negativity and hostility that is so often portrayed about the Diasporic experience, the continental African student sees no need to identify with it.

This juxtaposed reading of continental Africa and the Diasporic reality is intended to stress the continuity and inseparability between the continent and her peoples, irrespective of where they are currently living. My argument is that it is through a definition of the spiritual bonding that youth learn about the connections of the self to the other. Spirituality and spiritual knowledge have implications for rethinking African education and the education of the learner. Within Africa today, critical educators are teaching youth to be spiritually informed and to think of themselves as Africans and as global citizens. Learning proceeds through the development of the African self and identity. Critical teaching allows the learner to stake out a position as African, one that is outside of the identity that has been and continues to be constructed in Euro-American ideology.

Education in Africa today is challenging the historical denial of African spirituality. Africa is seen as an important knowledge base with possibilities in the search for genuine educational and development options for the continent. Arguably, a major challenge facing contemporary education is the reconciliation of the secular and the sacred. Rather than shy away from spiritual dimensions of education, educational practices and teachings may reconcile mainstream secularity with individual and community understandings of spirituality. To successfully enhance learning possibilities, educators must tap Indigenous, traditional and culturally based knowledges as important resources for the learner. Looking critically at school systems, an argument can be made that specific educational initiatives should ask learners to situate spiritual knowledge in everyday practices and interactions of society and to relate common sense knowledges to schooling and education. Local knowledge references the social norms and values and the social, mental and spiritual constructs which guide, organize and regulate a people's way of living and making sense of their world. Embedded in such knowledges are theoretical and practical conceptions of what schooling and education should be and what it means to engage the self and collective for meaningful political action for educational change (see also Dei 1999c). Again local subjective knowings and voices are very informative.

Narratives

Interconnectedness of language and culture to a peoples' spirituality and values:

At the time of the study, Odom was nearing completion of his teacher-training program. He sees the importance of language, history and culture for learning in schools:

> Actually, language and culture [are] ... let me say equal in the sense that the language ... teaches us ... our norms and laws. And our culture too teaches us some of our traditional norms, and ... because of our culture, we easily say that this is what our forefathers did when they were there ... At times we may speak to someone ... and the man or woman may use proverbs and other words and so we see that the man [or woman we are speaking to] actually knows the language very well. If we want to know [what they mean] we may even ask the elder, what is the meaning of this? And that man or that woman will teach or correct the meaning of that [proverb]. It will guide you in some way in your life. Yes. So culture and language at times go together ... The history aspect at times also teaches you [about your] origin, where you came from. At times your forefathers, even my father has done that ... At times he called us and then told us how we came to stay in a particular town, the way we moved to this town, what happened ... So history will tell you what happened in some years past and how [your] community came about. (09/10/97)

Odom points to language as important for the transmission of cultural norms and social values of a people. Proverbs carry powerful meanings and their use allows for the sharing of knowledge about a community's history and social existence. The respect for elders is important as they are known to possess spiritual and ancestral knowledge by their "approximation" to the dead and the world of spirits. This is why gerontocracy is a very prominent aspect of Ghanaian cultures.

Onipa, who is also in the final years of her SSS education, discusses the value of learning culture from an integrated perspective. For her, culture includes music, festivals, marriage, births, death, economy, lifestyle and so on. She is encouraged that some students are taking history and that in the Junior Secondary (JSS) one learns about "history, culture and cultural studies." She believes it is important for students to learn about their cultures for self and spiritual affirmation:

> To learn about our culture is very important because it helps us to
> know things about our tribes ... I have learned [from] culture to
> know the importance of festivals ... Culture [also] teach[es] us
> [about] those who are not from your tribe—the way they eat, the
> way they dress, and other things too. It has led me [to appreciate
> these things] ... so I think it is important. (09/21/97)

Festivals are cultural activities that carry the social, economic,
political, spiritual and symbolic aspects of a community's life.
Learning culture has led Onipa to "know about music, how you play
it, how you sing music to a person." Learning culture not only helps
you to understand oneself and society, it teaches you about the past:
"If I don't know what they did in the olden days, through history I
[can learn about] that ... and [about] those who are not in Ghana,
those who have died and I [learn] what they did to help the economy
of Ghana" (09/21/97). Culture acknowledges the spiritual connection
between the living and the dead. This is an important link that is
revered in local cultures. The dead person does not sever her/his ties
with the living. The dead watches over the living by constantly
providing knowledge, guidance, advice and protection. To know one's
culture is to be spiritually informed. For the educator, this spiritual
grounding is an important pedagogic and communicative tool
employed to further the goal of effective educational practices.

Resistance is situated and contextualized through the use of local
languages that uphold cultural and spiritual values, personal ethics,
interests and desires. In 1997, Dankwah completed his studies at the
University College of Education. He is now a mathematics teacher in
the same institution as Donkor. He talks about how language and
culture have a role in the new educational reforms by developing
students' self esteem, identity and appreciation of history and
community values: "Culture is language and language is culture. That
is what I can see. Culture is taking active part in the new educational
system because they have a subject called cultural studies and over
there they learn the actual culture and they act, worship and [do] other
things. There, they act the musical aspect ... (08/28/97). Language is
important to understanding the self and one's education. It is a
marker of self-identity. Language brings meaning, relationship, self-
reflection and critical thought into the learning process. It is through
language that culture, values, norms and beliefs of people are
conveyed. When asked what it means to teach Ghanaian culture,
Dankwah connects the issues of culture, values and spirituality:

Okay, Ghanaians should be allowed to know the culture because there are some values and beliefs in our culture. They should be known to Ghanaians so that ... we can compare with others wherever we go. And then, second, Ghanaians should learn the culture because it is [through] the culture that ethics ... norms, values, beliefs and other things are derived. So before a child can learn and obey the rules [that are] convenient ... to society, he should be able to know all the values ... pertaining [to] society. (08/28/97)

Teaching values to the child is fundamental to future social engagement. In discussing aspects of Ghanaian culture, Dankwah points to the relationship between the "dead and the living" as a form of ancestral worship shared by most Ghanaian cultures. While agreeing that there is no one culture, his response to the question of which culture an educator should teach in school is very informative:

In fact, I don't agree with those who say that ... there are so many cultures ... Anyway that is because we have so many tribes ... But I think the sentiment of the culture when you try to analyse ... you could see that they are all trying to reach the same point ... in actual fact they become apparent. By getting to the peak you see they are all bringing the same idea. *[Can you give an example?]* Example? [Take] the Akans. The Akans celebrate what you call Addae. You see Addae is a type of culture where they worship the [ancestral] ghosts, calling on the ghosts whom they believe [have been] existing from time immemorial. They are calling them to come and guide them. You see they call them through the deities. The chiefs and all [the dead] should come to them and listen ... Yeah this is done by the Akans. So you see that it is specific, it is a grand ... historical festival. The Ewe also have their festival which is historic [and celebrates] how the ancestors brought the people [here from] where they migrated from ... they also call their ghosts ... to come together to guide them. They also ... celebrate the same thing. You see it is just a part, but getting to the point they are trying to be the same. That is why I said earlier they all relate. (08/28/97)

Cultural festivals serve not just to teach about history; they also teach the values and beliefs that connect individuals and groups to one another. These festivals become defining moments in a people's culture, history and identity. For example, the belief in the power of ancestors is ingrained in the minds of the youth and adults such that the connection between the living and the dead is continually maintained. Ancestors are believed to guide and protect the living.

They praise and reward good work but also punish those who go astray or perform deeds inimical to the well-being of the family and the wider community. Since not all the dead become ancestors/ancestresses except those who lead good and exemplary lives, the living are impressed upon to lead exemplary lives worthy of emulation.

Cultural resource knowledge is ancestral knowledge with its own cosmology of the living/dead. The commonalities in cultural and spiritual values are the things which Dankwah stresses to students when discussing Ghanaian cultures and ways of life. His intention is to show the connection among students as a people. Educators like Dankwah and others use culture to promote spiritual and intuitive learning. Spirituality is not necessarily an ascription to a high moral/religious order, but an understanding of the self/personhood and culture as a basis to engage learning. Education is anchored in a broader definition that encompasses its emotional and spiritual dimensions, cultural knowledge. A personalized, subjective identi-fication with the learning processes makes it possible for the learners to be invested spiritually and emotionally in their education.

Religion and Spiritual Grounding: Accommodation or Imposition?

In Ghanaian schooling contexts, a discussion on spirituality necessarily evokes religion. This is understandable because for many spirituality and religion are powerfully connected. While this text makes the distinction between religion and spirituality, it is noted that some Ghanaian students and educators, particularly those in mission schools, do not see a clear separation. Educators and students in general have differing views on the role of religion in schools when spirituality is the subject of discussion. There are contestations around the spiritual and religious values and how they should be affirmed or (not) taken up in different schooling contexts. Otambo is a Religion and Life Studies instructor at the SSS level. He sometimes also helps out with the teaching of languages. He acknowledges the differences that exist in schools along spiritual, religious, ethnic and cultural lines. When asked if the school takes all the differences into account in the teaching, learning and administration of education, he is quick to note that in the case of religion and spirituality:

> Yes, they do. Because in terms of religion we have Muslims. We have people practising traditional religion. So we don't force them to accept a single religion. So we give them a general and open

forum. For example, religious and moral education; when you are teaching about the concept of God, you come in and tell them this is what the Muslims call Allah. These traditionalists are saying the Supreme Being ... is the one and only person ... So we talk about the good values in all religion and they are to choose. When it comes to the dialect [language] aspect of it, when teaching the children certain examples, we use English. Then we say, this is what the Akans would say, and [for those] who understand Ga, [we ask]: How do you call that person in your own language? So we cater to all spheres of languages. And when it comes to entertainment, too, when we have cultural displays, we give them the chance to display what they have from the various ethnic groupings. (08/11/97)

Otambo accepts the multiplicity of faiths and how spiritual values help the learner in developing an identity and a personhood. Agyena, a second year student in the SSS also insists that there is a place for acknowledging diverse cultures and practices of the various religious denominations at the school. To her "since culture is the way people live, everybody has the layman's view about culture. For example, singing, walking, dancing." She asserts that her school encourages each student to affirm her or his respective spiritual and religious experiences as an important knowledge base through which to engage the school system. The school, she points out, supports the spiritual and cultural development of the learner. In fact, she maintains that there is institutional support for all students to develop their culture, broadly defined and other extra curricular activities. She adds: "You see, [in] this school, they [students] normally converge here, share ideas too, all sort of things, so any activity that takes place ... is organized in this school" (07/10/97).

Agyena's classmate, Hana, interviewed at the same time, also sees some accommodation: "You [can] take a class after Mosque. Then on Friday they also go and worship. So they don't discriminate between any religion. You go to your church and in the evening all of us go for church service together (07/10/97). But there are differing and opposing views. Ohemaa, a non-Adventist who teaches at the local Teacher Training College, finds the discipline severe and the standards high at the College. Yet, she also critiques what she sees as religious imposition and discrimination. Asked about how the school addresses difference among the student population, she observes:

Ah ... I don't know. In my view, I think here, because it is an Adventist institution, they tend to use their doctrine [to] dominate, you know. And although every two weeks they allow them [students] to go to town and have their own church activities, I don't think they really consider the differences. Because basically when you come here, for instance, you are not supposed to put on earrings and other things. But at home people do put on all sorts of those things. [But] when you come here you have to go the Adventist way. That's how I see it. (08/20/97)

To Ohemaa, the "imposition" of a particular set of values challenges the freedom of self-expression. She credits the academic success of the school to the discipline maintained through the values of the faith. Yet, she critiques the restriction placed on personal and cultural identity.

Kidi, a student in the same institution, shares Ohemaa's concern with the imposition of religious and spiritual values: "The school should be free. There shouldn't be an Adventist thing there. They should allow every denomination to exist in the school. So if you are Methodist or Catholic they should allow [you] to have [your] way of worshiping God. We should be treated fairly and equally. And everything should be free not compulsory, if you want to attend" (08/19/97).

Both Kidi and Ohemaa speak of freedom of religious expression, which they find lacking in their particular school. However, other colleagues in the school disagree on this point. Boatemaa says she chose to come to the College because it was near her hometown. In responding to critiques made by some students of religious practices being "imposed," she forcefully expressed her views, conceding she is of the SDA faith: "I think that they are wrong. Because as a human being you have to combine everything with God. So if you study and God doesn't help you, it is going to be fruitless. So they have combined the studies. So that after getting the physical aspect you are getting the spiritual aspect as well" (20/08/97). But educator Koto, who teaches physical education in the same institution as Otambo and Agyena, is very adamant about the place of religion in schools. He strongly believes that religious beliefs should be private and not forced onto others: "because the school is a government school, it is not a Church school" (08/12/97).

These narratives show that there is a legitimate reason to disassociate the teaching of spirituality from any particular religious denominations or dogma. What is taken as "sacred" maintains its efficacy through a personal negotiation and understandings of the self and one's identity. Identity is linked powerfully to schooling and knowledge production. Educators and students of the SDA faith produce particular knowledges that affirm the practices and belief systems of their religion. They attribute school success to its grounding in spiritual and religious values. Within school systems, the sacred can be the connecting link that holds fragmented parts together. The sacred can be important in helping to create and understand "the sense of otherness of the things of the world" (Palmer 1999, 5). Otherness is a site and source of richness. Understanding otherness is to affirm interdependence.

However, the sacred can neither be institutionalized nor imposed through the political system of power, otherwise it loses the respect and humility attached to it and the power to connect individuals to a community. Palmer (1999) points out that "distortion happens when the sacred [is] vested in an institutional context or framework" (9). The respectfulness and humility of the educator are crucial in transforming knowing, teaching and learning. Such characteristics form the cornerstone for developing the educational values of community, ethics and compassion that make learning possible. Humility makes teaching and learning possible by respecting the knowledge, ideas and contributions of others (see also Palmer 1999). When the sacred is imposed, it cannot allow the learner to know, to learn and to teach from within. Nor can the learner recover the sense of community with others. The learner may not easily connect with the subject of study and the self who is teaching, especially when the sacred is imposed through a power relation. Every learner, like the educator, has a soul—the driving force of human action. The effective educator develops a sensitivity to the ways the body, mind and soul unfold within the learner to create a strong spiritual relationship with the community.

Affirmation is central in forming individual and collective identities and developing a sense of community belonging, pride, purpose and direction for the learner. For effective schooling some Ghanaian educators and students have tapped into the positive (solution oriented) aspects of inculcating spiritual values into individual moral codes. In the research study, this connection emerged more strongly in the school that is of the SDA faith. Monsa, an educator in the teacher training institution, admits that religion and spiritual values are integrated in the organizational life of the school. For example, on staff practices, he observes:

> If anyone goes to the mission schools you find that leadership [belongs] to whoever goes along with the faith and practice of that mission. So it is not peculiar to this particular College. If you go to any Catholic institution, to any Presbyterian or Methodist [institution, or to] any of the missions, you [will] find that the head, the assistant, house masters, senior house masters, senior house mistresses all belong to the same faith. (09/22/97)

To Monsa, leadership is key to laying a strong spiritual and moral foundation in a school. According to him, this is the basis for a demarcation of leadership roles along the criteria of faith. He vehemently insists that the school does not actively encourage the staff to be members of any particular faith: "No, it doesn't. You come to work. The school will not force you to become a member. But like I already said, there are one or two positions that one would not have if one is not a member of that particular faith" (09/22/97). Nonetheless, he recognizes the difficulty for some students and educators who may not share particular religious and spiritual faiths. But given the lessons from his philosophy of education, he asks that critics look at the "bigger picture": "My philosophy of teaching, I might say, is that I have been influenced by the philosophy of the Church, which is to teach wholeness, to teach an individual spiritually, academically, socially. You realize that man is an entity. It is not only one side. So all the sides of an individual must be taken into consideration in teaching" (09/22/97). The idea of seeing the individual as a whole is relevant for understanding learning. To ground spirituality in learning is to pursue and promote holistic education.

Holistic Education and Success

Miller (1999, 3) presents the view that the individual is "a complex existential entity made up of many, many layers of meaning." This complexity marks the uniqueness of being. Holistic education acknowledges this complexity of being by pointing to the cultural, political, emotional and spiritual implications for schooling. Holistic education sees the complex, multi-faceted and differentiated self as a whole being. This knowledge is a deep spiritual realization. It is a humanizing education which empowers the learner to fulfil her or his responsibilities to a larger citizenry, such as confronting and resisting oppressions and social injustices in their myriad forms. Included in holistic education is the cultivation of meaningful relationships. Through this form of education, students and educators are able to dialogue, connect and mutually create meanings and interpretations about their worlds (Miller 1989, 1997, 1999). As Groome (1999) also notes, holistic education engages individuals as whole beings to learn, teach, think and act critically for themselves and their communities. Spiritual learning as a form of holistic education integrates and synthesizes that which is sacred and that which is secular' (see also Shepard 1988) to constitute material and emotional success.

For example, in discussing what it means to promote holistic learning, educators and students integrate views about academic and social success. Arts educator, Mina, for example, takes a holistic view of success. She sees academic and vocational pursuits as constituting part of what can be broadly termed as students' success: "Success is not defined simply in an academic sense because it is not everybody who can be successful by the academic. Somebody who has extra curricular activities can be successful. Some of them [students] like the vocation. Some of them will be successful through the vocational aspect. Some like the skills aspect. So success is not determined solely on the academic" (09/18/97). Skills are not simply what one knows but how one applies what one learns. When probed further to speak about the social dimensions of school success, Mina brings an expanded meaning to the goals and purposes of education. She ties the learner to the broader community: "Okay. The social aspect of success, I think, should be classified as well because you see sociability should be achieved by everybody so that he [or she] will be able to ... contribute to society. If a child doesn't achieve the social aspect, I think society has lost and in fact it is not the aim of education ... so socially they should achieve equally" (09/18/97).

Otambo also places educational success within the wider community context: "Educational success is measured after schooling, when the child is able to apply what she or he has learned to carve out her or his niche in society and make a living. It doesn't matter if he has a high qualification or not. But if he is able to make ends meet, then I think [that means] he has been successful" (08/11/97).

There is a powerful spiritual domain in the educational process, for example, helping learners develop a sense of self, collectivity, community, and a consciousness of being and place (see also Shields

1999). Students and educators use the spiritual understanding of personhood as an entry point to teaching and learning. They engage knowledge production and validation through the entry point of understanding the self, spiritually, emotionally, materially and politically. Particularly, educators bring an understanding of self, individual and collective to their teaching practice. Classroom teachings stress the society, culture and nature nexus and the need to cultivate a peaceful co-existence. Learning happens across differences. Rather than detracting from learning, group-focussed teaching and learning emphasize individual creativity, resourcefulness and collective empowerment. It also encourages divergent and multiple thoughts and ideas. The evocation of the spiritual in education also has implications for understanding power and authority and for teaching mutual respect in student-teacher relations. Collective and collaborative learning allows the learner to display dependence, interdependence and independence simultaneously (see also Hoffman 1999, 1995). The teacher's authority is enhanced when the learner reaches an understanding without the exercise of authority to maintain compliance.

Local Knowledges and Learning from the Past

Donkor teaches vocational skills (sewing and leather work) at the local Teacher Training College. He argues that the community has a body of knowledge which is indigenous and this knowledge has a role to play in the school reforms. Referring to culture and history, Donkor notes that local knowledge is neither static nor frozen in time and space:

> We should also refer to [knowledge] as something that was there and you see and try to start up from there and improve. You don't go back and say use that ... Why is the African man not improving upon what he did? ... You see that is a problem ... We have some talent, some knowledge [that] started from here; that knowledge is stagnant, [it] is not moving and that's what we have to think and improve upon—indigenous knowledge ... There is a whole issue of whether you see knowledge as static or knowledge as something that is dynamic, and that is always reforming itself. (08/28/97)

While he questions the failure to use existing knowledge to build on what society has, Donkor is also conscious of the need to see knowledge in its broader application as dynamic and reforming. Education must help the learner understand the dialectic of self and society. In seeing "knowledge as something that was there," Donkor is gesturing to the self as being part of a culture and a society. Similarly, Ini, who teaches literature at the Senior Secondary School shares Donkor's views. When asked for his conception of indigenous knowledge, he is emphatic:

> Indigenous knowledge ... is what they [educators and students] do in cultural studies. The student needs to know what was [here] before we were colonized. It is very necessary because the past tells on the present, and that would tell on the future. If we don't tell our children the values of our culture, it is like they don't have a past. Where did they start from? Where did I come from? If it is negative, you teach it, but you tell the person it is negative. You tell them that this is what is not good about our past. If it is positive, you can learn from it. (08/13/97)

Starting from where one came from means knowing the self and the history of one's social existence. Knowledge has a purpose in teaching a people their history, their cultural past and present. Ini later discusses his past educational experiences of learning about external knowledge. He argues that colonial education is still happening. Students are learning about things that have no direct bearing on local environments and conditions. But, he also sees some changes taking place today:

> What I realize is that in the English [class] in elementary schools, they brought us passages from the outside. We learned so much about other lands, but not our land. But when you take an English language book now, the writers make sure that they have brought us passages that are more relevant to our situation ... I think that they are focussing more on what is happening to us now. Like these days, geography teachers have to take their students out [to the field]. So if they have to learn about waterfalls, they have to go to the Volta Waterfalls. If they have to learn about lakes, they have to go to Volta Lake to see what it looks like. So I think that we have broken away, but not completely, from what we [learned in the past]. (08/13/97)

Spirituality and questions of ecology go hand in hand. Land as a place of abode transcends the physical with the metaphysical realm. Knowing about one's lands is to acquire knowledge about the spiritual and material connections between society, culture and nature. African spirituality connects the physical with the metaphysical world. Educators do not simply teach about rivers, lakes and waterfalls as physical structures but as natural entities imbued with human qualities.

Generally, these narratives speak to issues about the importance of self, culture and learning. Learning proceeds from knowing the self, history and culture. Local knowledge is significant for this learning process to be effective. It is this learning that helps to ground the individual and community spiritually and to develop a people's sense of purpose and direction in life. It is argued by these educators that indigenous/local knowledges have maintained their viability in the face of the colonial encounter. Rather than remaining static or frozen, local knowledges have survived and adapted to changing social, political economic, emotional and spiritual conditions of peoples. However, while different epistemologies may conflict foundationally, the view of indigenous knowledges as dynamic resists the epistemological chasm of Western/non-Western knowledge formulations.

Criticisms of the call to reclaim the past are based on the linearity and the circularity of reasoning, meaning that to claim a recourse to the past is to claim the past as uni-directional and frozen in time and space. Indigenous knowledges challenge the idea of linear reasoning in favour of circular arguments which speak of transformation. Such knowledges retrieve the past, but a transformed past. While different knowledges may conflict foundationally with each other, Indigenous knowledges call for an epistemological shift away from linear circularity to emphasize a dialectic relation among points in a circle without presupposing a static point of origin or a simple repetition of the past (see Turner 1999). The past is never lost but transforms itself. There is no possibility of going back to a frozen past. Nothing repeats in its original state. As the old is reclaimed, it is transformed and becomes a new reality. The spiritual self is part of the past, present and future. The past can also be reclaimed through the use of proverbs as historical knowledge which continues a dialogue with the ancestors and the spiritual worlds.

Proverbs can be used by educators in the form of ancestral and spiritual knowledge to promote learning for youth. Rima, who wants to be a Home Science teacher someday, speaks about her teacher's pedagogy as one that connects spiritually with her learning. For example, in articulating the importance of history, she remembers her teacher retelling a saying from an historical ancestor: "History too is important ... then he [referring to ancestor] also talked about the girl child saying; "If you educate a man you educate a husband; educate the girl you educate the whole nation." So this is also history for the whole of Ghana" (09/21/97).

This is education as pursued from the position of its importance, not simply to the individual but also to the larger community. There is an expressed spiritual tie between womanhood and nationhood. Another student, Kuse, refers to the personal and social importance of choosing one's peers and recalls a proverb that emphasizes the interconnectedness of individual character and how it is perceived as indicative of a good moral code. Good friends are said to be symptomatic of one's inner strength, being and character as in: "show me your friends and I'll tell you your character" (09/21/97).

Relevant Teaching

In answering why he went into teaching, Jojo, a Social Studies educator mentions the changing role of the teacher in society:

> When I entered the University of Cape Coast ... I could also have gone to any other of the industries ... But during the second year I developed a love for training youth in the way they should grow, so that when they grow they will not depart from it ... It's not only the academic work that I do in class. [But] anytime there is an opportunity, I give some sound training to students. What I often say is that seeing they are all Ghanaians and I am also Ghanaian I would like to train them in the way they should grow, so that by the time they have grown and I am an old man they will not give me problems in my old age. So I tell them that I'm confident that while I'm training, even if I don't meet them when I'm old, I may meet some other people and I believe that the work that I have done when I was young will benefit people ... So I believe that, that is why I chose the teaching field to help train students of Ghana. They are my own people ... That's my philosophy, so that they will grow to become responsible citizens of this, our dear country. (09/21/97)

Jojo speaks of responsibility and accountability and the importance of making education count in the lives of the learners. He went into teaching to make an impact, to ensure that he can provide education to youth who one day will serve the wider interests of the community. To him teaching is not simply a materialistic undertaking but a task imbued with spiritual understandings and interests. Jojo connects the self, individual and person to the group and the collective. Teaching must encourage students to develop a connective capacity with their teachers, student peers, and the subjects being studied. Ghanaian educators within that framework stress to students that the community is made up of individuals, and that "whatever happens to the individual happens to the whole group, and whatever happens to the whole group happens to the individual" (Mbiti 1969, 108). They work with a concept of relationality which says that community is structured around interpersonal relations. To enhance the community is to strengthen the individual. The individual is strengthened by the community, not necessarily subsumed by it. The individual is enriched by her or his culture. With culture understood as shared values, aspirations and concerns, so classroom teaching and learning are rooted in shared assumptions about community, society and nature. Classroom teachings also stress rights and privileges of the individual and groups as matched with corresponding social responsibility. Part of that responsibility includes that the privileged who exercise the right to learn and receive education in turn need to put their education to the good of the individual and the wider community. As an educator, Jojo has developed a sensitivity to the students' and the community's needs and aspirations. His form of spiritual teaching is helping students to know and feel about the community and to develop a sense of belonging and continuity.

Spirituality as Self-Discipline

To ingrain these thoughts in the minds of the learner requires spiritual discipline. Thus, for some educators and students, spiritual values are understood as self-discipline. The acknowledgement of the positive aspects of spirituality is held by Odom, a student in the final year of his teacher training program. He clearly sees the importance of integrating culture, language and proverbs in the education of youth. He applauds the integration of religion and spirituality in his life and in the College. Odom received financial assistance throughout his schooling for which he was very grateful, given that his family was of limited financial means. He interprets the assistance as being the help of God:

> Well, the main thing is the discipline ... because as a man or as a human being, if you are not disciplined, you cannot fit into society. So for me, for instance, I like the discipline very muc, so that I will be able to fit into any society ... So [this] College is one of the best in Ghana. That is why I like this place very much. Moreover, it is

an Adventist school and mostly they force us to always pick the message of God. As we learn the message of God they teach us religiously. (09/10/97)

Later in the interview, when referring to his father who could not financially help further his education beyond JSS, but who was there to support his son's learning through advice, Odom adds:

> What I like about my father, though he couldn't further his education ... I actually appreciate that when I am going to school, he tells me, "[Odom] you know the problems we have in our home, please don't go and make friends with the rich man's son or daughter, but always learn. When you are learning too, remember your God always." Always when I am going to school my father tells me this. In fact, I am grateful to him for this advice and I always stick to that advice. (09/10/97)

The reasoning in his father's advice is that religion can provide a strong spiritual base on which to ensure school success.

Conclusion

Spirituality supplies the context of meaning for society and regulates thought and behaviour of individuals in everyday life. Learning and teaching must generate relevant knowledge base in collective resuscitation, spiritual rebirth and cultural renewal of all learners. Effective schooling cannot be dismissive of the spiritual as an important knowledge for the development of the self, the inner character and personhood. In spiritual education, teaching and learning are geared towards the cultivation of the inner level of self. Such learning is connected to the collective for social action. In spiritual education there is also an interplay of the sacred and secular since spiritual traditions are embedded in educational thought and practice.

Hoffman (1999) draws on the distinction between individuality and individualism when speaking of Japanese education. While individuality attests to the strength of inner character—an ability to negotiate the collective on the basis of an understanding of the self and one's place in a collective—individualism drives the self to disconnect from the collective or group. Within Ghanaian education, there is a degree of both individuality and individualism. Individuality, as pointed out in the foregoing discussion, is an affirmation of uniqueness and distinctiveness. Individualism, on the other hand, is the competitive spirit that seeks to avoid the collective in the sense of perceiving the group as a threat to individual power, survival and accomplishment. Competition in schooling can take the form of individuals competing for top grades, or aspiring to reach the top at the expense of group interests and wishes. Individualism is a market-driven ploy that cherishes competition at the expense of group solidarity. By itself individualism is not a detriment if it harnesses individual creativity and resourcefulness for collective use. It becomes a problem if it ascribes knowledge to individual acumen and negates the degree of dependence and interdependence in knowledge production.

The maintenance of the bind between self and other and individual and group is significant in teachings about social relations in African contexts. For example, African spirituality embraces the "complementarity aspect of the male-female relationship or the nature of feminine and masculine in all forms of life, which is understood as nonhierarchical" (Dove 1998, 522). In other words, every life form of knowledge exists as indispensable pairs, such that the self is connected with the other, inner with outer, individual with group, subject with object, reason with emotion, culture with nature, mind with body, and the abstract with concrete. To posit these as distinct from each other is to show the "ahistoricity of all such dichotomies" (Harding 1998, 385). There are no neat distinctions in life.

Space and location, like history and culture, are also significant to understanding African spiritual sense of self. As the foregoing discussion shows, there is a historical-social-temporal location of the personal and indigenous subjectivity. African spirituality defines the "space" as both geographic, connected and sacred. Land as a physical space is embedded in metaphysical meanings that are sacred and spiritual. Land and people are inseparable. Land is knowledge, and not a mere possession. It is key to human survival.

In broaching wider theoretical implications, one needs to be aware of the problems of "abstract universalism" that downplays the specificities of local situations; "decontextualized learning" that allows no recourse to the importance of local experiences, histories, cultures and identities in the learning process; the problem of "consensualism" that does not acknowledge conflict, tensions and ambiguities in claiming a role for spirituality in education (see also Hatcher 1998 in a different context). As this chapter has pointed out, there are contestations around spirituality, identity and representations of values.

The intellectual engagement of spirituality and African education leads me to argue that Africans, to paraphrase Ifi Amadiume (1989), need alternative terminologies and new terms of reference to speak about our identities, histories and social existence. The African spiritual identity, like all forms of identity, is embedded in and constituted by particular social practices and prevailing ideologies. Resisting imposed identity in the African sense is a politics to construct an Africanness which is outside of that identity which continues to be constructed within Euro-American ideology (see also Muteshi 1996); that is, the capacity to project oneself into one's own experience, culture and history instead of continuing to live on borrowed, external terms (Mazama 1998).

Culture, history and origin emphasize the uniqueness as well as the interrelations of spirituality, ethics and human values. Yet, we need to escape the quagmire of relativism by acknowledging that individual ideas about spiritual knowledge, while located in place and within historically specific contexts, can still be shared with others. Writing on African womanism, Dove (1998) points out that for all peoples of African descent "there is a belief that we, despite our different experiences, are linked to our African cultural memory and spirituality and may at any time become conscious of its significance to our Africanness and future" (p. 516). In other words, while we do acknowledge the diversity among African peoples, "such diversity does not preclude sameness" (Dove 1998, 518). Gyekye (1995) also cautioned against taking the African diversity falsely as purposefully exaggerated by the European "invention of Africa" to the extreme. It should also be added that even these values of African spirituality discussed in this text can and are shared by other populations.

The future of education in Ghana, as in Africa, must move beyond the fetters of an externally-imposed and sanctioned agenda to one defined in relation to locally relevant and meaningful visions of the equilibrium between change and historicity. As Ghanaian education addresses indigeneity through ongoing implementation of state reforms, striving for equitable access and inclusive social participation, education must validate not only diverse human resource knowledge bases as productive agents of change, but must re-humanize knowledge production and human "capital" in spiritual, ancestrally-linked terms, negotiated on local terms.

The narratives of educators, teachers and students show how spirituality connects to education by linking identity to schooling and knowledge production. Identity, defining the self and one's place in the group, is not just a spiritual identification. It is also a site from which to engage educational practice. Spiritual and intuitive learning enhances individual creativity and resourcefulness. It creates spaces for local knowledges to enter the school system and to engage in the process of educational delivery.

African spirituality does not value the individual over the collective or vice versa. In fact African spiritual values shun an individualistic, autonomous, self-centred subject as much as it despises an uncaring community. Rather, the concept of "relation" is employed in making the linkage between the self and the group and in understanding social interactions within and between groups. The individual and the social cannot be posited in "antagonistic disrelation" (Turner 1999). The self is intrinsically and conceptually connected with the community. An individual develops her or his sense of self through relationships within the community or collective (see Harding 1998, 364). Furthermore, African spirituality emphasizes cooperation and group validation as key to individual accomplishments. Individual creativity emerges from dependence and inter-dependence. The self can neither be individualistic, separated from others and nature, nor threatened by a close association with others. Similarly, in the knowledge seeking process the self cannot separate itself as "impartial, disinterested [and] dispassionate" (Harding 1998, 364). Learning is a process that creates the individual self, for example, learning for individual spiritual self-activation. By engaging the individual learner as a person, her or his inner self is touched/ affirmed, leading to learning.

The individual is a cultural conception (see also Hoffman 1995, 1999; Tobin 1994; Shields 1999). Within every community there is a cultural knowledge embedded in what the individual and self mean and can accomplish. The individual can be the site of strength, creativity, knowledge and resistance. Ideas of spirituality affirm the individual as an inner being, inner spirit and character that can use embodied knowledge as a starting base to engage schooling. The inner world of individual and collective consciousness offer guidelines to human action. The self is multiplicated and the individual is a symbol of difference. Difference is understood as variety, as a site of strength. It is the particularity of (individual) experience that in practice becomes the contextual basis of knowledge. Educators in their teaching and students through learning stress the relationship of the self to culture (e.g., upholding group cultural values, norms, beliefs that govern individual actions).

The concept of the individual also speaks to the interface of body, mind and soul. There are different conceptions of the body, mind and soul linkage that can be relevant for creating alternative forms of schooling. In one conception, the mind and soul direct what the body can do, including teaching and learning. The mind and soul provide the spiritual guidance for action. The individual learner as active agent can also be a resistor to group conformity without necessarily being individualistic to the extent of shunning the group. An educational perspective and practice grounded in a Ghanaian spiritual traditional worldview promotes individual creativity that is well aware of the need to let individual talent flourish.

It takes an individual with a strong spirit to know the world of the unknown. Culture teaches that the living is emboldened by ancestral knowledge and the wisdom of the dead. Learning culture and spirituality thus enthuses continuity between the world of the living and that of the dead. Thus ancestral spirits are living knowledges. They are acknowledged as guardians of the living. They provide knowledge, wisdom and advice and regulate living practice.

Within modern western school systems the issue of spirituality as a particular body of knowledge is not seriously examined. In fact, spirituality (if discussed at all) is very much part of philosophy or theology. Both private and publicly-funded religious schools have tended not to formally examine the spiritual world/s of knowledge, despite the fact that alternative and competing visions of spirituality, community and religious faith persist. Officially, there is a secularized push to schooling, one without the recognition of the spiritual and of different ways of seeing. This conventional worldview has indeed served to impose hegemonic knowings on the views of others. Yet, in reality, spirituality and spiritual ideas have always been "present" in our schools, and the search for genuine educational options must retrieve these "subjugated knowledges" to enhance learning for all. The Ghanaian case study offers important insights.

As already noted, while the focus of the study (on educational reforms) was not on the issue of spirituality, aspects of local perspectives on spirituality emerged directly and indirectly from different entry points (e.g., from the perspectives of religion, from how students of different religions find their voice of difference in the schools and from students' conceptions of the self, culture and community and the individual's place in society). It is from the latter that the reader gets a broader view of spirituality as one outside of religion. In other words, students, teachers, educators and parents have different views of spirituality and there are different ways that spirituality is expressed. The possibility of analysing a broad view of a grounded local spirituality can, therefore, be developed. Local spiritual views are expressed in the common sense of the place of the self within the community. In some cases spiritual values are expressed within, outside and around the specific religions. It is in identifying the sites in which religion, community, local and the self are spoken of, that a people's articulation of their spirituality emerges.

It is worth repeating that while theoretically one ought to make a distinction between religion and spirituality for some students, in historically mission schools or schools with a particular religious slant, spirituality is tied to their religious faith. From the perspective of established religions, one could argue that the coming of these religions has strongly/differentially impacted on local spiritual practices. Colonialism silenced some traditional cultural practices. At the same time traditional African practices strongly reflected imported [colonial] religious beliefs. Today, traditional cultural values are still expressed in community life and shared memories largely outside the faith community. Even in communities with different faiths, common spiritual values are shared across local differences because there is a sense that people are connected to a place, to a history and to traditions. It can therefore be argued that Western formal education has colonized the spiritual traditions of Africa, but not without resistance and not without African peoples themselves appropriating these other religious and spiritual traditions and making them theirs. Within some established religious structures, there are myriad ways in which local peoples voice a spirituality that goes beyond the imposed structures and reaches out to other spiritual expressions across religions.

In effect, what the present study shows is that there are significant students', educators' and parents' narrative voices speaking to beliefs within particular religious structures that cannot be excluded from a discussion on spirituality. To do so would exclude students who identify themselves with a particular religion from making the connection of their practice to a broader collective spirituality. To do so will also prevent us from seeing the way in which students struggle to transform their religions from colonizing practices by integrating local views of spirituality and spiritual consciousness. It is very evident that the local, the community and the social and educational values offered the greatest source of data on the broader more interconnected sense of spirituality (that is, spirituality that is not necessarily attached to a religious institution but rather to the spirit and sense of community and values of a people). The broader, more grounded sensibilities of a people from a place seem to filter through the lens more freely than that of religion which tends to separate people into their differences rather than their common sense of belonging to a place and history with a collective sense of indigenousness.

Note:

1. Increasingly the important role of spirituality in African education is being recognized. Within the context of Ghanaian schooling, the subject matter is broached in some depth in specific related works (see Dei 2002a, b, c)

Chapter 6

Local Knowledges and Languages

The relevance of local, indigenous knowledges for understanding and implementing educational change in African contexts cannot be overemphasized. However, many who have assumed the mantle of leadership in addressing African development and educational concerns have usually devoted little analysis or attention to the ingenious contributions and untapped resources potential of diverse local African knowledges to the development process. An increasing number of studies have looked at educational policy and reform. There is also a number of writings on the process of educational transformation within African countries at times of national development from a participatory research perspective (e.g., Tanzania, Guinea-Bissau, Cape Verde) whereby the processes of restructuring the nation and its educational system are documented in action as policy makers, educators and communities reflect and act on the challenge of establishing an anti-colonial national education system/program (Freire & Macedo 1987; Hall 2001). However, except for a few studies (e.g., Buchert 1998), there has been little systemic qualitative interview research that considers how local subjects (i.e. teachers, students and parents) understand and engage reform and educational change and how educators respond (in their classroom instructional and textual discursive practices) to the diverse needs and local/indigenous knowledges of students under difficult conditions. Conducting this kind of research allows those engaged in education to step back from the reality in the reforms and begin to reflect on it with the researcher in dialogue.

In identifying the important role education plays in national development, educational reforms must focus on local educators', students' and parents' understanding and assessment of the impact and consequences of change and the ways to enhance learning for all students. This requires a basic underlying assumption that recognizes difference among individual students and groups of students which, in turn, also means understanding how difference is perceived and acted upon by all educational stakeholders and specifying the implications for formulating viable educational options. The sense of urgency in the present search for viable educational options rests on the apparent contributions of education to the development process. However, part of this search for educational alternatives entails a need to problematize the uninterrogated assumption of a universal, direct and immediate linkage between education and development. And it must also problematize and interrogate what kind of development and for whom. Educational change must be undertaken in terms of the maximization of human possibilities in the development of critical thinking skills and for social action within the local context. The legitimation of local knowledges will help to transform the relations of power within which people produce, interrogate, disseminate, value and apply different types and forms of information, different knowledges and ways of understanding. One of the ways to gain insights into how those involved in education are actively or passively engaging these issues, is to ask them. To enter into a dialogue with them, whereby, these questions are posed and reflected upon.

An important component of genuine educational change is the application of local indigenousness popular learning and teaching to address human concerns, needs and aspirations. As previously stated, indigenousness here means "knowledge consciousness" that arises locally and in association with long-term occupancy of a place. Such consciousness emerges from an awareness of the productive forces exerted by indigenous knowledges in local norms and social values, and in the mental constructs which regulate African ways of living. Indigenous knowledges differ from conventional knowledge (see also Fals-Borda 1980, p. 37 for a discussion of the valorization of popular sciences engaged as dissent to dominating epistemological and political relations of knowledge production). People who over time have been subordinated or marginalized use these knowledges to make sense of their worlds in ways that are continuous and consistent with traditional world views and principles. In other words, these knowledges are distinguished by an absence of colonial and imperial imposition. This contrast is instructive. The notion of indigenousness highlights the power relations and dynamics embedded in the production, interrogation, validation and dissemination of global knowledge (Dei 1999a). I view indigenous knowledge as unique to a given culture or society, reflecting common sense ideas and cultural resource knowledges of local peoples concerning everyday realities of living.

At one level, educational reform in (many parts of) Africa portrays the dissonance of theoretical intent meeting harsh reality and highlights the practical constraints associated with a lack of political will (on the part of governments) or material support to back well-intentioned state policies. While there has been a shared desire for change, the means to arrive at such change have not always been cultivated. In many local contexts, international finance capital and donor agencies (such as UNDP and UNCED) in defining the educational agenda have magnified the impotence of the state in supporting and implementing locally defined priorities. For example, Banya (1993) points out that educational change has been "ambiguous and ambivalent," such that the British educational system which was designed to generate cheap labor has been permitted to remain intact (p. 168). Moreover, while military expenditures have continued to dominate Sierra Leonean budgets, educational provisions have steadily diminished. The case of Sierra Leone is a recent example of a more extreme dissonance between the needs of local peoples and the policies of national governments in relationships with international financial and market interests. The situation in Ghana is different. However, the pattern of dissonance between the needs of local peoples and national policies has some pattern of similarity albeit to a much lesser degree. When prioritization has meant the redistribution of resources, the state has been found wanting. Not surprisingly, in the eyes of many ordinary Ghanaians, the governing leadership has been losing its legitimacy and credibility to "rule."

Fortunately, a few local educators are exercising the power of human agency. In the midst of educational hardships they are using local knowledge and innovative skills to promote educational delivery. There are important theoretical and practical lessons. In the search for genuine educational options critical research must focus on how students, teachers and administrative staff work together to understand themselves and their social and material world in the face of hardships and despite the lack of material support. This focus leads to a more comprehensive understanding of how students, teachers and local communities imagine and act in creative and innovative ways to enhance the experiences of schooling and learning for all. This chapter shows how local teachers, students and parents understand reform and the challenges, limitations and new possibilities for educational change. The examination of instructional, pedagogic and curricular practices of educators demonstrate the limitations as well as possibilities of promoting genuine reform. The specific practices of educators and the strategies of engaging school by students may well offer crucial lessons for re-conceptualizing schooling and educational change in diverse African contexts. For example, how do teachers teach and learn from students and how do students learn from each other?

From this Ghanaian case study, there emerges a recognition of the importance of local knowledge and culture in the implementation of reform. In classrooms, teachers and students are seeking to use local knowledges to understand and transform the social world they inhabit by speaking, reading and writing about that world in order to further co-operative and collective teaching and learning. With assistance from their teachers, parents, peers and local communities, students are seeking out ways to empower themselves in order to succeed in school the best way they can. If academic learning is to be successfully integrated and sustained, schools must devise ways to ensure that students', educators' and parents' concerns about educational reforms are heard and understood. Learning strategies that emphasize the importance of centering the learner and his or her community of peers in their education and teaching approaches that start from the known to the unknown are crucial to the transformation of education in different African contexts. In such learning environments (school settings) students learn from the familiar, from experiences in and of their communities. They are taught to locate themselves, their identities, subjectivities and histories in the processes of learning. From such a situated pedagogy, they can make the connections to and see the relevance of their daily experiences of producing, interrogating, validating and sharing knowledge. Similarly, many Ghanaian teachers are working to educate with the tools available to them. They often have to improvise to deal with scarcity and hardship. The study reveals that teachers' classroom practices are influenced by a number of factors such as: teachers' assumptions about knowledge and of knowledge transmission; teachers' and students' perceptions of each other and their respective roles and responsibilities; and the goals and objectives of schooling and education (see also Tabulawa 1998). The continuous affirmation of the idea of multiple knowledges and the collaborative dimensions of knowledge production make learning and teaching possible even when there is a shortage of physical and material resources. The goals of collaborative and reciprocal approaches to education must ensure that students can identify with teaching and learning processes. The theoretical lesson is, perhaps, that the task of educational transformation is not simply to reform existing curricular, instructional and pedagogic practices. It needs also to address issues of relevance, meaning, social survival as well as bias and inequality in schools by creating spaces whereby alternative readings of our worlds are an integral part of learning that is open. Over two decades ago, Ali Mazrui (1978) extolled Africans to build a genuine partnership between indigenous cultures and educational systems. He argued that the "full maturity of African education will come only when Africa develops a capacity to innovate independently" (p. 352). Educational reform initiatives that fail to tap local creativity and resourcefulness are doomed to fail. Such reform can only further external dependency (see also Lindsay 1989).

Research aimed at soliciting local subjects' perceptions and views of the educational reforms are significant for informing on the impact of the reform initiatives on individuals and communities. At heart, Ghanaians who participated in this study (educators, parents and students) want the reforms to work for them, for their communities and for Ghana as a nation. They see local/indigenous knowledges as a relevant part of educational change. How they voice and narrate their subjective experiences allows the critical educational researcher to tease out the complexities, nuances, ambiguities and subtleties of implementing reforms on them, a specific population. From their subjective accounting, we begin to understand the human and practical dimensions of how educators, teachers and parents are experiencing the reforms. Responses to and interpretations of educational reforms demonstrate the intellectual agency of the participating subjects/citizens as they make sense of local conditions and offer insights and knowledge on dealing with educational hardships, constraints and failures. Readers begin to learn and understand how schools, educators, students, families and communities are reacting to the harsh climate of economic decline, austerity and structural adjustment and its impact on education. We learn from educators that the problem with the colonial system of education operating in the past was that it was too "foreign," "intellectual" and "abstract." It was not geared to meet the immediate needs of Ghanaian society, but rather it served external interests. This form of education was too intent on producing school graduates who had no deep knowledge of their environments and situations they would encounter. Yet they could summon enough vocabulary to expound on external issues. Mathematics teacher, Dankwah, rightly critiques past colonial education: "Well, I think it has been too academic for me. All the education that we had was too academic. At least if we knew some practical aspects that would have been better" (08/28/97). Redressing this imbalance of theoretical over practical schooling has been one of the overriding challenges propelling the educational reforms. Many teachers, students and parents share a vision of an education that is meaningful and practical. In the face of hardships and obstacles, they are resolved to do their best to improve upon the quality of the current system. This resolve lies behind some educators' desire and zeal to improvise in the face of inadequate or lack of textbooks, material resources and other logistical supports. Most teachers, students and parents have had to rely on their creativity and resourcefulness to deal with those issues that are within their immediate control and power. In their efforts to address the problem of a lack of textbooks and other material supports for vocational education, many educators are improvising in their teaching practices. They have to depend on the surrounding local environments as cultural resource sites for teaching and learning. In speaking about improvisation, Osei, the head of the science resource centre, remarks: "Before the science resource centre ... was improv-ising. We were taught to improvise. I said I'm a professional we [are] taught to improvise so I was really improvising and it [is] helping because we have large numbers of students" (08/21/97). When asked to describe the nature of the improvisation he practises, he explains: "First, stones could be used as weights. Second, sand could also be used as you know little particles. Third, wood could be shaped in the form of a metre ruler. We have some metre rulers that are just to measure. You shape the wood in the form of a metre ruler. A fluorescent tube could be cut and then used as resonance tubes for experiments etc." (08/21/97). Educators have to look to their surrounding environments for local alternatives to educational resources and materials to use in their classroom teaching. Dankwah speaks about some of his particular pedagogic practices in the classroom:

> Well in terms of chalk if there is no chalk, there is no chalk. But in terms of textbooks at least [you] make an effort and try to go to a library or to go to a friend in a school where [you] can get at least one textbook which [you] will use ... [to plan and develop] ... assignments ... The students will not be able to read from the textbooks [individually] but at least the teacher will have it for teaching. (08/28/97)

Teachers are having to find alternative curricular content, materials and teaching approaches to educate youth. They are sharing knowledge and pooling scarce resources. They are using accumulated local knowledge to educate. With respect to the information that is traded and circulated in the academy, Amaadee, an instructor in general science, points to the importance of seeing students as part of the process of knowledge production. Acknowledgement of their active involvement ensures that students develop a sense of identification with and ownership of knowledge. It also allows educators to learn from students: "I think it is sharing knowledge ... Like I said earlier on, we learn to give and take sort of thing. And I think the more students are involved the better it is for them because they will be able to retain more [knowledge]" (08/21/97).

Local knowledge begins with the self. Local knowledge is indigenous to the self, group and community. Experience and practice are the contextual basis of such knowledge. Personal identity and collective histories are implicated in the making of knowledge. Donkor, who has taught vocational skills (sewing and leather work) in his school for over seven years, believes that one's identity is relevant to knowledge production. He sees this connection as an important aspect of the ideology behind the school reforms since the reforms have the stated objective of ensuring that education speaks directly to local and Ghanaian issues, concerns and aspirations. In light of such reasoning, he concludes that the background of those preparing curriculum and resource materials is significant, particularly in the teaching of vocational skills. He thinks that schools and teachers should have books written by Ghanaians:

> A non-Ghanaian will be using ... maybe tools and equipment which [are] mentioned in the textbook but which in fact he may not be familiar [with]. But if the person, the writer is Ghanaian he will be using familiar tools ... and ... the [text] written in the country will be more practical and comfortable for the students. But education is in part dynamic and is going out so maybe [one] will be training here and find ourselves somewhere. So we [educators] try in fact to compare and bring the similarities between maybe ... the US, Britain and [here] ... So we try to teach all these things but we normally want the pamphlets or the books written by Ghanaians. (08/28/97)

While he concedes that all knowledges have contexts, he also argues that in a system of meaningful, practical education which is the anticipated result of the reforms, the pursuit of knowledge cannot simply be self-referential. Knowledge must always relate to what is happening both internally and externally. This means that there is a synthesis of knowledges affirming the multiple, collective and collaborative dimensions of "knowing."

Parents, community workers and elders have a responsibility to ensure that community knowledge speaks to the complexities of experiences and social realities. In fact, the many challenges posed by ongoing educational reforms require that all educational stakeholders perform their duty to ensure the effectiveness of educational outcomes for youth. In creating and developing educational programs and knowledges that are relevant, the importance of parental engagement cannot be overestimated. Education is too important to be left in the hands of school authorities alone. No reform, no matter how extensive, well-intentioned or well-executed, will produce effective educational outcomes for youth without consultation, support and assistance of parents, teachers and the local community.

From what I learned in the interviews I conducted, it seems that students, teachers and parents are generally critical of school reforms. While they applaud the goal of providing practical education to all learners, they also disparage of the implementation process. Donkor[1] holds a diploma in education. As noted above, he has been teaching vocational skills (sewing and leatherwork) at the college level for over seven years. The experience of his long service, he believes, places him in a position to offer an assessment of the reforms. Although he lauds the spirit behind the new changes, he wants to see reform initiatives directed at addressing the perennial problem of educational discontinuities and the lack of resources, including trained personnel. When asked to reflect on the reforms in general thus far, he lists a host of issues impinging on the challenge of effective implementation:

> I think the idea [reforms] is very good [but the way they are going about it is not good] ... I think if we are reforming the education system ... we should start from the primary level to the JSS and then to SSS ... [T]eachers must also be trained for all these subjects ... [T]here should be facilities, the equipment ... and tools must be there for students to use ... [T]hey want the teacher to go and then improvise but in this system what we used about 30/40 years ago may not be the same thing. (08/28/97)

For Donkor, consistency is the key to educational success. He speaks from practical, local experience. In his view, it is important for administrators to commit to sustaining any new educational initiatives. He appreciates the objective of equipping all students with hands-on, practical skills. However, to his mind, new initiatives must start from the primary level and continue into secondary and post-secondary education. In other words, the goal of making each level (Primary/JSS/SSS) in part a self-contained terminal stage is not enough. There must also be some continuity in the system in order to achieve intended benefits. He works with a knowledge base that emphasizes the importance of continuity and learning from what has preceded from the indigenous ancestral past. But what we have seen is that the new reforms again continue the same problem of not taking into account the reality of local needs. Those engaged in education in the different communities know the resources which are available and those which are lacking. However, they have not been brought into the process other than being informed of the new initiative to be implemented by them.

Donkor's colleague, Dankwah, teaches mathematics. He is a recent graduate, having completed his university education in 1997. By drawing on his own personal schooling experiences, Dankwah presents further insights into the problems of implementing the reforms. He highlights the issue of textbooks and the fact that teachers of new subjects lack adequate training and preparation. Sometimes teachers received their training in different subject areas. In his opinion, this mismatch can only be detrimental to students' learning. It constitutes an inappropriate use of human resources and talents. Moreover, it is clearly indicative of a failure in plans to work with the idea of practice and experience as the contextual basis of knowledge:

> I think we have a lot of problems. You go to the schools and ah they're supposed [to] get textbooks. [But the] books are not there... [In addition, we] don't have enough teachers. And those who are ... qualified, ... they may have a full degree or a certain degree but the subject he/she is teaching may not be his area of specialization. For example, some people are teaching mathematics who did a [different] course, you see. This ... and ... they ... may not know the ins and outs of it. (08/28/97)

As a young parent, Dankwah shares the economic pain of most Ghanaians as they struggle to meet multiple family demands. The problem of severe economic austerity is compounded by the perception and realization that the government has reneged on its responsibilities to provide education at the basic level to all youth. Rights and responsibilities are intertwined. The teacher's duty to teach must be complemented with the responsibility of the state and local community to ensure that the educator has the tools and resources to undertake the task. For Dankwah, meeting one's responsibility is key to successful leadership:

> ... Well you look at the nation as a whole. We have a problem with the economic situation of the countryside ... every parent is suffering. When we take children who are going to school, parents are supposed to buy books [and they] need [other] materials but [these] resources are such that they cannot afford ... At times those relevant materials which the students are supposed to get, they [do] not ... And when they go to school those which are to be supplied by the government [are] also not available. So, in effect, they see pictures in the [dark] ... Those items are mentioned but

they don't see [them]. ... This is what is happening in their education. (08/28/97)

Even when parents do have the means, educational materials (e.g. the new textbooks intended to support the integration of indigenous knowledges) are not readily available. This, in Dankwah's view, impedes the reform process. For their part, students raise similar concerns. They fully recognize that current educational initiatives offer possibilities for individual and collective learning and advancement. Yet, students see the big picture. Educational opportunities are welcome if the tools exist for students to take advantage of them. The students' experience teaches them that learning cannot take place in a vacuum. In the following extracts of students' voices, concerns ranging from lack of textbooks and professionally trained teachers to the failing physical infrastructure can be heard. Students speak of the importance of all educational stakeholders' developing and then fulfilling personal and collective commitments and responsibilities. They realize that success means working hard and taking education seriously. But they ask: How can students achieve success under these reforms when the promised textbooks are not in schools? What happens to learning when students have to worry about the breakdown of the educational infrastructure?

> You see, the main problem [im]posed on us is on our educational system. The educational system [is such that] if you don't try to become successful, you don't learn. [If] you don't stick to your books, you don't make good friends, you become... end up being unsuccessful. You can't earn a living. (female student, 10/24/97)

> We lack textbooks, some of the teachers are not trained well. (male student, 10/20/97)

> If I [had] the chance of changing the school, I would propose that they [raise] funds for the school [to] build a new dormitory. (female student, 10/24/97)

> They [teachers] are giving all their best. (male student, 10/20/97)

> I would like to change the time of completing school ... to at least 4 years (from the current three years). (female student, 10/20/97)

Like many others, these students have interests, hopes and desires as well as fears and anxieties. They welcome the goals and objectives of the reforms but are aware that it takes more than good intentions and policies on paper to achieve favourable educational outcomes. Students are grateful to the teachers who persevere against all odds. They are also "unforgetting" of those teachers who come to class ill-prepared. Students have their own ideas about changing their schools. And they accept some personal and collective responsibility for ensuring school success. To apply local knowledge is to be creative, skilful and resourceful. From speaking at the ground level in communities to those delivering, receiving, and supporting education it becomes very clear that they have critical insights into the problems of educational reforms that are imposed from a centralized planning system that does not take fully into account the very real local needs. If they were to do so, the reform process would be more participatory and ongoing. Discussions with the participants make it clear that the people in school communities are a source of knowledge of both the needs and the strengths within a locality. Understandings derived from these dialogues can inform educational reform processes that are more transformative and participatory, whereby those in communities continuously reflect on the local resources, problems and visions for an education that meets individual, local and national needs of the people of Ghana.

Educational Innovations: Local Knowledge, the School and the Community

On a hopeful note, it can be said that in order to address the challenge of educational reforms, school communities are finding ways to tap the immense creativity and resourcefulness of teachers, students and parents, thereby confirming peoples' spirit to be active agents in their world. Educators are rethinking classroom teaching practices and pedagogic and communicative methods to ensure that learning is culturally and politically relevant to students. Innovative educators are using local knowledges and improvising with available local resource materials. They are finding ways to draw out local community interests. Such educators work with an understanding of individual and community empowerment. Bonsu, a general arts instructor and community worker, knows fully well the power of social and community knowledge. His critique of educational reforms is tempered by an enunciation of positive (i.e., solution-oriented) aspects of educational change. He speaks about the extent to which ongoing reforms have helped to usher in a sense of community ethics among teachers, students and parents. Local communities are, in turn, striving to fulfil their responsibilities to the educational process:

> The only thing I can say is that this [reforms] ... has created community already. Now when you go to every community and they see the need that the school should provide ... the community ... contribute in terms of physical cash, materials and then their labour to put up school buildings. And now [some communities] have provided bungalows with ... institutions at least for supervision course. (08/11/97)

Admittedly, the practice of pooling community resources and skills to ensure school success is not new in Ghana or for that matter Africa in general. For example, there is literature on community involvement in education in Tanzania (see Buchert 1994, Kaduri 1997). However, the idea of community being evoked in a new context brings different insights. For example, English and history teacher Ohemaa, with eight years professional service, draws on school-community relations in her classroom pedagogy. To her, building and maintaining such relations allows students to develop a sense of identification and connectedness to the school. Students are able to articulate their responsibilities to local neighbourhoods. Thus, maintaining the ties between school and community should mean that students continuously seek to be grounded in communal practice. The quest for knowledge in the interest of personal gain is thus to be tied to collective learning and development. Elaborating on her pedagogic and communicative practices with students, Ohemaa adds: "We normally teach the relationship that should exist between the school and the community and what goes on between the school and community ... because the school is situated in the community and the students are also going back to the community to teach so we should teach some cordial relationship to exist between the two" (08/20/97).

Similarly, Amina, who holds a Bachelor degree in Social Science and a diploma in Education, states that, to be effective, a teacher must know and understand her or his community. A mother with two children, she has taught social studies for seven years. She argues that teachers must use the community as a site for and source of knowledge. Students must be taught to define their responsibilities to the wider community. Within Ghanaian cultures, it is understood that the community sustains and nourishes the individual and her or his personal growth. Amina provides a comprehensive definition of what community must mean in the cause of promoting genuine educational change. Implicitly, she speaks about the importance of having a local perspective on knowledge.

Directly, she refers to textbooks, curricular and instructional materials in use in schools and the roles of local communities in producing their own knowledges. She points out that for far too long national educational policy has given only lip service to the notion of "local community knowledge." She credits the current government for trying to change this "mentality." But she adds that if the effort is to succeed, official support must be forthcoming at all times. When asked to expand on her critique, she chooses the case of school textbooks:

> For example, I don't know. But sometimes I think that the books that are written by our people, I tend to like them more than those that are written by others; Europeans. Sometimes I argue that we are here and they come and tell us something. So, me personally, I believe those that have been written by our own people … If it is history, I prefer the book written by them [our people] to those by foreigners. (08/20/97)

In local contexts, the success of educational innovations depend on the sharing of knowledge on developing a sense of community and place. Many educators recognize that local knowledge can be an important teaching tool. Such knowledge is acquired by virtue of long-term occupancy of a place. It is knowledge expressing social norms, traditional values and the cognitive processes that guide, organize and regulate local peoples' ways of living and making sense of their worlds. The contextual basis of such knowledge is practice and experience. In their classroom practices many Ghanaian educators use local knowledge to engage students today. Amaadee, an instructor in general science, describes in succinct detail a classroom pedagogy relying on local knowledge. Hers is a pedagogic/communicative strategy that starts with what is known within familiar surroundings and then projects beyond this initial focus to the outside/external space. To explain what is taught, she first finds concrete examples from the local setting so that the student is able to grasp the concepts, the context and the content of the lessons. This pedagogic practice complements and is part of the broader approach being espoused/utilized to decolonize African education. It is intended to ensure that the student leaves school well-informed about her or his own local society and environment and is able to use such knowledge to analyse critically received, external knowledge to move beyond colonial education.

> Now we are hammering on the known to the unknown and we are still ... we are insisting that at least they should start from the immediate environment to the outside world. So we normally concentrate let's say on what is going on in the campus ... We extend it to [outside]. From [mentions name of town] or the nearer environment to the whole of Ghana and maybe compare it with other countries. So now we are concentrating solely on what goes on in the environment. Teachers are even being advised to use materials for experiments and those things that are found in their localities ... Yeh, so now it seems it is quite better now than at first when we were in school. (08/21/97)

Osei, previously the Acting Head of Science and now the Co-ordinator of the Science Resource Centre 3 in Amaadee's school, concurs with an anti-colonial education grounded in local Indigenous science. Osei is a Physics instructor who insists on the idea of teaching from the Indigenous knowledges to the unknown external knowledges to promote discussion and student comprehension of the subject matter. This also means that the student can more easily relate this acquired knowledge to her or his concerns, needs and immediate environments.

However, it must be emphasized that in the context of today's educational reforms to use local knowledge in the practice of contemporary schooling and teaching is to improvise. In the absence of textbooks and other curricular materials, teachers depend on the surrounding natural environment as a cultural resource/site for teaching and learning. Donkor, the vocational skills teacher, attests to this practice:

> Here, we improvise a lot especially with tools ... We haven't got the right type of tools. We know how it is. So that maybe you carve it out of wood or maybe plastic and then the students will be using them ... We have been improvising a lot and sometimes instead of using fabrics we tend to use ... cement paper and some others and work with them ... When you get improvising like the tools, when it comes to drafting that's where you need the tools for the work and we use that tools to teach them [students] how to cut maybe trousers, a shirt maybe a suit, you have to practically go and cut and this way ... But when it comes to the brown paper maybe you are going to sew a ... shirt. The fabric is not always available and is

> costly. Maybe they can't afford it immediately. So you have to use brown paper, demonstrate to them and they also will use it the paper too. After that they later purchase their fabric … then work on it. So that's what we normally do. (08/28/97)

Such pedagogic practice is relevant for delivering education in the face of a scarcity of resources (e.g. textbooks, laboratory equipment and workshop facilities). The practice may have its drawbacks, but it does move instruction away from over-dependence on "external" resources and assistance. It forces those involved in schooling to look within communities for local substitutes. It also engenders Indigenous initiative into the educational system as a means for solving pressing problems. In fact, it is in the area of science and technology that Indigenous/local knowledges offer genuine educational options for African communities. Kofi is a highly respected young community worker who, utilizing his university education in science, teaches chemistry and core science. He enthuses about the implications of ongoing reforms for science education in Ghana:

> Reform in science education entails … the science in Ghana today, it seems more Indigenous than Western. That is, now [we are] taking all almost everything from the environment [and trying] to solve the problem that Ghana has. I use … soap as one of the examples. Our Indigenous people who are not scientists have been manufacturing this soap, local soaps using these raw materials …. (08/13/97)

The national introduction of Science Resource Centres in some school districts and regions has been a way to promote Indigenous science, knowledge and culture. Local science teachers bring strong insights and contributions to the discussion of Indigenous science and community resources. Many parents support the idea of maintaining and enhancing our local languages, culture and Indigenous knowledges in schools. They also make strong contributions to the dialogue on the teaching of Indigenous science and the role of the resource centres to the process, but not to the degree to which the teachers do. For parents the central issue is equitable access to these resource centres by students in more isolated communities and by students who are not in the science program as a major.

Osei is the head of the Science Resource Centre in his school. In his narrative, this teacher who is also a father of two implies that teaching science should include both Western and local Indigenous science that relates education to the local economy, to botanical knowledge and to the knowledge local farmers have of the soil. Students' learning of science is not abstract. It needs to be hands-on in the fields and in the labs. If it isn't considered relevant to the local context of the learner, the connection is not made and learning is reduced or does not occur. Therefore, Osei is strongly supportive of the establishment of Science Resource Centres but advocates greater access by all students and the community, which would necessarily entail more resource centres and resources within each centre: "You don't become a good scientist by just seeing pictures of equipment and then learning them by heart. That is one of the challenges that I see in Ghanaian science. However, the government of Ghana has done something about it by establishing these Science Resource Centres, so there is something being done" (08/21/97). In explaining why and how his school was chosen as a site for the resource centre, he points to how schools deal with the lack of physical infrastructure and the help that parents and local communities can offer to alleviate such problems:

> Normally when the [Ministry of Education officials] come to these schools, they look at the structure [of the school and determine if a resource centre can be located] there. The government hasn't got funds to build new science blocks so they come to a school and [if] they see that this school would be ideal for the Science Resource Centre for that particular area, [they choose it]. So that's why we were chosen ... The Science Resource Centre has come to solve a lot of problems. But the ... students are many and some of the equipment cannot go around to all of them. That is a problem ... If you are taking it as an elective [that is, specialized physics, chemistry and biology], you get to use the equipment. But if you are taking it as a core ... you don't handle the materials often. The teachers take the equipment to the classroom and [use it to demonstrate, but] it's not as in-depth. *[So what do you think?]* It is not [good]. We have told the teachers who teach the core science to come for the equipment and demonstrate for the students. If you want students to sit down and perform experiments then the whole period will be gone. You will not teach that and the syllabus too. So these teachers will only show the equipment to the students and demonstrate for them to see and then give them the notes. (08/21/97)

When asked about the extent of local community participation in and contribution to the science resource centre initiatives, Osei responds:

> What we have been told is to appeal to the local communities, the municipal assembly. Since we have spent only one term of three months, we have appealed to them and they promised to help us—especially fuelling the bus to convey students from the satellite schools to the resource centre here at our school. The bus is a very big bus and it consumes a lot of petrol so we have appealed to the local municipalities. They have promised to help us. But yearly the Ghana government gives us 500,000 [cedis], which is [not enough]. (08/21/97)

Local investment in supplying needed resources by the community puts into strong question the issue of limited access by community members to educational resources.

The views of Kofi and Osei point to the power of local knowledge and its contributions to rethinking classroom pedagogy and instruction. Indigenous knowledge cannot be dismissed as "unscientific" or "invalid' knowledge." Both educators are aware of the differences as well as the shared principles and methodologies of multiple knowledge systems. They work with a broader definition of science that includes the "Indigenous." They believe that the synthesis of knowledges augurs well for Ghanaian and African education. The making of educational knowledge has multiple and collaborative dimensions. The promotion of knowledge in schools (production, validation and dissemination) is seen as a collaborative process involving multiple stakeholders. This understanding implies multiple responsibilities in the processes of schooling and education. Local peoples have their own conceptions of what it means to be "involved" in the schooling and education of youth. In advocating the reforms, educational stakeholders recognize the vital role played by parents and local communities. Parents, teachers and students each have their different ideas about how parents and local communities ought to fulfil their roles and meet their responsibilities.

Mensa, a father actively involved in the local parent-teacher association has three children in the school system. He is encouraging them all to take science because, as he reckons, there is a "future" in majoring in science subjects. He insists that a parent must act as a sounding board to the child and should communicate all "deficiencies" with teachers and educators so that help can be secured when and where necessary.

To ensure that students, teachers, parents, and communities play their respective roles, Amaadee, an instructor in general science, calls for a redefinition of school/educational success. She offers an alternative reading of "success": "I think that exams shouldn't be the only yardstick. That's why in a way I tend to like those continuing assessments ... because ... the teacher deals with the students and you can really know what they stand for rather than a whole year end in an examination" (08/21/97). By what "they stand for," Amaadee is alluding to students' discharging their responsibilities to their communities. This adds strength to the position that parents and local communities all have a stake in the well-being of the student. A student's accomplishment is not for the good of the sole individual but for the wider community. Therefore, all parties must be supportive of one other. As students undertake community and family responsibilities and obligations, local communities and parents must be there to support these students

Keepers of Language and Culture

For many teachers, parents, and students, teaching indigenous Ghanaian languages is a way of achieving a more comprehensive understanding of knowledge. In responding to the question of whether or not local languages should be taught in Ghanaian schools, Mansa, a teacher, who is married to Kofi, states:

> [*Should Ghanaian languages be taught in the schools?*] Yes ... yeah I think
> so ... Even though we all speak our own languages if we don't
> continue to learn how to write them the time will come ...
> Language is dynamic, things will continue changing ... and we will
> no longer have a language and our language ... [and culture] ...
> will be a mixture of everything even when we are writing, so I think
> our languages should be taught, they should be taught. (08/13/97)

There is an awareness that language is significant for the maintenance of cultural identity. Cultural identity is part of defining the indigenous sense of self and personhood. Language carries cultural values and collective identities as well as social and ancestral histories. Language helps articulate this definition. Language is, therefore, seen as dynamic and in its more encompassing content. It is integral to indigenous knowledge which, as mentioned in the introduction, is tied to a place. It is not separated/abstracted from the local. The language, the culture and the natural world are interconnected physically, intellectually, emotionally and spiritually. Throughout the interviews (the data), there are dialogues filled with strong emotions of support, need and a desire to base/include Indigenous science, local cultures and languages in the curriculum, in the culture of the school. However, there is less tension/struggle in the dialogues on how to develop a science program that is grounded in local knowledge of the natural world that also includes Western knowledge (Indigenous & Western science) than the issue of languages. This is because there are many local languages spoken by students at a school. Also, although the issue of language/s is tied to the people's sense of local identity, it is also balanced with a view of and desire for Ghana as a nation with a language that unifies and for the need to develop proficiencies in a language/s with international marketability. The issue emerges as more complex for the participants. Yet there is no doubt that they fully support the learning of Indigenous languages in the schools. It is the question of how that presents them with more questions.

The success of promoting local languages and culture in schools depends on active community involvement. When parents, educators and students express their views on the importance of teaching the local languages and cultures in the schools, their knowledge is informed by an urgent sense of ensuring the survival of the broader community and their different and yet connected histories and identities. Tano, a parent-teacher, explains the trials and tribulations of teaching local Ghanaian languages in schools:

> We teach the Ghanaian languages. At first it was only English that could be used as the medium of instruction. Then the students would write their exams and fail in Twi. None of my children passed Twi. At first we were whipping children who spoke Twi in school. Then, we realized that we have to learn Twi at the Training College in order to teach it to students. So they started teaching Twi even at the kindergarten level. Kindergarten children started using Twi nicely but then we were asked to stop. So now children start learning Twi at Primary One. I think we have to teach Ghanaian languages because the students sit for it at the SSS final exam. (09/15/97)

The inherited colonial educational system did not teach local languages. Consequently, the system produced learners who could be seen as "successful educators" yet had lost proficiency in their local language to the extent that they could not write well in the local vernacular. Thus, as the noted educator Momoh explains, it is important to teach Ghanaian languages in schools as resistance to colonization and as a way to encourage decolonization:

[We use] the English language ... so that they can use the language and be able to write it because [English] will help you to gain higher heights ... But in our country here, you see everything of Ghanaian origin, everything of African origin, [and] we have been made to accept that [as] satanic. It is even prestigious [to speak] English and [to speak] it quite well. You see in our set up, that is what is happening: If you ... go into any institution at all, whether for studies or for work, without a credit pass in English you will be marginalized. We have stifled a whole lot of skills. So it is something that we have taken upon ourselves. In some countries they use English side by side with their local language and they are doing very well. We [threw our local languages] away and it is having such a bad effect on us. (08/11/97)

Parents take on the role of teaching local languages in the homes. That is used as a basis to facilitate children's learning in schools. Bonse, an educator and grandmother, attests to the importance of teaching local culture:

In the first place, the cultural studies we learned in the school embraces all the cultural practices of the country. So for example, if we are learning about Dagbani, whether you are an Akan, Ewe or any other tribe [cultural group], you learn about the culture of Dagbanis. When we come to the turn of the Ashantis, we do [the same thing]. On puberty rites, we learn and compare that of one tribe to another. In so doing all the students are learning about the different tribes of Ghana, so that helps. (09/19/97)

In order to instruct effectively on these cultural practices one has to be well-versed in the local culture. Bonse's long narrative on the specific issue of language is worth reproducing here as it reveals a clear understanding of the politics of language and communication and its importance in fostering a sense of self, group and national identity/ies in the myriad of different ethnicities and cultures:

Well in the school, speaking Twi is more or less prohibited and that restricts the Akans or other people from using their local language. For that matter, everybody is compelled to speak English [and] English becomes the medium of instruction. Whether you are an Akan or from a dominant or minority tribe, we all speak the same language and that helps to [bring our] cultures together. When we are choosing our cultural practices, we do not think of a majority tribe. We think of a suitable tribe. Sometimes, we invite somebody from a minority tribe and he comes to teach [the students]. Recently, we had a cultural troupe dancing in Ga. Whereas even though they are Akans, there was no Akan dance. So that is how we go about such things. One thing more I would like to talk about is that people like the Japanese; they developed rapidly because of the use of their local languages. I have a friend who stayed there for sometime and according to him they wanted to know whether Ghanaians did not have their own languages at home. [When he questioned that], the [Japanese] replied that all the Ghanaians who have come there, nobody has used any other language apart from the English language.

So Ghanaians must be interested in their own culture. Sometimes, we talk about culture [and] development and what not. But, it seems we are not interested in our own culture. One of the components of culture is language. So far nothing, if anything, has been done at all. I don't see anything done about Ghanaian languages in terms of the reforms. You see, everybody thinks in his [or her] language before translating it into English. So the child must develop in his [or her] language before he grows so that he will be able to speak freely without thinking of it. So if we help our people develop their own language, it will help them develop in any area of learning. Since the inception of the reforms, no Ghanaian language book has been written nor Ghanaian language teacher has been invited to any forum to write books or to develop the language. But in all the subjects, subsequent teachers have been invited to write books and find ways of developing that particular subject. Before we are able to make any headway we must develop our own languages. It is very important. (09/19/97)

This narrative points to the challenge of teaching difference in the context of different ethnicities, cultures and languages. The challenge is compounded by the dominant perception that education's goal is to promote social and national integration and the building of common citizenship. This view can persist to the extent of subjugating differences.

The discussion of language is complex and needs to be placed within the history of what has been and continues to be the primary language of the school, English. The language of the school is itself socially contextualized within the multi-lingual nature of Ghana, the interconnection between language and culture and the reality of the home language of children from poor and rural families/homes being different from the school language. The importance of learning Ghanaian languages is underscored by many study participants in the context of what is perceived as a unifying common language, English.

The language situation in Ghana (and in fact much of Africa) is different from that in other countries where the official national language was tied to a modern nationalist project of an earlier period. For instance, at the present time in Canada, it can be said that on the whole uni-lingual, bi-lingual and multi-lingual activists want to include ways of teaching, maintaining and developing native/aboriginal languages and other immigrant languages as part of Canada's evolving national project. Given the current international context, there is a need for common dialogue among Ghanaians to include at least one of the dominant colonial languages in the repertoire of the school official languages; in this case most likely English. Any anti-colonial nationalist project for educational reform and change must recognize that language is key to unifying the modern state. In Ghana there is some concern that some students are not being sufficiently immersed in English to learn it proficiently. This problem needs to be addressed given Ghana's insertion in the modern globalized world.

There is power in schools cultivating local languages and other ways families and communities communicate with each other. Therefore, schools and educators cannot be timid on the issue of language. Within global contexts, language is and must be approached with assertion. The role of different languages in global education is tremendous. Generally, the issue of language needs to be fully explored. Students need to have a very broad and positive view of languages which includes the language of music, the language of physical theatre/dance, science, and spirituality. In using local/indigenous languages in Ghanaian schools, the pedagogic project should not be one of antagonism and fear. Rather the option is to be positive (that is, solution-oriented) to open up the possibilities of language/s for debate. For educators not to take language seriously risks undervaluing and under utilizing Ghana's linguistic cultural resource base. The context of language use does not have to mean a narrow focus on students' home language. Of course, this is important but we must appreciate how we can learn each other's languages. Ghanaian students spoke of learning the language/s of the community/ies where they might go to live and work. Teachers and students spoke of the connectedness of language/s to culture, to voice and to identity. The context of how languages can be taught posed questions and problems that need to be taken up. First and foremost schools must officially recognize the existence of different languages spoken in the school and in the regions. The extent of the diversity of languages needs to be known. The numbers of languages spoken and percentages of student population who speak or want to learn to speak a certain language will help to develop differing strategies for different language groups. The linguistic resources that can be accessed and developed for communication, teaching and furthering the development of local languages need to be researched. It is critical that the local community, parents, teachers and administrators be involved in discussing the language/s question and in proposing different ways of approaching the development, teaching and promotion of local languages. By working in partnership with elders, cultural workers and other community educators, schools are acknowledging the significance of language as a primary source of culture and identity. They also recognize the many indigenous/local languages and the possibilities and difficulties of working with the linguistic situation/reality within Ghana.

Although complex, the task need not be viewed as overwhelming and distant. The path to longer-term goals can begin through tasks that are within easy reach and close to home. For instance, the classroom teacher can examine the different writing systems and languages based on similar or different alphabets as well as the etymological roots of words. Teachers and students can learn the different language and sign systems of people through the study of fables, tales, proverbs, myths and mythologies. Teachers, parents and community workers can work collaboratively to discuss the messages conveyed in proverbs, tales and fables. Local writers, educators, students and others can collect these into different forms of text to be shared in schools and in communities. The different ways of conveying information would be explored, i.e. through graphics, arts and sculptures. The teacher can explore the meanings of visual culture in different groups. Students would seek to learn and understand storytelling, theatre and dance as alternative forms of communicating. For example, in Ghana talking drums convey several messages. The teacher could have artists from the local community come to their classes to perform for students, discuss the meanings of such performances (e.g., the use of drumming as a form of speaking, communal music making) and actually teach drumming (the music) and the making of the instruments. Teachers could be invited to attend and participate in community activities (cultural performances, popular culture and arts of local groups) to learn and introduce non-book techniques into the classroom. The teachers can learn to integrate these ideas into their classroom practices by extending invitations to local cultural workers, artist and performers to attend their class discussions and contribute to knowledge production. The way local communities engage in public conversations suggest that there can be alternatives to the teacher-led classroom discussions, a notable example of which is the use of the circle format for discussions (e.g., as in aboriginal communities of North America). Here each person talks for as long as they want on the problem under discussion without interruption. Sitting in a circle as a symbol of unity and collectivity participants have an opportunity to speak if they want until the problem is solved. All voices may be heard within such a structure. These ideas can be imported into the classroom and used as alternative learning structures. The community as an extension of the school becomes a salient source of cultural knowledge. These approaches counter textbooks as the sole mode of communicating knowledge.

In Ghana (as in much of Africa) colonial education was "successful" in educating students and keeping them out of touch with their local culture and community. The task of post-colonial education is to counter such dominant viewpoints. The lesson here is that without strong local community support, the objectives of making education practical and relevant to local community needs and aspirations will come to naught. Relying on the government to pull communities out of years of misguided education can be problematic when the state itself relies on external sources to fund its projects. It is important that different structures at the local community level, the national government and the schools (through/with the PTAs) work together to find solutions that will address the educational needs of all Ghanaian children—from a local and national perspective that fosters an understanding of their place in the world today.

Note

1.   As Cruikshank (1992, 8) points out, we must also be aware of the pitfalls of essentialism that attribute "ideas and concepts to the 'indigenous voice' even when the words are actually being supplied by a[n] Eurocentric ideology."

Chapter 7

Difference and Inclusive Schooling

Can one talk about inclusive schooling in the African context in the same way in which others, for example, have discussed inclusive education in the Canadian or North American contexts (Dei and Razack 1995; Banks and Banks 1993)? One of the problems of theorizing minority and inclusive education in Africa is that not much work has been done in the area (at least not until recently). Nevertheless, as pointed out elsewhere (Dei 1994), it is important to recognize from the onset that scholars like Fanon (1963), Memmi (1969), Du Bois (1965a, b), Rodney (1972), Cabral (1973), Nkrumah (1970), Said (1979), Garvey (1986), wa Thiong'o (1986), Amin (1989) and Freire (1990) have to varying degrees raised the issue of education that would recognize the variety of experiences and the history and achievements of all peoples. It should also be noted that concerns around equity and social difference (class, gender, ethnicity, religion, culture and language) have been articulated by many educationists writing on Africa and African peoples (see Asante 1987, 1988; Banya 1993; Bloch, Beoku-Betts, and Tabachnick 1998; Heward and Bunware 1999; Myers 1993; Obenga 1992; Shujaa 1994; Tedla 1995).

The discussion of inclusive schooling is complicated by the fact that terms, concepts and conceptualizations that are essential to a theoretical discourse on minority education are themselves usually subjected to different interpretations and analyses. This is usually the case with the use of conceptual and analytical categories, which are themselves social constructs (Samuels 1991, 2). I use the notion of "inclusivity" as evoked in the North American contexts (see Hilliard 1992; Anderson and Collins 1995). That is, inclusive education is education that is capable of responding to complex and nuanced concerns of a diverse school body defined in terms of ethnicity, class, gender, race, region, sexuality, religion, culture and language (McCarthy and Crichlow 1993). Such an education also draws on the accumulated knowledge resources and capabilities of its constituent members (Asante 1987; Mazama 1998). Explained in these contexts, the connection between inclusive schooling and minority education becomes clear: inclusive education targets the needs and concerns of those who are minoritized and disadvantaged.

The notion of inclusivity brings to the fore certain key questions. It calls for a broader understanding of learning, teaching and administration of education and the relation to social development; it focuses on both the process and content of educational delivery that produces differential outcomes (Dei and Razack 1995). In other words, inclusivity involves asking what students learn, how and why; what educators teach; who is teaching, how and why along with the issue of educational relevance. In order to deal with certain questions, the place and role of qualitative studies of schooling become paramount. We need to understand students' and educators' experiences, their perceptions and understandings of difference and what this body of knowledge means for rethinking schooling and education in Africa.

Within pluralistic contexts, educators are continually struggling with the challenge of providing inclusive education to meet the needs of a diverse student body. African schooling is not oblivious to this objective. Among many things, Africa must confront the post-colonial challenge[s] of education—that is, education in an era celebrating difference and diversity. There are five key questions that need to be addressed in discussing inclusive education in the African context. 1) How do local peoples understand the nature, impact, and implications of "difference" for educational change? In other words, how do local educators, policy-makers, students, parents and community workers view and name, from their respective standpoints, their conceptions of difference and diversity and its implications for schooling? 2) How do schools themselves view difference and diversity among the student population? That is, what are the specific educational practices pertaining to pedagogy, instruction, curriculum, texts and discourse, that address difference and the intersections of gender, ethnic, class cultural, linguistic, religious and minority issues in education? 3) What particular educational initiatives in schools link identity with schooling and knowledge production, and how do school systems address the issue of representation in education? 4) What supports and resources are needed to assist teachers and learners to deal with the question of minority education? 5) What are the implications of difference for schooling, for peace education and for "democratic citizenship participation" in Ghana?

To ascertain the specific roles of ethnicity, culture, language, religion, sexuality, dis/ability, class, age and gender in African schooling, we need to examine the linkage between questions of identity, knowledge production, representation and schooling (Bloch, Beoku-Betts and Tabachnick 1998; McCarthy and Crichlow 1993). For example: What meanings about social difference do students and educators bring to school? How does knowledge of culture, language, ethnicity, gender and class inform schooling? How would taking into account difference and diversity in the student population contribute to the search for viable educational options and alternatives for "post-colonial" Africa? Furthermore, we need to examine broader theoretical questions about the pursuit of transformative learning in an epoch that is remarkably different in its celebration of social difference and cultural diversity. For example, how are ongoing global debates around issues of educational equity and academic excellence being conducted? To what extent are discussions about global poverty and social injustice situated within a critical framework for examining the structural processes of schooling and the delivery of education? How can progressive and radical educators ensure that the structures of schooling address questions of social responsibility, fairness, justice and equity? Is it possible to achieve global notions of educational excellence without comprehensively and simultaneously addressing concerns of educational equity and justice? And do all educators share a common understanding of what constitutes academic excellence and success? To answer these questions, it is important for research on

African education to tease out the nuances and complexities of difference structured along the lines of gender, class, ethnicity, regional differences, culture, language and religion in the local schooling contexts. In this chapter, I focus on gender, social class, ethnicity, culture, language, religion and regional differences to help us understand the barriers against and advancements made in achieving inclusive schooling.

Gender

There is today a critical reduction in national fiscal expenditures and global economic supports for education. This, has generated an urgent effort to relocate adequate resources that support and encourage girls and women to participate in formal education (Beoku-Betts 1998). But how much do we know about gender and schooling in African contexts? Dei and Connelly (2000) argue that new research must contribute to developing a body of knowledge that analyzes the schooling of girls and women within Africa's changing educational system. In rethinking education and schooling issues in Africa, critical scholarship must consider an ethical approach to understanding the social construction of male and female relationships. Rethinking African schooling requires a critical understanding of how gender is lived and experienced in the local contexts of schooling and educational challenges.

There is a challenge in speaking about gender relations, experiences and issues in African education without reproducing or reiterating phallocentric/patriarchal language and ideologies. I am striving for a discussion that will support serious considerations of the relations of identity, power and difference in African education. In considering the multiple voices addressing gender issues in schooling and education, particular interest lies in building a discursive critique around alternative ways of interpreting female participation in education within the Ghanaian context.

There are limitations of contextual spaces in which Ghanaian and African women have been inscribed inimically in educational discourses through subject/ object relations of disempowerment in schooling. It is important for us to examine the disjunctures and tensions within women's historically situated knowledges and the knowledges imposed through community-based praxis of formal and informal schooling and education. For example, Csete (1998) has stressed the importance of helping African women articulate indigenous knowledges about their everyday needs, resources and experiences. Throughout Africa, there are cases of local women advocating for themselves and for their children's rights to education and social services. Their politics and social knowledge suggest the importance of possibilities for social transformation beyond a mere reliance on formal/institutionalized hegemonic interventions by states, local governments or even donor agencies (see Bloch, Beoku-Betts and Tabachnick 1998 in the area of education).

The problems of low female enrolment, lower retention rates and poor school success among girls have repeatedly been noted (Stromquist 1998). Anderson-Levitt, Bloch and Soumaré (1998) have also presented an analysis of how girls' subordination and voicelessness in African classrooms is constructed through both female and male teachers' and peers' abusive and dismissive interactional behaviors - behaviors that have normalized the alienation of young women's learning contexts through the reiteration of gender stereotypes about women's inferiority. Classroom interactions are situated within power relations that sustain tacit gender/power hierarchies in the social construction and regulation of African girls and boys. The cultural politics of schooling suggest that what goes on in school compounds this imbalance and that classrooms are never gender-neutral or "gender-equal," which ruptures the common sense notion of students' equal participation. Yet we have evidence of local resistance in school settings. As Foucault (1980) aptly noted, within every power relation there is resistance.

There is a growing critical consciousness among African women of gender identity and the possibilities for social change that comes with gender equality. Local women do not gain access to power and privilege by performing themselves in ways that are "male." Those who have argued the contrary fail to recognize the problematic of a patriarchal/phallocentric gaze as a normalized point of reference regulating women's activities (Dei and Connelly 2000). There are today many sites of women's resistance as well as sources for their political, economic and educational transformation (see Bloch, Beoku-Betts and Tabachnick 1998; Egbo 2000). Educational research has identified African women's everyday lives as a dynamic process of creating spaces and possibilities for social participation and as a negotiation between individual and collective interests (Kiluva-Ndunda 2000).

The policy and legislative implications of such knowledge is that there is a need for a "decisive and pro-active collective action" to create substantive shifts in gender relations to support gender equity through education (Gordon, Nkwe and Graven 1998; Kiluva-Ndunda 2000; Okeke 1994; Egbo 2000). Policy-oriented research must, however, explicate how women's voices are constructed and regulated through the normalization of male knowledges in order to appear equal to men's. Research must examine the implications of what struggling for "equal voice" in decision-making means for the knowledges that can be publicly spoken and represented in a domestic context. As Mbilinyi acutely observed, it is not enough for research merely to tell us that local women know all about their problems and yet to ignore the ways they have "learned to be subordinate, to have lower[/higher] expectations for themselves, to lose as well as to resist and struggle" (291).

No doubt patriarchy continues to dominate power relations in African contexts, and little attention (e.g., educational research) has been paid to forms of intervention that reproduce the alienation, oppression, marginality and exploitation of women (see also Okeke 1994; Obbo 1980; Kalu 1996; Etta 1994). It is important to read the multiple, shifting, dynamic voices of African peoples across borders of gender, class, race, ethnicity, nationality/regionality, and culture while at the same time supporting possibilities for African women as actors and agents of change with reference to ancestral histories, traditions and local knowledges. To this end, I believe it is vital that qualitative studies of African education focus on how local women, through the power of individual and collective agency, take advantage of the limited opportunities to challenge and rupture patriarchal ideologies and structures.

Research on educational reform for gender equity in Africa must seriously consider the implications of how African women make sense of their everyday experiences. Research must problematize essentialism while explicating and centering African women's experiences to permit the reading of African women's experiences through shifting female African subjectivities. To create spaces for maximizing human capacities and capabilities for social justice critical research must seek diverse representations that upset the normalized sense of an African woman as a constructive and productive subject who is complicit in and resistant to her everyday existence (See Dei and Connelly 2000).

The examination of gender relations in schooling requires an analysis of how patriarchal ideologies permeate the processes of educational delivery, that is, the structures for teaching, learning and administration of education. Such analysis involves developing critical knowledge of the content and quality of instruction, the structural processes that keep women in gender stereotypical roles and the explicating ideologies that continue to create and perpetuate oppressive gender relations in schools (see also Mbilinyi, Mbuguni, Meana, & Ole Kambiane 1991, 46; Malekela 1983; Mulugu 1999; all cited in Levira 2000). Put succinctly, the analysis should involve a study of school texts and curricular content as well as pedagogic, instructional and communicative practices of schooling. No doubt structures of educational delivery implicate the broader questions of educational access and equity along lines of gender and other forms of difference. Gender must be understood as a site of difference as well as a power relation. To understand this in the contexts of schooling relations, it is important to tease out how students internalize and resist patriarchal ideologies in their personal and collective attitudes, perceptions and views of gender relations in schooling.

We begin by exploring the meanings Ghanaian students and teachers bring to social difference, questions of identity and knowledge production. Gender is recognized as an important aspect of identity. However, students' understanding of gender shows some ambiguity to its status as a salient marker of difference that needs to be seriously acknowledged in schooling. For example, the common initial response to whether social difference is vital to understanding schooling is that "we are treated the same because we are equal." The notion of equal rights (i.e., that students are treated the same to ensure equality) is taken at face value. Yet as students examine actual practices, they note differences in the expectations of behavior and in how the females and males perceive gender issues and schooling. The perception of gender equality being equated with receiving the same treatment does not recognize how gender affects schooling in profound ways.

In fact, male students point to how their teachers work with "difference." Fela has two other siblings pursuing Senior Secondary education. His father is a police officer. Fela is studying chemistry and Physics to become an engineer. He claims his favorite teachers are "approachable," and that all students are treated the same. Yet he observes that in the classroom "boys are sort of disgraced before the girls":

> ... there is not much differen[ce in] treatment. But at times when a ... simple problem is given to the boy [to solve] and he is not able to do it, the master (i.e., teacher) will at times ... punish the boy in front of the girls maybe to show [his] power ... When you are a boy and you're not able to do something, say [solve] a simple problem, the masters like to disgrace you in front of the girls. Who knows what the masters have got with the girl ... But the girls, ... they don't treat them like that. And when we go to the dining hall [and] a boy [doesn't] come to the dining hall, when the master comes in he'll try to [punish him] ... But when a girl comes and doesn't eat [the teacher] actually says, "Oh, she doesn't feel like eating." [If] you're a girl they leave you [alone]. But when you are a boy, they find something for you to do. *[I see. So you see some differences in the treatment of the two sexes?]* Yes, I do. (09/21/97)

To Fela, teachers use their power to mete out punishment differently to students. He sees that male and female students "get away" with different things because of their gender. At times, the perception of "preferential treatment" for females is explained by male students' interpretation of the teacher's relations with the female student. Thus, while on the one hand Fela asserts that the schools treat all students the same, his concrete examples reflect a reading of differential treatment. This is a contradictory stance. When pushed to explain his standpoint, Fela argues that theoretically male and female students are simply "students." This generic understanding of the "student" runs through the thoughts and interpretations of many students.

Ayoso is a seventeen-year-old in SS2. It is her hope to become a lawyer. She does not believe it would be different if she were a male coming to her school, "because I think we are the same." Asked if the school treats the female students differently, she claims, "No, we are mixed in a class so they teach us equally" (08/14/97). In clarifying why the female residence has an enclosed wall as a security precaution, she perceives differences in students' behavior and actions along gender lines: "They [the boys] have a net. But the boys normally destroy it and then put their head [out the windows] and shout [at the girls]" (08/14/97).

Ayoso attributes the structural difference of the dormitories to male behavior. She disputes male assertions that there is differential and preferential treatment of female students. To the males, the misconduct of female students go unnoticed. Riti, an eighteen-year-old boarder in a co-ed institution, is studying mathematics and commerce at the SS2 level. She disagrees strongly with a male counterpart's view that female students misbehave and consequently do less well academically. As is often the case when asked how girls and boys are treated at school, the immediate response is to say "we are treated equally." However, when the discussion moves to specific events or activities such as living arrangements, Riti notes some differences based on gender. She argues that it is because of past incidents at the school that the girls' dormitory has a wall around it. If anything, she thinks the school keeps a closer eye on females than males: "Yes ... they treat the girls [differently] than the boys. Some of the boys if you treat them [that way], they won't take it. But the girls, we are afraid of some of the teachers in this school" (09/21/97).

Riti thinks educators do take advantage of female students' respect for authority while allowing male students greater latitude. She continues to say that girls normally obey school laws more than the boys. She interprets male truancy to mean the possession of power to flout authority: "The girls obey the laws more than the boys in the school ... The laws are equal for both boys and girls. But the girls obey the laws more" (09/21/97).

Onipa, an eighteen-year-old in the final year of his Senior Secondary education is studying geography, economics and French. He wants to be a pilot or a French teacher someday. His father is a herbalist and his mother a shopkeeper. He was born in the region of his school and claims the reason he likes his school is that the "teachers are serious." He disagrees that males and females receive differential treatment at school. However he notes some differences when it comes to the work assigned to males and females:

> [In] this school we don't separate the boys from the girls, so if anyone did something the treatment that the school authorities would give to the boy would be [the same one] given to the girl ... In terms of teaching too, it is the same ... We do the same work but there is some work in this school that girls don't do like ... [cleaning] gutters, constructing gutters and ... other things. Girls don't do that. (09/21/97)

On the point of work assignments, Adobea, a sixteen-year-old who attended her current school because "my sister is here," disagrees with Onipa's observation that males do the hard work in the school. She reasons that the different sexes "do the same (work) [and] are given equal treatment." In fact, she adds forcefully, "What a man can do a woman can do" (07/09/97).

Adobea is alluding to a gender consciousness that is crucial for engaging the school system. The female student must believe in herself and challenge patriarchal ideologies in order to succeed. Boatemaa is twenty-eight and studying life skills at the teacher training college. She likes the fact that the school is close to her hometown and is accessible. She sees gender as an area of differential treatment in many aspects of schooling: "I can say that [teachers] don't treat us equally, because there are certain ways they consider difference ... When they give us work, like weeding, there are some types of places that women cannot reach. So, they will give those places to the men and they will give us those places that would be good for the women" (08/20/97). When it comes to physical activity educators assign different tasks to men and women. When questioned if she feels there are other differences she retorts: "Hmm ... also at times they consider the women to be weak [and] with little effort they [can] push us" (08/20/97). In later interviews she concedes that the division of labor may follow patriarchal, sexist attitudes and ideologies. But she does not see that as a major problem if a student believes in her own capabilities. Boatemaa also acknowledges that female students in some ways internalize that the males are the ones who "know." They go to them for help only to find that females do better: "... At times ... we, the women, are always going to the men for them to teach us, we will not talk, but we will listen to them. But at long last the males see that during the examination we come out with flying colors" (08/20/97).

Gono, a twenty-three year-old male student taking vocational skills and graphic design, is following in his parents footsteps to become a teacher. He is in the final year of his teacher training education. He also sees difference in terms of the allocation of physical resources to students. In Gono's school, there are more males than females. He thinks space is an important consideration when admitting students of the opposite sex: "The men outnumber the women because of the dormitories. We have two blocks for the men ... And, we only have one dormitory for the women. So in the admissions they consider that. So the men outnumber the women" (10/09/97). The lack of physical space means educators have to take into consideration the number of female students who can be admitted in the school. This practice has perpetuated inequities in male-female student ratio. Rather than ensure or insist on the building of additional infrastructure, administrators simply see structural limitations of physical space as a reason to restrict female admission into schools. Gono also concedes that female students fare better academically than their male counterparts: "... The women do rather well, better than the men. In the initial stages you will see them [males] performing well. But we have study groups and these study groups help the women a lot. So after we have written the examination at any time the women will do [better] than the men... " (10/09/97).

Odom, who is twenty-one years old, is a strong practitioner of the Seventh Day Adventist faith. When he graduates he wants to be a mathematics teacher. He likes the pedagogical style of his "favorite teacher" which he describes as "open, confident and secure." He also notes that there are fewer dormitories for women than for men, thereby, limiting the numbers of women admitted to the college. But he also adds an interesting perspective beyond what he calls the "accommodation problem," pointing to how gender and class intersect in schooling to influence social action and policy:

> That [accommodation] is the main problem. But I can also say that as the school is an Adventist school. It is religious. So I think they thought twice [about] admit[ing] the men more than the women... When they admit equal numbers, that is of men and women ... you see as soon as we [men] see ... that is the opposite sex, it is very attractive or it attracts the men especially to follow them [women] ... So I think [for] the administration that is a reason why they admit more men than women ... Well the men, most of them, they will do their own things. But mostly, I have noticed ... [that] it is mostly the rich men's sons and daughters... because the men [outnumber] the women ... we have something of the rich men and the rich men's daughters at least about thirty per cent over there. If they want to ... they just cheat for them [women] with their money. But we the poor men, we sit, we always learn.... (09/09/97)

Clearly, this narrative is laced with a problematic understanding of the intersections of gender, class and religion. The school administration wants to avoid problems around male-female interaction that can undermine the religious ethic of the school. Hence, it undertakes a deliberate policy of favoring male over female students in the school's admission policy. But Odom also notes how class intersected with gender to establish differential advantage.

Students bring different interpretations to why there are more females than males in the co-ed institutions in the school district. One possible reason is that there are more "all-male schools" in the area than "all-female schools." Iso, who is in SS3 and has three other young siblings in the school system, is taking business courses "because there is money to make." He provides an explanation for the unequal ratio of male to females in his school:

> In [this school] the authorities used to admit girls. And they have admitted girls more than the boys. So as of now, one of the boys' dormitory has been given to the girls because the boys are less than the girls ... So the girls ... have been given another dormitory and they have shifted the boys to the nurses' dormitories. The ratio of the boys and the girls is bigger on the girls' side. (08/13/97)

He sees a preference for female students. He provides a sexist, patronizing interpretation as to why he thinks this "deliberate" practice is unfair:

> Because girls are somehow difficult to [educate]. There are some girls who don't come to school with the aim of learning, they come to school to do some social things, which are not good. And, at the boys' schools there's a challenge in learning whereas in the [co-ed] school ... when someone wants to say an answer, because of the girls, he feels shy, he [thinks] he may get it wrong, so at school they don't usually [answer] ... [I]n the boys' school we are all boys. So if I get it wrong ... we all laugh at ourselves and go away. But some girls will go to dormitory and converse about some habits of some boys in the classroom ....(08/13/97)

No doubt, Iso rationalizes his preference by drawing on what he perceives as differential actions of male and females students. He believes the school treats females differently from males and reasons that the actions and behavior of female students justify the constant scrutiny of teachers. He articulates strong disapproval of certain behaviors by females but does not find it as problematic when males do the same thing:

> ... because girls are so bad that some could go outside to their boyfriends and others go home ... They always organize some roll call ... and check the rules because some girls go to their boyfriends to sleep with them and others go dances ... So they used to check the girls. *[How do you know that?]* Okay, the boys they also used to go to town a bit but not too much. Whereas the girls they go ... Boys used to go to mining [mining means studying deep into the

night], when the girls [are supposed to] sleep. When you check a room and a girl is not in the dormitory, she may be either at home or have gone to her boyfriend's. But if you go to check a roll call at the boy's dormitory and you find that there is one boy missing there, the implication may be either he has gone to the dance or he is [studying] .... (08/13/97)

Gender stereotyping is a major problem in schools. Ado is a seventeen-year-old currently in SS3. His mother is a trader and his father is a university-trained educator. When responding to a question about his favorite teachers, Ado provides a stereotypical view of female teachers that is very disturbing, to say the least:

I prefer the male teachers than the female teachers. *[Why do you say that?]* Because a female ... teacher may get pregnant and she may not be able to come to the school, so the students at that time [won't] get any teacher to teach them. They will sit in the classroom and talk, talk, talk. But the male teachers, they are always punctual in the school. *[Have you ever seen a male teacher who comes to school late?]* Yes. *[So when you say that the female teachers are always coming late, you do also have female teachers who come to school on time?]* Yes, the female teachers, some of them, come to school on time. (08/12/97)

Obviously, Ado is reflecting on a particular case and generalizing the experience to all female teachers. This sexist view can be interrupted if educators take the meaning and implication of difference seriously in their teaching and instruction. Ado has some interesting views on why there are more girls in his school. He feels that boys are more serious students than girls and that female students are pampered because there are more of them than boys. He points out why he would prefer an all-male school:

because in a boys' school, we shall have much [more] time to learn than [in] the girls' school. *[So why can't you have more time to learn here?]* Here? *(silence).* (08/12/97)

While female students generally would say they prefer a mixed school to an all-girls' school, males were more likely to have a preference for an all-boys schools. In her narrative, Ayoso points out that if she had the choice between coming to an all-girls' school and her current co-educational (co-ed) institution, she would still have chosen to go to her school. In explaining why, she touches upon group socialization and hints that there are some benefits to a mixed student population:

"Because it is easy to communicate with boys. Because we are all equal. But if you go to an [all] girls' school maybe it will be difficult. Maybe if you come out it will be difficult to talk with a boy or something like that. But I prefer coming to the mixed school." (08/14/97)

Hana, an eighteen-year-old student leader, is taking geography and economics as majors with French as an elective. She insists she likes her school "because the teachers teach well." She is in SS3 and both her parents are teachers. Hana exhorts that female students must fight for equality and for their future through education. She notes that while the school may profess to treat all students the same, there are some subtle differences that have consequences for learning outcomes:

> ... Umm, we are treated equal! At first, the time for studying was different. Even now, the time [is] very short. At first we closed [night studies] at 8:45 p.m. The girls would leave, leaving the boys. And they can [study] for an extra [thirty minutes] ... So they break us first. But now the lights are put off around 9:30 p.m. But still, we the girls, we always leave before the boys. And so, the boys beat us in the hours for learning. *[I see, why is it that the boys are given more time than the girls?]*... We have to fight for equality because actually we are learning for our future. Before we finish we all move to our hopes and so they must make it in such a way that everyone will get equal time for studying. But they are saying that they want the girls to leave for our dormitories before the boys ... so that they can control [loitering at night] ... I don't think it is fair. (07/09/97)

From Hana's viewpoint, social interactions between males and females at the school contributes to the learning process. In particular, she notes gender differences in student behavior and how joint socialization can change individual action:

> [we] are better behaved than the boys (laughing) ... Okay, the teachers and the staff, I think they've noticed that. They say that during the [prep times] when we got the time for studying ... during that time when we stay together in the classroom some do discussions and some of them talk. It is prep time so they think that separating the girls from the boys will solve the problem during the prep time ... You come to school to learn how to be sociable, so if you sit together ... that will also make us fit in society. (07/09/97)

However, effective social integration does not efface conflict and power differences. Ayoso believes things are not done differently for males or females at her school. She thinks the school pampers both sexes. In this conversation she observes that although quite a few times she has run into trouble with males, she works perfectly well with both male and female students. It is important to notice that in the earlier conversation Ayoso spoke of males as less well behaved than females. Here she alludes to some tensions in male/female interactions:

> ... sometimes I argue with them. *[Why do you argue with them?]* Maybe I'll ask a boy to teach me something and when he refuses to do it ... I will talk against him. *[So what are some of the things that you say?]* Maybe you think you know it and don't want to teach me. *[Do you ask female friends to help you with your school?]* Yes, sometimes I ask [them] to teach me something I don't know. When it is something I don't know I contact one of my friends and we discuss [it] together. (08/14/97)

Students see such male and female interactions as significant to their learning. Ayoso finds that she relies on both male and female students for academic help. The perception that one sex is [in]capable or superior or inferior is part of patriarchal and sexist ideologies that may persist in a local culture, even though such views are not supported by facts. Unfortunately, parents, students and educators may consciously and unconsciously live and work with these ideas and consequently restrict the life chances of girls/women. An example is the traditional idea that female students do not do well in some hard subjects (e.g., science and mathematics). Although contrary to the evidence, the power of such a view may be such that those parents who hold that view alongside a valuing of these subjects over others may see no point in sending their daughters to school. In some cases, educators may also steer female students away from these subjects. Also, some teachers may reinforce stereotyping behaviors and practices on gender roles. These, in turn, influence female students' academic attainment or interests in schools (Delamont 1990). What needs to be interrogated are the structures that deliver these subjects to students and how the delivery can result in male and female students becoming disinterested in them. As Mulugu (1999, 161) observes, within schools the "learning process is influenced by how women are perceived, identified, positioned and treated by the [larger] society" (cited in Levira 2000). Within homes, different demands on the time of females (e.g., household chores) may mean girls will have less time for school work (see Mbilinyi, Mbuguni, Meana, & Ole Kambiane 1991).

The narratives provide lessons for our understanding of gender relations in schools. Gender differences are socially constructed, and are enforced through existing structural barriers and structured relations to create gender inequities in the educational delivery processes. In order to deal with such systemic inequities we must first understand just how gender relations in schooling contexts are structured and see how students themselves understand, articulate, engage, navigate and resist the differences that they bring to school.

Social Class

While many students may deny gender (and as we shall see later, ethnicity) as a site of salient difference ("Because the school treats everyone the same. Because we are all equal"), students do acknowledge socio-economic class to be a political site of difference. It is clear that despite efforts to assist poor students, this difference continues to have major implications in schooling. For example, students acknowledge that, because of differences in family socio-economic backgrounds, they do not all have equal access to educational resources (i.e., textbooks) and not all parents can afford to send their children to boarding school. There are additional requirements that come with boarding school (e.g., payment of meals, accommodation and higher fees) The student life of a boarder differs from that of the day student. Boarders are said to have more time for their studies (that is if they choose to spend their time studying).

Ayoso considers herself "lucky" because her father is an accountant and her mother is a trader. She does not have many financial worries compared to other students. But she maintains it is "tough" coming to school if you are from a poor home; "Because maybe if you are from a rich home there are some textbooks that you can buy. But if you don't have money and your parents cannot afford it, it is very difficult to buy the textbooks" (08/14/97). When asked if she knew students whose parents could not afford to buy textbooks, she adds, "I know a friend who is ... always learn[ing] from other friends' books" (08/14/97).

Ayoso's parents can afford her textbooks because they are both employed outside of the home. They have the necessary financial resources. But for the student from an economically poor home, there can be additional pressures at school that illustrate how socio-economic class creates powerful differential factors in schooling. Along with access to material resources, socio-economic class also leads to students in wealthy families having parents who are perceived to be "powerful" and thus have their voices heard. The ability of wealthy families to support their children's education means career choices are opened up for students. In showing how a student's socio-economic background helps tremendously in school, Riti connects wealth, power and school success using her own family situation: "My family is helping me a lot in my education. In my family we are not rich and we are not poor ... We are in between the two. So they [family members] are all educated [and] they will advise you to be in the school so in the future you get a good job" (09/21/97).

Educators concur with students on their perceptions and views about socio-economic class and schooling. Akoto, who teaches physical education at the SS level, has a diploma in Education from the university. She is keenly aware of the impact of social class of the youth on schooling and learning outcomes. Throughout her educational experience, she has watched as youth from poor families have struggled through their education while privileged students simply have made use of the available opportunities. She provides an example of how in an era where there is a lack of textual and other physical resources, children of poor families are very disadvantaged: "Regarding payment of fees, those who are from rich homes are able to pay all the time. But those from the lower class they always wait till they've been asked to go home and pay the school fees. I think this tells you a lot" (08/12/97). When students are sent home, it takes time to report back. In the meantime, teaching continues and students return only to struggle and catch up. Akoto detects class differences in the material possessions of students: "... [also] the way they dress, there are differences. Some will come ... at times barefooted because they don't have the canvass shoes and they cannot work with classroom footwear. So, they have to participate barefooted" (08/12/97).

Students and teachers make judgments about socio-economic class affiliations on the basis of material possessions and individual actions and behaviors. Ini notes that class is visible in the conversations the students have among themselves and with educators:

> You can tell. They talk about each other or they talk about their homes. They'll say, "My father is in London. He thinks I should come and receive a call soon. So can I have a letter to [go and] receive the call?" [or] "My father just sent me some money, can I go to the bank?" That kind of thing. I even have a girl who keeps her money with me. I keep telling her, "Hey, you are a student, but you are richer than I am." ... There is a locker in my bedroom. I lock her money in there and give her the key. The other day she told me that her two parents are in America and that they sent her money. Sometimes the money goes directly to the school and sometimes she keeps it with me. So from those things we know who the rich ones are and the ones who are not. (08/13/97)

While Ini's narrative attests to the relationship a teacher has with her students, her narrative also points to how money and social class interplay to regulate school lives. Student whose needs are repeatedly met do not have to worry about school fees. They have all the time to study if they so choose, unlike students who are constantly in fear of being sent home to their parents to collect school fees.

These economic differences are seen not just from the visibility of affluence but also from the difficulty of the poor to pay the fees and purchase textbooks. Ini concurs with Akoto:

> When it comes to the paying of the fees, the headmaster [would] realize that some people owe [the school]. Some people have to pay in instalments, in bits and pieces until the term ends. So the authorities take this thing into consideration. If the parents are not well-to-do, they make arrangements for you to pay in bits and pieces. (08/13/97)

The school tries to accommodate students by maintaining an awareness of their parents' financial circumstances. But there is only so much that school authorities can do. Many times, they have to enforce the payment of fees with the sole recourse of sending defaulting students home to their parents and families. There is a recognition that some students leave because of the inability to pay the fees, to work and help with the family finances.

In interviews with teachers and students, there are frequent references to the students from poor homes being more diligent and not getting into trouble as much as students from affluent families who are described as spoiled and who know they can get away with doing poorly and misbehaving. Otambo gives testimony to this:

... but what I have realized is that those who come from the rich families, they come for exhibition ... because their performance are not all that good, [they] are rated high because of the foundation [they have]. But at certain times too, some come here, especially the girls, just [to hang out] with the boys. Every weekend [some girls] want to go home and see Mummy and Daddy and get some more money to spend. But someone who comes from the less [affluent] family will not be thinking about going home. So they will not break the school rules by not attending social gatherings like [going to the] dining hall to eat. (11/08/97)

While boarders are viewed more positively in terms of their inherently class-based social advantages, the feeling is that students of wealthy parents are prone to breaking school rules and paying less attention to their academic work. They have the financial means to engage in non-academic activities that may actually hinder their educational success. As wealthy families can afford to have their children board, schooling problems play out differently for students depending on their status as day students or boarders.

Most day-students are locals and repeatedly refer to the need to study hard. They are described/categorized by their families in terms of how hard they work. Boarder student life also highlights different conditions between the girls and the boys in terms of accommodation, chores, study times and social activities. To deal with some of the problems around the economics of school access, the government has been encouraging community schools to allow students to attend schools within their home regions. The more traditional boarding schools, however, continue to operate with important differences perceived by teachers, students and parents.

There are other ways in which students perceive class as a barrier, especially when speaking about favoritism, nepotism and differential access to education. In a lengthy interview extract, Ado (a seventeen-year-old student in SS3 and whose father is a university-trained teacher) offers the following insights into some of the "unjust practices" of schooling that are structured along the lines of socio-economic class. This is the experience of a student from a non-affluent family. He is a day-student because his family cannot afford to send him to a boarding school or fulfill his desire of going to an all-boys school. Ado identifies very specific unjust practices and insists that it's "tough" for someone to attend school if they come from a poor home:

[Why do you say that?] If, for instance, a person has got maybe a very bad grade, he likes the school but due to the financial problem he may not have money to come to the school for the admission. But if a rich person with maybe average of twenty, he may pay administration to get a transfer to the school: *[Do you know someone who came to the school because their parents were rich, that's why they came here?]* Yes. My friend. *[Does it mean that he didn't pass the exam or he wasn't qualified?]* He got maybe twenty-two. *[And, you can't come here with aggregate twenty-two?]* Yes. *[Can you or you cannot?]* Okay, you can. *[You can come here with an aggregate twenty-two?]* Yes. *[So why do you say that your friend came here because he was from a rich family home?]* Silence. *[Is it difficult to come with an aggregate twenty-two?]* Yes, it is difficult to come with a grade twenty-two. But he paid some amount to that administration. *[To get in?]* Yes.: *[Did he tell you about that?]* Yes. *[Do you know whether this happens a lot?]* It happens a lot. *[Do you know who gets the money?]* I don't know. *[But the students talk about it?]* Yes. *[Have you reported it to anybody?]* No, please. *[Do you think it is right?]* I don't think it is right. *[Why is it not right?]* Because ... we come here ... and others come here and can go straight through ... and if they had got twenty-two here they would laugh at us. They would say this school is stupid. *[I see what you mean. But it's also that if someone comes here with a grade twenty-two, it is possible that someone who had aggregate ten may not be able to come because the one with twenty-two took the space?]* Yes. (08/12/97)

Aido is concerned about corruption in the school system, specifically how money buys educational access. He is aware of and concerned about the stigma that will follow his education if the system allows money and power to dictate standards and procedures.

Ethnicity, Culture, Language and Religion

It is in the discussion on ethnicity, language, culture and religion that the value of knowing about difference is made explicitly clear by students in particular. Kuse was born outside the school district in the Volta Region. Both his parents are civil servants. Business is his favorite subject. Interviewed on the same day with Riti, he enthuses about the need for individual students to learn other cultures and histories:

You see culture is the way for people to live ... in society. It is good to learn culture ... you learn about [the] historical background of ... the country [and] the different religions in the country. We learn to move about or move with other people and then you know other

people from other religions and other tribes and it will help you
develop morally and as a person. (09/21/97)

Fela, whose mother is a trader and father a police officer, attests to
the importance of knowing about different cultures. To him,
difference is a source of knowledge: "There are ... some taboos in
other cultural or ethnic groups. But when you learn about others, you
are able to know your left from your right in those ethnic groups. So,
I think it is better for us to learn the culture and what other groups
are doing" (09/21/97). Hana, the eighteen-year-old studying
economics and geography, adds: "... as a citizen of the country ... I
think it is somehow good to know something about the past ... [and]
our ancestors and other things. It also helps make you a good citizen"
(07/09/97). On the understanding of culture and cultural differences,
Hana seems to present the view that the means to cultural
membership is access to locally validated knowledge: "... Yes, and we
all come from different towns and places. Then, to know the culture
is also very advisable. As you know, to go to a town or to somewhere
you need to fit into that society" (07/09/97).

Ayoso also acknowledges that culture, language and religious
differences are pronounced in her school. The school is located in an
Akan district. Some students come from the north. Some are Asante.
Some are Ewe or Ga. And many are Akan. She herself is an Akan and
was born in the nation's capital, Accra. Similarly, some students are
Catholics. Others are Methodist, Presbyterian, Muslims or of the
traditional African faiths. However, when asked if these differences
are important to be taken account of, she is emphatic: "No, I don't
think so ... Because, I think, if you come to school we are all equal.
We all learn together. So I think it is not necessary (14/08/97). Yet,
the follow-up conversation is informative: "*[Look at someone who is an
Ewe, do you think things are going to be difficult for him or her in your school?]*
Okay, I can say yes, maybe someone will come to school and we
students are like speaking our language which is Akan. And, if you
have a friend who is Ewe it will be difficult for that person to
understand easily" (08/14/97). She acknowledges that language
differences can create some "difficulties" for a student. When asked if
one particular language should be a compulsory subject for all
students, after a long pause she comments: "I don't think it is. It is
not compulsory to study Twi. It is only those who do the elective that
study Twi. At first it was compulsory but now they've cancelled it, so
now only those with the elective study Twi" (08/14/97). In her

response, the reference is to Twi, the dominant language of the Akan. For the most part, students see language as a medium to create cultural and ethnic bonds with each other. Hana reasons: "Okay, in everyday life... when we move around we always communicate through language [with those] besides us ... As a student, you must be able to learn the languages ... because in everyday life and even taking examinations everything is given out through language. So you must learn [language]" (07/09/97).

Recent changes in educational reforms have recognized the importance of teaching Ghanaian local languages. However, unless handled with care, the emphasis on the languages of the dominant groups can also lead to a further marginalization of linguistic minorities in the school system. Students express a view that language accommodation must be encouraged in the same way religious differences are observed. As Hana notes:

> Okay, on Sunday ... we go to our various churches in the morning from seven to nine, so if you attend church, you go this or that church ... They've allowed those who are Moslems to attend their mosque in town or take a classroom [as a] mosque. Then, on Fridays they can also go and worship. So they don't discriminate between any religion. You go to your church alright. And, in the evening all of us go to church service together. (07/09/97)

Having a place of worship is vital to meeting one's spiritual and emotional needs. Religion and spirituality is part of the individual's identity and acknowledging the self as a site of difference is crucial to school success.

Twenty-three year-old Gono's reading of regional, ethnic and cultural diversity is interesting in that it describes how the majority population dominates at school which leads to a perception of unequal treatment of minorities, despite the official notion and philosophy of "equal treatment." Gono's school is located in the Akan region dominated by the Asantes. Given their number, students who are Akan and Asante dominate:

> The fact is that, most of them in [school] are Asantes. Some people from Kumasi and others are also coming here. Whenever the admissions are ... conducted, you will see that at the end of everything, the Asantes will dominate. Even though we have a large number of Gas and Ewes here. In the end the Asantes dominate. (10/09/97)

Gono argues that in spite of their large numbers, the Asantes are not treated any differently from the other cultural groups:

> They are not treated differently. Everybody [has] certain things. Everybody does [what] he is asked to do. But the fact is, [we have] the Ewes, Fantis, the Asantes and the Gas ... [and] ... you have most of them being the prefects, [that is] the Asantes and the Gas. Let us say that there is something going on ... concerning allowance and other things, you will try to tell [all students]. But [sometimes] one wouldn't tell [another] because he belongs to a different [group]. And when they are doing things, they will try to call their friends. The Gas, etcetera, they will do things together. And the Asantes will do things together. But when it comes to the student body as a whole, when we are doing something [as a whole], there is no discrimination. (10/09/97)

This narrative tells us that even though the official policy is one of non-discrimination and equality, informal practices are different. Students display favoritism towards friends and members of their own ethnic affiliation. Gono also problematizes the fact that school leadership is often held by members of majority groups.

Educators generally show concern about how cultural, ethnic, religious and linguistic differences are evoked in schooling. On the one hand, educators recognize the importance of understanding these differences. Obusu, a school administrator who has an extensive record of teaching and administration in the Ghanaian Educational Service, likes his school because colleagues "despite a few complaints, are committed to the work they are doing." He acknowledges the extent of linguistic, cultural, ethnic and religious diversity as well as regional differences in his school. However, to him these differences should not be allowed to complicate the schooling experiences of students. His approach to schooling is to accentuate the commonalities rather than the differences:

> Well yes, especially for those who are boarders, we have associations which are for people from very different cultures in this school. And, we don't very much emphasize this cultural thing in the school. We want to create some sort of homogenous atmosphere where they feel they are students and nothing else— Ghanaian students and nothing else. (10/09/97)

The school supports cultural and ethnic associations or societies. However, there appears to be a consensus that it must not encourage differences to the point of upstaging the common link of students as

Ghanaians. Obusu feels that accentuating differences creates and intensifies tensions at school unless differences are understood in terms of the connections with others:

> You see, we don't ascribe to cultural groups, tribal groups. Let me put it bluntly, we don't ascribe to that. I don't think that we can sanction that. We sanction groups that are made of different tribes [cultures], like religious groups, other social groups which are formed by students with different cultural backgrounds. And I think that is healthier. (10/09/97)

Tensions and contradictions, which seem to come up frequently in discussions around differences, highlight the fear of students becoming divided or thwarted from forming a uniform student culture or from coming together first and foremost as Ghanaians. Yet those who are boarders do have cultural associations as extracurricular activities. These are regulated in the school area but occur after the formal instruction period. Because in the students' narratives on culture understanding one's own cultural group and others is often highlighted as important, Obusu's insight into how tensions can be reproduced is interesting. Accentuating differences for the sake of creating divisiveness is no virtue of diversity. Differences must be understood as sites of strength and the promotion or accentuating of differences cannot be sacrificed on the prism of basic commonalities. Differences mean variety and multiple sites of strength. Difference is a circle to which everyone brings a contribution.

Kofi, a chemistry teacher and youth worker, spoke about his school taking into account religious differences, thereby allowing for many denominational services. Afterwards, he commented further on why it is important to downplay ethnic differences: "But on ethnic background ... I don't think the school takes that into account and I think it is better that way. Otherwise it will bring the kind of divisions on ethnic lines which is not good for the school ..." (08/13/97). Kofi goes on to speak about language and how and why it is appropriate for students to speak their different local languages. Again, his narrative highlights some of the tensions and the differences in the popular discussion on culture, religious and ethnicity, depending on how the narrator understood or interpreted the context.

Pepa has been teaching English in the local teacher training college for five years. On regional diversity, he says:

> I see differences as a strength because we believe in unity and diversity ... I will start with the student. For example, some come from the Northern Region, Upper Region, some from the Volta region ... They come on campus [and] we see a mixture. We see a diverse display of culture. And on some occasions, we have activities like cultural night displays. We see student groups displaying their various cultures from their regions. You see such very encouraging, very challenging [activities] that one can learn from. And, by the end of the three years you find that some students have positively learned something that they did not know before coming to college. (08/22/97)

In his pedagogical practice and instructional style, he uses the self as a knowledge base. He recognizes the importance of sharing knowledge and learning from others. The educator, he believes, should begin with where students are and allow room for growth in knowledge. Difference, as Pepa rightly says, is a source of strength, not something to be feared, especially when pedagogically engaged in the process of knowledge production and use.

Regional Differences and Ethnicity

Regional differences and disparities in Ghanaian schooling go back to colonial times when authorities concentrated schools in the southern parts of the country. A post-independence approach to national development and social integration has sought to rectify the regional differences by creating incentives for northern education and to encourage and support youth from different localities (less resourced) to attend schools. The latter has meant that students from different cultural, ethnic, religions and linguistic background attend school together. When questioned as to how the diversity in student population is taken into account, Fela shows how ethnicity can also be a ploy for favoritism:

> Okay, at times maybe when there is a problem concerning a master [teacher] who is maybe an Ewe and ... a student who is also an Ewe ... at times when the Ewe person has a problem with the [Ewe] master, the master doesn't take the problem to the higher authorities, that is for example the headmaster. But maybe, when an Akan or a different person gets involved in certain [trouble], the [Ewe] master normally sends the problem to the higher authorities to be dealt with. (09/21/97)

To Fela, the teacher may show favoritism to the student who comes from the same cultural group. Fela insists that regional diversity raises issues to be addressed and uses the case of students attending schools outside their home localities. He argues that certain "priorities or advantages" should be given to people from other regions attending his school. For example, when a student falls sick or is in need of emergency funds:

> The authority should [assist] because some [students] are from maybe the northern region coming to this place. At times ... they do not have provisions and will be short of money. So when certain things happen and maybe [the student] is from far away, he can approach the authorities. [They] can give the fellow the help that he needs. Anyway, if the fellow is from this town and he is from here ... to go to his house is close, not far. So he may be able to go back. Someone from the northern region will find it difficult to go there. So I think that those people should be given [more of an] advantage than those staying around. (09/21/97)

Fela would like to see his school extend assistance to students who are coming from outside the community and who cannot easily seek assistance from their parents because:

> [T]he fellow could be well prepared. But he may not know what will happen tomorrow. Maybe he will fall ... sick and then the amount he is paying will be much. Because of that he would be down, and because of that the [school] should [help]. But someone [who] is from this town ... he will be sick at home, since the parents are in this town they will be able to provide whatever he needs. (09/21/97)

He draws a clear distinction between meeting the needs of a student who attends a school located in her or his own region and the student from other parts of the country.

Noting that many cultural, religious, ethnic, linguistic identities point to a student population that is very diverse, Iso is not in favor of accentuating differences at school and critiques the practice of students getting together around regional, ethnic and cultural groupings. She uses the lessons of seating arrangements in the school dining hall to make the point of accentuating the commonalities:

> No, they treat all students as one. They don't group them as Ewes, Gas and Akans. ... We're treated as all together. When the boys go to dining hall we don't have Gas' table or the Akans or Ewes ... similar with the girls. Through that you learn how to live in a

> community. Because if you group boys on one side and girls at
> another side there will be no [community]. So they used to mix the
> boys. And some of the boys also feel shy eating with the girls. So
> when they are mixed together they will learn how to, because ...
> boys are so bad that when they are eating they will interact in some
> ways which are not good. So if they are mixed they will eat gently.
> So that's why they used to mix the girls with the boys in dining hall.
> (08/13/97)

From the official standpoint difference is not accentuated. However,
the students themselves form social groupings along the lines of
difference:

> [Schools] don't consider [difference]. It is the students who usually
> organize themselves. Okay, some students come from one place
> and there will be some boys who come from the same area, let's say
> Accra. So, when they come to the boarding house they ... organize
> themselves and when they are in dormitories they ... eat together,
> some bring food and ... they help each other ... The teachers treat
> us all together. It's the students who organize themselves into
> ethnic groups in their own dormitories. And, they speak their
> languages. (08/13/97)

Students bring ambiguous meanings to difference. While Riti
acknowledges the extent of cultural, ethnic, linguistic and regional
diversity in her school, she maintains that this is no reason for
"differential treatment" of certain groups. In her narrative, she makes
reference to the "possibility of conflict" based on regional differences
or perceptions of privilege. The way school authorities deal with
difference can itself create conflicts if students perceive they are being
differentially and unequally treated. To Riti, there is "the danger of
conflict" as educators begin to treat students differently, depending
on where they come from: "... it will bring about conflicts in this
school. Let's say, when someone is sick and the one is from the
school region and you say you won't give the person money to go to
the hospital. The person can go home maybe he won't get to the
hospital ... [So] he is supposed to go and [that] can cause a lot of
problems to the school." (09/21/97)

Kuse acknowledges diversity in his school but also declares that
different treatment could lead to problems and discrimination. Within
the context of receiving help or recognition for being from a different
area of the country, Kuse disagrees with Fela in terms of the need to
be aware of difference due to situation and contexts. To him

"different treatment," even if needed, can possibly lead to difficulties: "We come from all over the country we have to be treated equally. Wherever you are from, around here or afar, you have to be treated equally. Anybody from here can go to other district" (09/21/97). Responding to Fela's earlier assertion about dealing with emergency situations (medical and financial), Kuse argues that students who come from places outside the school district should not be treated any different: "No. We have a clinic in the school, so if you are sick [and come] from near or afar you have to go to the clinic for medical check up. If [the school] is to give priority to those who come from away it will lead to corruption" (09/21/97).

Kuse is concerned about teachers playing favorites by arbitrarily deciding whom to support and whom not. However, Onipa recognizes the situation of students coming to school from outside the local regions may require a differential response:

> Yes, I think so because some ... from outside ... who came to [the school] say they have to give them fair treatment because the person leaves his parents and comes to this school and maybe he doesn't know anybody in this town ... So if a person doesn't have money on him or her the school authority should give the person the money, and also when they are sick the school authorities should take them to the hospital and care for them. (09/21/97)

But Onipa would set boundaries that would ensure that rules and regulations, and school punishment, are enforced equally: "If you commit any offence in this school, I think the punishment they give to those from this district [should be] the same for those outside the [district]. Because when they take advantage that they are not from this town, they will treat them in special way ..." (09/21/97). To Onipa, unless rules and regulations are uniformly enforced, there will be disrespect and disobedience as students take advantage of any exemptions from the rule. Students have the view that any exemptions mean differential treatment especially when it is decontextualized.

Understanding Difference

Difference both fractures and strengthens the educational community.[1] The understanding of difference as simply diversity is embedded in the local knowledges of study participants. But a critical take on difference must allude to tensions, contestations, contradictions and ambiguities in claiming knowledge about "sameness." The understanding of difference is relevant beyond a critique of colonial/patriarchal education. The recognition of difference symbolizes the multiple strengths that different actors bring to a collective undertaking. Unfortunately, in contending with the challenges of educational reform, educators and schools often work with a problematic understanding of singular and separate differences (i.e., ethnicity, class, gender, religion, culture) and of the implications of difference for schooling and education. Narrative accounts of teachers, parents and students reflect the struggle of schools to deal with minority education in light of prevailing discourses of nationhood and citizenship. In an extract of the interview with Amina, a social studies teacher of seven years, the extent and nature of the problem is revealed, particularly in terms of schools' desire to accentuate commonalities by denying difference:

> *[How does your school deal with differences among the student population?]* ... we take them all to be equal because you can't say that because this person is from this region or that [region] you give some preferential treatment or [not]. You take them as one. You teach them in a book and you are off. You don't give any preferential treatment to any. Even at times ... even in this college when you are rather an Adventist and you misbehave your punishment is even more severe than ... [others] ... because they say the school is for you so you should set some good example for the others to follow. We don't discriminate, from my perspective. *[So what if someone is to argue that say given that these students come from diverse backgrounds it may not be actually appropriate to say that we should treat everyone the same ... [but] that we should take into account these differences that the students bring from their diverse backgrounds?]* It wouldn't be the appropriate way because then it's going to bring some diversities in the whole thing and to bring up a lot of things. We try as much as possible to take them as one irrespective of their home background, their religious background or whatever it is. We assume they are all equal. Once you have been able to enter through the required grades and made the entrance with a pass, we feel they are okay so you can cope with everything that goes on ... yeh. (08/20/97)

Quite evidently Amina, who has two children in the school system, is not reading difference as a site of identity and knowledge production. That is, she is not seeing different students' embodied identities in schools as carrying diverse and multiple knowledges that can be tapped to strengthen the process of educational delivery. By insisting that schools treat all students the same, teachers may adopt an approach to schooling that is "blind" to ethnicity, class, gender, religion and culture. Such an approach is often recognized as vital for the child to succeed as a learner. It builds on and connects the child's capabilities to the learning context in school and in community. Dominant knowledge espouses a view that students go to school as disembodied youth. Working with hegemonic knowledge, teachers and students may deny difference by affirming that all students be treated equally. Anything short of this, according to this perspective, is "bad." Difference is not read in terms of the particular identities, subjectivities and histories that students bring to school and how these specificities impact on the schooling and knowledge production process. When described in terms of subjectivities, identities and histories, educators are more at ease in admitting that ethnic, class, gender, religious and cultural differences have a significant impact on the schooling process. This is why, in one discursive space, Amina acknowledges that religion can be a basis for meting out unequal punishment to the students at her college. Yet in another she insists that the school treats everyone the same. In fact, when pressed further on the issue of differential treatment along religious lines, Amina is quick to add:

> [I]t is an Adventist institution [and] they tend to use their doctrine ... to dominate... Although every two weeks they allow them [students] to go to town and have their own church activities ... I don't think they really consider the differences in [religion] because basically, you know, when you come here for instance you are not supposed to put on earrings and other things ... but at home ... people do put all sorts of those things. When you come here you have to go the Adventist way ... that's how I see it. (08/20/97)

Conventional "observance" of difference belies the perception that teachers can and do treat all students the same. Difference is inevitably, although not overtly, recognized. It is recognized in such a way that problems are invariably created. For instance, Dankwah, the 1997 university graduate now teaching mathematics, reveals that teachers continually have to challenge negative perceptions of what course subjects males can do well in and females cannot. He has a more nuanced perspective than is usual on how the relations between gender and education have been broached in Ghanaian contexts. The gender imbalance in schools needs addressing. Having been designated a Science Resource Centre for the region, his school is noted for its strengths in science education. Dankwah admits that a good number of female students are taking science subjects:

> "*[So, how do you explain the fact that if you look at the student population we have more male students than female students?]* Well I think that is from our cultural background. You see, in the past our forefathers thought that girls' education was not all that useful, [but] that mentality is now [such] that it has begun to change ..." (28/08/97)

In his account Dankwah alludes to the school's attempt to break some traditional barriers, one of which has to do with girls and science education: "well ... [in the past] ... the notion that the science and maths are difficult [and] that [those subjects are] an experience for boys ... I think we have another ... social stigma ... hindering girls from taking mathematics in some cases." (08/28/97)

On the other hand, his counterpart, Osei, the co-ordinator of the Science Resource Centre, acknowledges difference only in so far as it relates to the teaching of particular subjects:

> I see the school treat[ing] every student on the same basis, with facilities, as far as teaching is concerned. [Through such] teaching and learning processes, students gain the same way. *[But do you think that there are some differences that have to be taken into account when you're teaching students?]* Oh ... probably more periods should be allotted to the sciences because it is a little demanding. We do practicals and you realize that the same number of periods are allotted to the sciences [as the] number of periods ... allotted to the arts, but we do extra practicals [in the sciences] and that is not [right]. (08/21/97)

These expressions point to the multiple ways in which schools can work beyond denying difference. However, the idea of uncontested culture, place and identity remains at the heart of educators' views of schooling. Culture, place and identity shape the production of knowledge. Teachers do not acknowledge that the approach of accentuating similarities by denying difference is problematic since it entails the silencing and non-affirmation of difference as sites of strength and knowledge. Within schools, not only is culture assumed to be homogenizing, but there is also a tendency to privilege dominant groups' cultures. Furthermore, the power differences and contestations around ethnicity, class, gender, religion and culture remain unresolved. Hence certain knowledges can be privileged while others are deprivileged. This is particularly evident when students' and educators' narratives affirm the discourse of the dominant. Such narratives lead one to conclude that issues of ethnicity, socio-economic family background, gender, religion and culture do not have particularly salient implications for understanding difference in the context of schooling and education in Ghana. For example, when asked about any gender differences in attitudes and actions that she has perceived or experienced in her teaching and school experiences, English and history teacher Ohemaa explains how gender is problematically viewed and understood in the schooling process:

> No, not so. I feel we are all treated equal provided you do the work that is expected of you. I don't think there will be any qualms about your teaching or something. But it seems, let me put it this way, because the females ... due to some family problems like children and a husband and the rest ... it seems the effort we put in may not be up to the expectation as the men. Because even at times when it comes to say that we should rally the students around, you see it's only the male teachers who will be working with us [women teachers], just giving some minor help ... except when we are assigned specifically [what] to do ... When we are assigned we can do it. But when it's a general thing it seems to me that ... it is mostly the males who are doing the greater part of the work. *[So you don't get a sense, for example, that there is a perception that say female teachers are say less capable or more capable than male teachers, you don't get that kind of attitude?]* I can say in some respects that the men are more capable. But generally, I feel the females are also doing their part ... I believe so. I think every teacher ... is capable. But sometimes the problem [is that] people have different views of other people just because they are different. (08/20/97)

She points to gender differences in the overall working conditions of women teachers. However Ohemaa does not translate that understanding into an awareness of the important distinction that must be drawn between the position that advocates that all students and all teachers be treated the same and the differential impact that ethnicity, class, gender, religion and culture actually has on the everyday work/life of teachers and students at school.

Inclusive Schooling, Equity and Social Justice

Students' awareness of social difference, equity and fairness is significant for rethinking schooling and education. Within many contexts students understood difference primarily as needing to treat everyone the same because being treated the same was perceived as being treated equally. When difference was acknowledged, it was done so mostly in terms of what is perceived as differential and unequal treatment that disadvantaged students on the basis of class, gender or ethnicity. There was a prevailing view that accentuating difference could create problems and that focusing on the shared commonalities was healthier for the students, the school and the nation. Yet when speaking of their ancestral past, of Ghanaian history, of local geography, of local languages and cultures and of developing local African/Ghanaian centred texts, differences through the local were affirmed and understood as important to learn. Although this talk was oftentimes separate and distinct from the participants' views of equating difference with potential conflict and same treatment with equality, dialogues about what was "local" point to the possibility of seeing difference as significant and as sites of strength and power. Difference here means knowledge. Class, gender, ethnicity, language and religion inform the understanding of the self and other. Difference speaks about identities that connect to how we come to know ourselves, understand the world and act within it. All learners should acknowledge their identities and the social differences that exist among the school populations. Identities are linked with schooling and with knowledge production. The question students, teachers, administrators must grapple with is how students negotiate these identities at the school site and within themselves.

Arguably a more detailed analysis of study participants' voices within each site of difference can be attempted under a general rubric of social difference and schooling. In-depth analysis delving into the specifics of each site of difference may reveal pertinent details to inform a general discussion on difference that can be specifically located.

Ghanaian educators generally uphold the ideal of a democratic pluralistic society which both recognizes community and advocates empathy for all individuals and groups on the basis of a common humanity. Educators emphasize goodwill, tolerance and under-standing of all differences. Diversity, while an acknowledged site of strength, for the most part is not emphasized as a site in need of attention. In other words, most educators work with the notion of our basic humanity and downplay difference by accentuating shared commonalities. But gender, ethnicity, class, religion and culture are important markers for claiming identity. Students and educators occupy and defend spaces on the basis of these markers. Identities are linked with schooling and knowledge production. To transform education to serve the needs of all students, there is a need to identify, challenge and change the values, structures and behaviors that perpetuate power and dominance and create hierarchies of knowledge. For example, many studies have highlighted persistent gender inequities (see Bloch, Bekou-Betts and Tabachnick 1998; Herman and Bunware 1999 for the latest of such studies). However, we also need to pay additional attention to other inequities perpetuated along the lines of class, ethnicity, culture, language and religion. The Ghanaian case study points to sites and sources for the manifestation of the problems of bias, discrimination, exclusion and marginality. The mechanism for redressing these inequities through education, sharing and exchange of ideas must extend to the fundamental structural change in schools and society. All students do not start from a relatively level playing field. They do not all have access to similar resources and neither do they have comparable values, aspirations and concerns.

Study participants' responses to questions of class, educational access and the negotiation of social difference in schooling should be contextualized in the prevailing discourse on cost-recovery and cost-effectiveness, which not only affect youth education, but also, help shape public attitudes towards education. Parents who cannot afford to send their children to school, to pay the high fees or to provide textbooks are socially disadvantaged. Schools may be dis-proprotionately concentrated in urban centres with implications for the rural poor. Perhaps the rural poor cannot afford boarding education for their children. And, if the student is a girl, the chances are that the parents will decide on educating the males and sacrifice their daughter's education. These matters cannot be lost in the critical discourse on difference.

Similarly, access to participation in the educational process must not be limited to a discussion of class and economics. Effective participation in education must include active involvement on the part of individuals and groups of different ethnic, cultural, linguistic, religious backgrounds to have their realities reflected upon with their participation in knowledge production. The varied knowledges that diverse peoples bring to the educational process help shape the communities in which they live. In other words, these social differences bring to the fore new questions of individuals and groups' participating in the educational process as equal partners, particularly in the generation of knowledge.

In emphasizing the goal of national integration, post-independence and "post-colonial" education in Africa have long denied heterogeneity in local populations, as if difference itself was a problem. With this orientation, education has undoubtedly helped to create and maintain glaring disparities and inequities that persist and grow along constructed lines of difference. This pattern can, however, be disrupted. We are reminded that "the effect of schooling, the way it alters a person's capacity to behave and do things, depends not only on what is learned, but also on how and why it is learned and the environment within which it is learned" (Dore 1976, 8; cited in Nwagwu 1997, 94). Inclusive education can acknowledge difference and diversity while, at the same time, highlighting commonalities, even among peoples with conflicting interests. Ultimately, it can contribute to both national integration and social reconstruction.

Admittedly, the discussion has not dealt with a host of issues emerging around the processes of knowledge creation and use by different bodies. Instead, my intention has been to look at the role of culture, religion and language in education and the challenge of dealing with educational equity and social difference in schooling. To promote inclusive schooling, the requirements of enhancing minority education must be understood. For example, there is a need for comprehensive curriculum development at the elementary, secondary and post-secondary levels (Obanya 1995; Sifuna 1992). Curricular change must respond to the question of relevance by applying knowledge to local needs, concerns and aspirations (Jegede 1994, 1997). This may require local input in curricular development to ensure that diverse local subjects develop a sense of ownership and control of the educational process. Curriculum must speak to fundamental questions of social justice and equity (see also Hickling-Dyson 1994; Bracy 1995). Classroom instruction must teach about ethnicity, difference and global citizenship. Educators must use the differential knowledges of a diverse student body emanating from homes and communities in their classroom practices in order for the students themselves to develop some ownership and control over the learning process (Banks 1993).

Inclusive education should expose how such power relations impact on students' learning in terms of identity with and alienation from the school. How existing socio-economic inequities in society impact upon students' learning and their sense of connectedness and belonging to the community should be a part of classroom and other educational discourses. Inclusive education should help African students reclaim the positive elements of their culture and cultural values as sites of empowerment and for developing a collective consciousness (see also Steady 1990; Dei 1994).

Inclusive education should incorporate the individual and group lived experiences of students and teachers into critical pedagogical practices in the schools so as to understand social reality/ies (see also Henry 1991). Educators must use relevant and critical teaching materials in their curricula and also secure institutional attention focused on ethnic bias, classism, and sexism in the schools (Higginbotham 1990, 15; Anderson and Collins 1995).

The search for a more inclusive body of knowledge in school will entail tapping the diverse local cultural resource knowledges of African peoples for classroom instruction and pedagogy. It also requires interrogating indigenous cultures as primary vehicles for educational and social transformation. Such local knowledges can be interrogated and applied in the resolution of tensions, needs and wants of local peoples (Dei 1999b, c).

Inclusive education must challenge the structures of power in society that control the educational system in order to transform the system so that it is fair to all students. Since transformative change encompasses more than the reform of existing curricular and pedagogical practices, educators must respond to problems of discrimination, prejudice and alienation within their schools and focus on the social and cultural values that support reciprocal considerations. To promote inclusive, non-hegemonic social participation and provide lasting solutions to human problems, education in Africa must acknowledge and affirm difference and diversity within the context of pursuing equity and social justice.

Note

1.   Given the great complexity of our world today, academic and discursive practices must be sophisticated enough to account for the tensions, contradictions and structural ambiguities that pervade claims for particular identities. To claim community is to engage in a powerful linguistic, cultural and discursive practice. As Price (1998, 3-4) further identifies, we can speak of community in some multiple, non-exclusive combinations of 1) "spatial community," in which boundaries (as spatial, localized settings) are defined for the pursuit of socially meaningful interactions; 2) "affective/relational

community," in which community draws on some bonds of affinity and community becomes a mutually shared experience of the values, attitudes, beliefs, concerns and aspirations of a collective; 3) "moral community" as defined in meaningful participation and belonging in a citizenry to achieve common goals defined as the "collective good." Within these various conceptions of community, tensions, struggles, ambiguities and contradictions are captured and articulated, and yet the integrity of a collective membership is maintained. As members of community/ies, individuals have multiple rather than single, affinities and allegiances resulting in profound complexities that defy/ challenge easy categorizations and designations. Yet, each community also maintains and reinforces certain processes of inclusion/exclusion in order to ensure that identities and histories are not obliterated.

Chapter 8

Rethinking the Role of Indigenous and Local Cultural Knowledges in Schools

In broaching the subject of Indigenous and local cultural knowledges and the relevance for educational reform, I want to highlight the discursive position that local knowings are crucial and relevant to implementing effective change. My argument is that we need a critical discursive lens to imagine and construct viable educational alternatives for Ghanaian and African schooling. In the discussion I use "Indigenous" and 'local' interchangeably to denote the complexity, dynamism and variegated nature of knowledge systems. I also place the discussion in a more broad context as a way to rethink schooling and education in varied communities. This is not just about schooling and education in Ghana and Africa. It is about rethinking schooling and education in global contexts. The ideas presented in this chapter also apply (albeit to varying degrees) to the Western academy, as well as to schooling in African contexts, as the latter by most accounts is heavily implicated by Western colonialism and colonialist practices of educational delivery. While I am aware that we cannot transport wholesale ideas and practices in Euro-American education to other contexts, I also believe that there are important parallels and points of convergence that must not be lost. The challenge is to work with such general ideas in the specific historical and contemporary contexts in which we find ourselves.

Local peoples ought to be at the forefront in the search for solutions to their problems. They can critically interrogate and utilize relevant knowledges from their own histories, Indigenous traditions and culture to devise lasting and working solutions to their current problems. Their knowledges cannot be discarded as irrelevant. They must be interrogated and the sites of empowerment identified in the search for genuine educational options. The current discourse of African renaissance or rebirth can be located in the need to reflect on past experiences and African history and to utilize locally contextualized, cultural knowledges to respond to contemporary pressures. This does not mean a recourse to a mythic or romanticised past but rather the realization that the past, history, culture and local knowledge have a role to play in fashioning modern solutions. The assertion of local voice is a necessary exercise in resisting domination and colonial imposition. Friedman (1992) speaks of the "existential authenticity of the subject's engagement in self-defining projects." The epistemic knowledge of local subjects is embedded in an awareness of the self and one's place within the collective. Knowing the self is important in order to appreciate the challenges and how we respond. Since indigenity and issues of identity are powerfully linked, we cannot dismiss the power of Indigenous and local cultural knowings. In fact, struggles over identity have serious implications when local peoples lose both their ontological and epistemological foundations. While culture may be negotiated, questions and issues of identity are not negotiable for local peoples. In articulating a new paradigm to schooling and education in Ghana and Africa, I adopt an anti-colonial lens as a decolonizing project that affirms the power of Indigenous and local cultural knowledges.

Indigenous knowledges rupture the sense of comfort and complacency in conventional approaches to knowledge production, interrogation, validation and dissemination in schools and other educational settings. Within institutions of learning, conventional/traditional paradigms, differential social locations and the relative positioning of intellectual subjects constrain many of us from being subversive, resistant and challenging of dominant or "stable" knowledges. To speak about Indigenous knowledges and the decolonization of the academy is to take personal and collective risks. By 'academy' I mean schools, colleges and universities.

My argument may be read as a provocation or as an invitation to engage in a dialogue about education and the ways in which our academies produce and legitimate knowledge. Education, as I have defined it, includes the varied options, strategies and ways through which people come to know and understand the world and act within it. The collective "we," to which I refer, includes readers of this text and those who share in the politics of decolonizing schools, colleges and universities so as to recognize the legitimacy of different forms of knowledges.

It should be reiterated that in this chapter I present a normative argument. Nonetheless, it is acknowledged that empirically one can point to spaces and sites (albeit a few) within the Western academy where some of the ideas presented here are being implemented. The focus on providing an empirical basis for the discussion could be subject of another text. Furthermore, while I concede that there may be multiple uses of Indigenous knowledges (e.g., using such knowledge to maintain a way of life that serves specific interests of gender, class, ethnicity, religion), my work engages in an explicit political project that must not be lost. I want to use Indigenous knowledges for the political purpose of decolonizing school systems. My educational journey was replete with experiences of colonial and colonized encounters that left unproblematized what has conventionally been accepted in schools as "in/valid knowledge." My early schooling history did not emphasize the achievements of African peoples and their knowledges, neither their own places and peoples nor their contributions to academic scholarship on world civilizations. Like many others, I engage in the topic of Indigenous knowledges with a deep concern about the historical and continuing deprivileging and marginalizing of subordinate voices in the conventional processes of knowledge production, particularly (but not exclusively) in Euro-American contexts.

Indigenous knowledges do not "sit in pristine fashion" outside of the effects of other knowledges. Rather than repudiate Indigenous, I bring new and complex readings to the term. Today we speak of the "hybridity" of knowledges. The fact that different bodies of knowledge continually influence each other shows the dynamism of all knowledge systems. Yet the Indigenous is never lost. The interplay of different knowledges is perhaps one of many reasons why Indigenous knowledges must be taught in the academy. The goal of integrating (i.e., centrering) Indigenous knowledges is to affirm this collaborative dimension of knowledge and, at the same time, to address the emerging call for academic knowledge to speak to the diversity of histories, events, experiences and ideas that have shaped human development and societies. If we recognize that knowledge is not static but rather constantly being created and recreated in context, we can see that Indigenous knowledges need to be an integral part of this ongoing co-creation and re-creation.

Furthermore, as an African scholar teaching in a Western academy I see decolonization as breaking with the ways in which the African human condition is defined and shaped by dominant Euro-American cultures and asserting an understanding of the Indigenous social reality informed by local experiences and practices. Bringing Indigenous knowledges into the academy, an institution of power and influence in this increasingly interconnected world, is ever more critical in this information era. At the same time, while it is important to avoid rendering a false binary or moral evaluation between good (indigenous)/and bad (conventional/Western) knowledges, the objective is nonetheless to challenge imperial ideologies and colonial relations of knowledge production that continually characterize and shape academic practices. There is also a realization that knowledge is operationalized differently given local histories, environments and contexts.

The exclusion of Indigenous knowledges from the academy within the current context of knowledge production in schools leaves the space for the colonization of knowledges and cultures in local environments and contexts unchallenged. Such a project becomes even more critical given the power imbalance between groups that own and have access to the technology of knowledge dissemination. The academy's privileged position in this regard entails a corresponding responsibility to include indigenous knowledges in the dynamic process of knowledge generation and dialogue.

Indigenous knowledges emerge in the immediate context of the livelihoods of local peoples as a product of a sustained process of creative thought and action within communities when local peoples struggle to deal with an "ever changing set of conditions and problems" (see Agrawal 1995a, 5). Such knowledge is dynamic, undergoing constant modifications as a people negotiate complex relations with nature, land, culture and society. Indigenous knowledges are relevant to the extent that they address the needs of the community. Although localised and context bound, these knowledges evolve and can transcend boundaries. They should not be understood as boxed into a time and space. All knowledges are in constant motion and the fluidity of interactions of different knowledges makes every knowledge dynamic. Purcell (1998, 266) also points out that "as colonialism uprooted Indigenous peoples it also uprooted their knowledge systems." However, these knowledge systems have continued to persist and adjust in new environments. The recognition of the specific situatedness of knowledge forms does not amount to a "fetishization of the local" (Ginsburg, 1994, 366).

Speaking about Indigenous knowledges does not and should not necessarily commit one to a dichotomy between "Indigenous" and "Western knowledge" (see Agrawal, 1995a, b). Indigenous knowledge does not reveal a conceptual divide with "Western knowledge." Indigenous is not strictly in opposition to "Western." To think of the concept of "Indigenous" is to do so in relation to Western knowledge. The concept of "Indigenous" simply alludes to the power relations within which local peoples struggle to define and assert their own representations of history, identity, culture and place in the face of Western hegemonic ideology/ies. Implicit in the terminology of "indigenous[ness]" is a recognition of some philosophical, conceptual and methodological differences between Western and non-Western knowledge systems. These differences are not absolutes but a matter of degree. The difference is seen more in terms of [cultural] logics and epistemologies, i.e. differences in the making of sense as always dependent on context, history, politics and place. Within communities there are certain key symbols of culture "which by their redundancies, pervasiveness and importance can be seen as capturing and expressing a society's focal cultural concern" (see Limon 1991, 118, citing Ortner 1973). Every community chooses certain values, norms and social mores to highlight in order to demonstrate the issues of primary [not exclusive] concern. Thus, acceding to the requirements of 'community and social responsibility' may be rewarded in one society as opposed to the affirmation of "individuality and individual rights" (see Dei 1993b). In other words, within different knowledge systems and/or worldviews there are particular understandings of the relationships between society, culture and nature that can be privileged and rewarded. Such understanding may form a legitimate basis of distinguishing between different worldviews.

The interactions of different cultures and cultural knowledges have always been part of human reality and existence. Such understanding ought to be distinguished from an uncritical postmodernist claim that what emerges from an articulation of two or more disparate elements is often a new distinct form whereby the former disparate elements [form] often lose their character, logic and identities. In a global context, when dominant knowledge forms usually appropriate other knowings and claim universality in their interpretations of society, there is a politics of reclaiming the Indigenous and local identities. This reclamation has a purpose in unmasking the process through which Western science knowledge, for example, becomes hegemonic ways of knowing by masquerading as universal knowledge. Hence, it is crucial to separate the politics and efficacy of disrupting/interrupting binary thoughts and the [en]coding of cultural differences from a positive (solution-oriented) affirmation of important differences that distinguish multiple knowledge forms by their unique philosophies and identities. Also, the world views of different knowledges may affirm some unbridgeable differences. For example, dominant knowledge forms (e.g. modern Western science for the most part) see the universe as something to be controlled and dominated while other knowledge systems (e.g. Indigenous and local cultural knowledges) speak of a search for peaceful co-existence with Nature. What all this points to is that it is important to acknowledge that in the intellectual and political project of affirming multiple knowledges the "normalization of difference" is distinct from the sheer rigid classification of "absolute differences."

The strength of Indigenous knowledges lies in their application to the lived realities of people. The relevance of Indigenous knowledges is that they speak to the practical and mundane issues of social existence. In the face of entrenched hegemonic relations and global economic and ecological threat, knowledge is relevant only if it strengthens a people's capacity to live well. It is concerned first and foremost with questions of survival. It is knowledge rested in "the livelihoods of people rather than with abstract ideas and philosophies" (Agrawal 1995b, 422). Indigenous knowledges cannot be simply understood in terms of their utilitarian purposes. Their existence signals the power of intellectual agency of local peoples.

They are symbolic (intellectually, politically and emotionally) in the projection to others that local peoples can and do know about themselves and their societies. They are about culture, identity and political survival.

Culture and language are very central to "Indigenous" for without these the concept of "Indigenous" is meaningless. As Purcell (1998, 260) again enthuses, there is a culture of science that is arguably unique to Western societies. Western knowledge is founded on a particular criteria of science that is too abstracted from any specific cultural genesis to be considered "Indigenous" today. While today we must be careful to ascribe 'Indigenity' to all knowledge systems, we should also note that Indigenous knowledges are not homogenous. They are demarcated by regional, class, ethnic, gender and religious differences. There are differential class and community interests when we speak of Indigenous knowledges. All knowledges are social and political creations that can serve specific interests. But we cannot idealize difference. There is interplay and exchange among and between cultures and communities and it is this process that harmonises differences within local communities and their knowledges. While there may be significant intellectual, cultural and political disagreements within communities, important lines of connection can develop across group boundaries and Indigenous communities with implications for knowledge systems.

Towards a Critical Discursive Approach: Indigenous Knowledges, Decolonization and the Anti-Colonial Framework

Recent trends in post-modernism and post-colonial theorizing represent a paradigmatic shift in the sense of rejecting universal, simplified definitions of social phenomena that would normally infuse a de-contextualized, essentialized reality. The focus is shifted to the complexity of lived experience. Rather than searching for broad generalizations, we must look for local, specific and historically informed analyses grounded in spatial and cultural contexts (see also Seidman 1994). In a sense (as many have observed), the post-modern discursive practice disrupts social and intellectual hierarchies and dismantles essentialism and foundational knowledge. Prah (1997, 16) states that post-modernity would defy "consensual rationality, hierarchy and order" that would act as "universal systems of thought." Whereas post-modern discourses bring to the fore questions of identity, difference and representation and the problem of decontextualized power, post-modern theorizing, on the whole, denies collective histories, except as "individualized renditions and interpretations of experience" (Prah 1997, 16). Thus, to use and yet challenge post-modernism that ends up over-subjectivizing, individualizing and privileging certain narratives and subject voices is important.

According to Sara Suleri (1992), there is also a distinction that needs to be made between those who control the discourse and those who resist (see also Bhabha 1990). Post-modernism neglects larger political-economic questions (see also Parpart 1995) and forms the world into separate enclaves/entities that have no connection, shared values and norms. For those of us who speak of a decolonization project, such a fragmented stance can be problematic. The noted discontinuities and fragments are, indeed, part of a unified experience.

It is within the context that the relevance of critiques of post-colonial theory[2] resides. Post-coloniality focuses on the interplay between imperial/colonial cultures and the colonized cultural practices. As a discursive framework, post-coloniality views "colonialism as an ideological and discursive formation ... an apparatus for constituting subject positions through the field of representation" (Slemon 1995, 46). An examination of colonial histories of marginalized communities is a necessary component of the process of decolonization. However, as a discourse, post-coloniality ignores the Indigenous histories of Southern Native peoples which must be the centre of any analysis of contemporary imperial relations; a transformative dialogue must centre on colonized peoples' understandings of their histories. We cannot shift that centre to the margins or to neutral ground, for if the focus of our work is to be anti-oppression, the understanding of colonization must be grounded in the colonized.[3] Ghanaian literary critic Ama Ata Aidoo is particularly blunt on this point when she argues that post-coloniality is increasingly becoming a "cover-up of a dangerous period in our people's lives" (Ama Ata Aidoo, cited in Zeleza 1997, 17).

Other interesting questions remain: Who is the post-colonial subject? Why is post-colonial theorizing appealing to Western academies unlike other critical emancipatory discourses such as Afrocentricity, anti-colonial theory and Indigenous knowledges? Post-colonial theory has become a metatheory by essentializing difference and thus risks idealizing and essentializing the human subject by privileging the individuation of the self. Post-colonial theory dehistoricizes and homogenizes human identities as totally/ completely fragmented, multiple and transient. In so doing, it negates/repudiates the repressive presence of collective oppressions, colonial exploitations and group marginality, as well as the shared histories of collective resistances of marginalized groups (see Zeleza 1997). Chisti (1999, 16) cautions against the dangers of "falling into the traps of complete unilateral fragmentation around difference," a discursive position that also shows so-called anti-essentialist discourses have the tendency to be essentialist positions. Post-colonial discourse is not immune to this critique.

Resistance is never autonomous. There is potential for resistance within the structures of power and knowledge (see Foucault 1980, 1983; Prakash 1992; Moore 1997). A knowledge of how power relations are articulated in societies, rather than the mere maintenance of power for itself, illuminates Indigenous forms of colonial resistances and how such knowledge retains relevancy in understanding contemporary social relations and social change. Frantz Fanon (1963) long ago insisted that decolonization can only be understood as a historical process that ultimately culminates in changing the social order. It is an initial violent encounter of two forces, "opposed to each other by their very nature, which in fact results from and is nourished by the situation in the colonies" (36). Moreover, Fanon adds that decolonization is a calling into question of the whole colonial situation and its aftermath. Thiophene (1995) also argues that decolonization is a "process, not arrival; it invokes an ongoing dialectic between hegemonic centrist systems and peripheral subversion of them; between European ... [imperial] ... discourses and their [anti]-colonial dis/mantling" (95). A decolonization project in the academy must be aware that the colonization process and colonizing tendencies accede a false status to the Indigenous/colonial subject through the "authority of Western knowledge" at the same time as indigenous knowledges are deprivileged, negated or devalued.

Regimes of power/knowledge work to position individuals in the academy differently. A critical reflection on all knowledge systems points to their sites and sources of possibilities as well as to their limitations. Indigenous knowledges (de)construct narratives of and about differences. The relevance of "identity discourse" in Indigenous knowledge production is that identity has implications, both within a discursive context and within the spaces/lenses we inhabit and through which we engage ourselves as historically situated individuals/ collectivities in social practices.

Therefore, Indigenous knowledges are appropriately discussed within an anti-colonial discursive framework. As argued earlier and elsewhere (Dei, 1999; Dei and Asgharzadeh, 2000), this framework is both a counter/oppositional discourse to the denial and repudiation of the repressive presence of colonial oppression and an affirmation of the reality of recolonization processes through the dictates of global capital. Like post-colonial theory, an anti-colonial framework is a theorization of issues, concerns and social practices emerging from colonial and imperial relations and their aftermath. However, anti-colonialism uses Indigenous knowledges as an important entry and grounding point. The "anti" is to register an opposition and resistance to colonialism that local peoples pursued. The practice of resistance to colonial domination is an important knowledge that can be gleaned from Indigenous and local communities to inform current political practice and social theorizing. As a theoretical perspective, anti-colonialism interrogates the power configurations and contestations around knowledge production, dissemination and application. It is an epistemology of the colonized, anchored in the indigenous sense of collective and common colonial consciousness. Colonial is conceptualized, not simply as foreign or alien, but rather as imposed and dominating. An anti-colonial discursive approach would recognize the importance of locally produced knowledges emanating from cultural histories and daily human experiences and social interactions. It sees marginalized groups as subjects of their own experiences and histories (see Memmi 1969, Fanon 1963, and also Foucault 1980). This approach would point to the relevance of using local languages and Indigenous cognitive categories and cultural logic to create social understandings. The approach would also draw upon and combine Indigenous literature with politics, culture, history, economics and understandings of spirituality. It draws and builds on work that is being done in communities and by minoritized, indigenous and local scholars in reintegrating local and native languages in the education of the young, in the study of language and literature, in publication of texts and in nurturing, supporting and publishing the works of indigenous writers in the academies and indigenous literary circles. An anti-colonial practice encourages these works not only to be reflective of their cultures but also for texts to be written in local languages (see wa Thiong'o 1986).[4]

An anti-colonialist approach is also a celebration of oral, visual, textual, political and material resistances of colonized groups—a shift away from a sole preoccupation with victimization. It offers a critique of the wholesale degradation, disparagement and discard of "tradition and culture" in the interest of "modernity" and the "global space." There is tradition, orality, visual representation, material and non-material cultures and Aboriginality that empower colonized and marginalized groups. A politicized evocation of cultures and traditions resonates with a genuinely decolonizing project. By according a discursive integrity to subjects' accounts (validating their voice/words/language) of their histories and cultures, colonial imperialist projects can be destabilized.

An anti-colonial discursive approach begins by questioning institutionalized power and privilege and the accompanying rationale for dominance in social relations. Such an approach acknowledges the role of societal/institutional structures in producing and reproducing inequalities that are based on race, class, sexual and gender location. A key argument is that institutional structures are sanctioned by the state to serve the material, political and ideological interests of the state and the dominant economic/ social forces that have influenced/influence its formation. However, power and discourse are not possessed entirely by the colonizer and the dominant. Discursive agency and power to resist also reside in colonized groups (see also Bhabha 1995). For example, subordinated/colonized populations had a theoretical and practical conception of the colonizer with which to engage social and political practice and relations. Contact between the "imperial order" and the "colonial" periphery continues to involve complex and creative encounters/ resistances (Ashcroft, Griffiths and Thiopene 1995). These forms of resistance help to sustain the local human conditions of the colonized "Other."

Ideas and notions of "nation," "community" and "citizenship" are not simply imagined constructs but are real in their meanings and evocations with profound consequences for colonized and marginalized groups working in Western/Euro-American academies. I agree with Homi Bhabha (cited in Parry 1995,43) that an anti-colonial discourse "requires an alternative set of questions, techniques and strategies in order to construct it." Anti-colonialism questions the practice of reading the histories of Southern peoples strictly in demarcated stages (i.e., periodization of pre-colonial, colonial and post-colonial epochs). It calls for theorizing Southern issues beyond their artificial boundaries. For example, seeing Africa beyond the boundaries created by colonial authorities and making the necessary internal and external linkages with local groups and Diasporic and other colonized peoples. An anti-colonial stance requires that the knowledge producer be aware of the historical and institutional structures and contexts that sustain intellectualism and intellectual projects. For example, whereas post-colonial theorists depend on Western models, anti-colonial theorists work with alternative/oppositional paradigms based on the use of Indigenous concepts and analytical systems and cultural frames of reference.

Indigenous Knowledges in the Academy: Basic Challenges

"Structural Hegemonic Rupturing": Knowledge and Representation, Curricular and Pedagogical Reforms

A profoundly challenging task in the academy is to facilitate the recognition and validation of the legitimacy of Indigenous knowledges as a pedagogic, instructional communicative tool in the processes of delivering education. The challenge starts with hiring a diverse faculty that includes members of ethnic, racial, linguistic, cultural and religious minorities and women to join teaching faculties and to integrate Indigenous and local cultural knowledges into the curriculum as well as into the instructional and pedagogic practices of educators and learners. The praxis of supporting diverse physical bodies and addressing the question of knowledge representation involve systemic change. Furthermore, to achieve a genuine synthesis of all existing knowledges, the academy must work with the idea of multiple, collective and collaborative dimensions of knowledge. In a more politicized sense, "synthesis" means shifting to a restructured and reconstituted space, where issues of knowledge content and physical representation are addressed in such a way as to recognize the multiplicity of human ideas. Synthesizing different knowledges will be an educational practice that leads to systemic change rather than to a remedial patchwork of unsustained efforts. Synthesis is not simply opening up the club to new members but examining the entire structure of the club.

In order to initiate the process, there are certain critical questions to be asked: Is the distinction between "traditional thought" and "modern scientific thought" false or relevant? What does it mean to "synthesize" two or more knowledge systems? What are the central concerns of each knowledge system? Are Indigenous moral and cognitive conceptions compatible with Western science? How do we arrive at meaningful and genuine theories (discursive frameworks) that take into account different philosophical traditions (e.g. Western and Indigenous thought)? Can we use another's language to attain a deeper conceptual and philosophical understanding of the "Other's" knowledge system(s)? These are relevant questions because, historically, Western philosophical traditions have provided the dominant theoretical frameworks for structuring social science knowledge and research.[5]

Currently, a small but growing number of Indigenous scholars are seeking not only to write and publish about the philosophical, literary, scientific traditions of their places but also to do so in their local languages (see for example Anzaldúa 1990; Philip 1989; wa Thiong'o 1986). Specifically in Canadian contexts, Native/Aboriginal communities and historians are rewriting their histories to (re)claim not only a past which was excluded in the history of the colonial nation (i.e., Canada) but also to name the colonial historical period from the perspective of their places and their peoples. Such decolonization activities also have direct implications for rewriting curriculum. Similarly, ongoing work presents education in Indigenous societies through a worldview that is integrated within the community. Education is not constrained by the age segregation of a classroom or the isolation of mother and child in the home; learning is imparted to the younger generations by elders such that it is an integrated part of a community's social, spiritual/ancestral and natural environment(s). Education in this context is intergenerational and part of a holistic, respectful communal view of belonging and learning. This perspective could be seen as moving beyond "opening up the club to new members" toward restructuring the view of education as it has been defined by the state in the classroom.

To integrate Indigenous knowledges into school systems is to recognize that different knowledges can co-exist and that different knowledges can complement each other yet be in conflict at the same time. As alluded to earlier, a false dichotomous thinking between Indigenous and non-Indigenous knowledges can be avoided by understanding that the past/traditional and the modern are not frozen in time and space. The past continues to influence the present and vice versa—continuity of cultural values from past experiences shape the present. Similarly, the present also influences the narration of the past. There are important reasons for working towards a synthesis of different knowledge systems. Aside from issues of partiality and uncertainty of knowledges, there is the inadequacy of scientific knowledge (both Indigenous and Western) to account for the complete histories of ideas and events that have shaped and continue to shape human growth and social development. The worlds of the metaphysical and the physical, of mystery and "invisible agents," and science and modernization are not oppositional realities (Prah 1997, 20). Different knowledges represent different points on a continuum and include ways people perceive and act in the world.

Different forms of knowledge (e.g., knowledge acting as superstition, a belief in the invisible order of things, knowledge serving mediation and intervention processes and purpose, and the question of what is perceived to be science) are all built upon one another in support of the idea of Indigenous knowledges as cumulative. Through daily social practice, human societies freely import and adapt customs and ideas from the outside to enrich their accumulated bodies of knowledge. Even as local peoples present their Indigenous cultures for external consumption, they are able to combine an intimate knowledge of their societies with the complexities and particularities of modern world systems (see also Errington and Gewertz 1989, 52). In effect, modernity is embedded in Indigenous knowledges. Western scientific knowledge also incorporate Indigenous thought. For example, Indigenous thought and knowledge have long been appropriated by Western scientific knowledge that Westerners acquired in contact with Indigenous societies and peoples but without acknowledging the collectivity and ongoing collaborative nature of knowledge creation in dialectic exchange. In the tradition of individualized ownership and land claims, Western researchers often integrated Indigenous knowledges into theories and claimed them as their own innovations.[6]

While not denying intellectual agency on the part of Indigenous peoples, we must deal with the historic inferiorization of Indigenous experience and the devaluation of their rich histories and cultures, or what may be called the "entrapment/enslavement of the human mind." The resilience of Indigenous cultural heritage as well as the local confidence in and customary usages of indigenous knowledges are constantly being undermined by a "Western cultural overkill" (Prah 1997, 18). The cultural imperialism of neo-colonialism exacts a psychological damage to the self/collective that calls for decolonizing minds (wa Thiong'o 1986).

A pedagogic, instructional and communicative approach to synthesizing different knowledges must first allow Indigenous peoples to produce and control knowledges about themselves, their communities and their societies. Indigenous peoples must own their past, their culture, their traditions and their present and future destinies. As Prah (1997, 21) again opines, the process of decolonization requires that indigenous peoples confront the "insulting idea that others know and understand them better than they understand themselves." The maintenance of local languages is crucial because the road "to authenticity ... cannot be reached in speech forms which lie outside the [Indigenous] cultural world of the writer" or speaker/narrator (Prah 1997, 21).

Resistance is a spatial practice. Homes, families, communities, workplaces and schools are differentially implicated in an exercise to integrate different knowledge systems in the teaching, learning and administration of education. It is within the academy that Indigenous knowledges may lodge a sustained critique of the dominance of Eurocentricity. Definitions of a place/locality and belonging are not fixed, but imagined and fiercely contested. Individuals and groups construct their own sites and spaces of resistance. Spaces are contested because they constitute places for producing knowledge, ideas, images and for imagining (see also Said 1993, 7). Using the academy as an important starting place, we can develop the following approaches in everyday classroom pedagogic, communicative and instructional practices (see also McLeod and Krugly-Smolska 1997, 16-17, in another context).

1. Develop an awareness of Indigenous knowledges (e.g., discussing the topic with students; inviting Indigenous guest speakers, parents and community elders to class and using Indigenous resource materials, posters, displays and films;

2. Targeting indigenous and local community concerns and issues in classroom discourses; undertaking research trips to Indigenous communities; planning cultural celebrations, placed in appropriate histories and contexts) to serve as a form of decolonized

education and to speak to the atrocities of the colonial encounters between the subject and the colonizer.

3. Develop advocacy and support networks to promote hiring a more diversified faculty, including Indigenous faculty; women and educators from ethnic, religious, linguistic, and cultural minority backgrounds; helping the learner acquire critical thinking skills to question the absences from the syllabus of Indigenous and local scholars writings/texts on the teaching and learning of Indigenous and local languages, myths, legends and philosophies.

4. Develop sustainable community action (e.g., memberships and linkages with Indigenous and local community groups; seeking guidance from Indigenous/local communities).

5. Initiate political actions (e.g., protests; submissions to university administrations; rewarding communitarian approaches to learning and schooling; holistic and intuitive thought, as well as varied ways of decoding information).

It is, of course, imperative that we clearly define the guiding principles, objectives and goals, establish a plan of action and develop a list of resources to use. We must also develop ideas about probable outcomes and who we see as crucial agents of change responsible for executing action plans (McLeod and Krugly-Smolska 1997, 18). Philosophically, some tensions and ambiguities in teaching Indigenous knowledges will also have to be addressed.

The Claim to Tradition and Authenticity

The claim to a "traditional past" and an "authentic voice," which may be implicit in Indigenous knowledges, has often been a point of critical interrogation. The interrogation is offered in two aspects: first, whether there is a voice of authenticity which is not open to challenge; second, whether there is a claim of Indigenousness[7] that invents a mythic, idealized past. I borrow from the discursive themes and ideas espoused some time ago by Keesing (1989) and Briggs (1996) to interrogate what could be called the "production/ construction of Indigenity." I am working with a knowledge of "invention," which engages the contexts and interests that inform the construction of the past in the present rather than as reference to the mere accuracy with which a reconstructed past reflects/represents historical events (Briggs 1996, 463; see also Hanson 1989; Hobsbawn and Ranger 1983). Also, by authentic I mean the claim to [re]present a "true or real" (not staged) culture, past, tradition or voice that is not subject to questioning.

There is little doubt that Indigenous and local peoples can speak about authenticity in more powerful ways than outsiders. However, there are dangers of unproblematically privileging the subject positions which we occupy. Even the learner as an Indigenous subject has knowledge that is intersected with Western knowledge. This is one of the reasons why any claim of authenticity must always be questioned. An interrogation is not tantamount to a denial, vilification or open dismissal of tradition. Admittedly, however, questions of culture, identity, home and location all have significant bearing on the production and legitimation of all knowledges (Trask 1991). As Briggs (1996) argues, there are broader political-economic contexts that could shape the designation of discursive authority. The discourse of Indigenous knowledges that recreate and reclaim tradition in the present actually reflects contestations of multiple interests (race/ethnicity, class, culture, gender) more than the "cultural essence of a purportedly homogenous and bounded traditional group" (Briggs 1996, 435). It is important that in a discussion of Indigenous knowledges and particularly on the issue of authenticity, we do not set up class, gender and power interests as more salient than race/ethnicity and color (see Keesing 1991).

The issue of an authentic voice is tethered to the question of who has discursive authority on Indigenous knowledges. It is a concern about the politics of representing Indigenous and local scholarship. For example, anthropologists and non-Indigenous scholars have lost ethnographic authority as Indigenous peoples increasingly redefine and reassess their relations with Western academic scholarship. The issues of misrepresentation and appropriation of local cultural resource knowledges have ensured that Indigenous peoples redefine the notion of ethnographic authority in their own terms (see also Clifford and Marcus 1986, Clifford 1988, Crick 1985). Indigenous and local peoples are demanding the respect for the right to tell and publish their stories. They are making these demands particularly in situations where authorship is seen as a marker of the unique creativity and resourcefulness of individual writers who, for the most part, have been and continue to be outsiders (see also Cruikshank 1992).

The Indigenous past reflects the history, customs, cultural practices, ideas and values handed down from one generation to the next generation. This past constitutes the group's cultural identity. How do we define the "real past" if we accept that culture is not a "passively inherited legacy" and that cultures and traditions are constructed in particular social and political contexts (Linnekin 1992, 249-250)? Recognition of situational, contextual, historical and political embeddedness of culture should lead us to the understanding that the Indigenous is not an undifferentiated category. It is a term that is contested and articulated in multiple ways, none of which implies that we cannot speak of the Indigenous.

Indigenous Knowledge as Counter-Hegemonic Knowledge

Within school systems Indigenous and local knowledges can be presented as counter-hegemonic knowledges. Keesing (1989) alludes to the Gramscian argument that "counter-hegemonic discourse pervasively incorporates the structures, categories and premises of hegemonic discourses ... because ... those who are dominated internalize the premises and categories of the dominant ... [and] ... also because the discourse of domination creates the objective, institutionalities within which struggles must be fought" (23). This is an unfortunate and perhaps an unavoidable situation. Yet the problem arises when the argument is overstretched: that counter-hegemonic discourses can themselves become hegemonic. How is this possible when critical discourses are still marginalized in our academies and do not have the same space and the institutional structures and resources that support and reproduce conventional hegemonic discourses? A case in point is the marginalization of oppositional discourses like Afrocentricity in the academy.

Keesing (1989) further argues that contemporary Southern representations of their own cultures and traditions have been shaped by "colonial domination and the perception of Western culture through a less direct reactive process, a dialectic in which the elements of Indigenous culture are selected and valorized (at the levels of both ideology and practice) as counters to or commentaries on the intrusive and dominant colonial culture" (Keesing 1989, 23). This claim may be closer to an argument that Southern intellectuals conduct selective (mis)capturings of elements of their own past, histories and traditions for valorization and celebration so as to strikingly differentiate the Indigenous from the non-Indigenous/West. In the contexts of African intellectual scholarship, this assertion is similar to the critique offered against Negritude and

Afrocentric theorists who decry the colonization and recolonization of the African intellectual space. While affirming the ideational as well as socio-cultural differences between alternative knowledge systems (see Horton 1967), we must guard against romanticism, over glorification and fetishization of the past as (sacred) anthropological truths.

While we need to be aware of this dialectic, we must correspondingly acknowledge the fundamental philosophical differences and distinctions in knowledge systems. The idea of ownership of knowledge is not a central principle of Indigenous and local cultural knowledge systems. Thus, for example, normative claims made of African knowledge systems do not mean that these cannot be shared by other Indigenous communities. To reiterate, Scheurich and Young (1997) highlight the ontological, epistemological and axiological positions that may characterize different knowledge systems.

The ontological position speaks to the primary assumptions that people (within given cultures) have about the nature of reality. In African systems of thought, the ontological viewpoint stresses that to understand reality is to have a complete or holistic view of society—a harmonious co-existence between nature, culture and society. The existence of the individual/ subject is only meaningful in relation to the community that she or he is part of. On the other hand, the epistemological position enthuses that there are different ways of knowing reality. In African systems of thought, knowledge is seen as cumulative and as emerging from experiencing the social world. Practice and experience are seen as the contextual basis of knowledge. Knowledge is for survival and both go hand in hand. While membership in community accords rights, there are important matching responsibilities. The axiological position maintains that there are "disputational contours of right and wrong or morality and values ... [that is] ... presumptions about the real, the true and the good" (Scheurich and Young 1997, 6).

In African systems of thought, therefore, cultural, spiritual and ideational beliefs, values and practices are evaluated in the history and contexts of communities as societies strive to set their own moral tone. These ideas may be shared by other Indigenous peoples, however, as has been mentioned in an earlier chapter, it is the privileging of certain core social values for "reward" (e.g., responsibilities over rights; community over individual; peaceful co-existence with nature over control or domination of nature) that sets different knowledge systems apart. An understanding of such differences and their dialogic dimensions is relevant in developing a basis on which to work towards a general synthesis of knowledge systems. For me and many others, the Indigenous past offers a means of staking out a position as African, which is outside of the identity that has been and continues to be constructed by Euro-American ideology (see Muteshi 1996).

There is a further contention that Southern, and particularly post-colonial intellectuals have themselves been "heavily exposed, through the educational process, to Western ideologies that idealize primitivity and the wisdom and ecological reverence of those who live close to Nature" (Keesing 1989, 23). In other words, in academic and political projects, Southern intellectuals promote Indigenous and local cultural knowledges and engage in problematic, fetishized representations of their cultures on the basis of false anthropological knowledges, which were instrumental in exoticizing their cultures. Indigenous scholars assert an identity based on an idealized romanticized past. As already discussed, the past is not frozen in time and place; tradition is not immune to criticism (Scanlon 1964). We must correspondingly acknowledge and speak about the sources of empowerment and disempowerment in the past and its cultural traditions. We must also acknowledge the Indigenous and local capacity to exercise intellectual agency and to engage in self-reflexive knowledge production. In this context, exercising intellectual agency means engaging in a process of recuperation, revitalization and reclamation of African Indigenous knowledge as a necessary exercise in empowerment. We cannot underestimate the power of ideas in terms of the role of social forces to generate relevant knowledge for collective resuscitation, spiritual rebirth and cultural renewal. A discursive project affirming the past cannot unproblematically be interpreted as a call to regress to a previous state of primitivity. It should be read as a political agenda to interrogate the African past, culture, tradition and history in order to learn from the sources of empowerment and disempowerment as African peoples search for ways towards the future.

On the whole, I believe Indigenous and local scholars should reclaim aspects about their cultures and traditions that can be narrated as whole entities and fundamentally humane. They need to do so in order to affirm and resist an amputation of their past from themselves. This ought to be differentiated from the exoticization of cultures and traditions of which anthropologists and non-Indigenous writers historically were guilty. Symbolic violence can ensue after Indigenous people reclaim their identities because once they have presented these identities they may have little or no control over how they are read, used and manipulated. In their relations with dominant society, Indigenous peoples have represented themselves in particular ways only to be labeled as inauthentic and deficient. For example, rather than trying to understand the practical meanings and theoretical relevance of such notions as holism, mutuality and spirituality, there are those who label these as essentialized categories or anthropological fictional representations of the Indigenous and the Indigenous social practice.

Contested Knowledges: The Politics of Place and the Re-Assertion of Indigenous Identity

The maintenance of cultural autonomy has been a "powerful resource in providing the ideological context in which [indigenous peoples] are framing their 'new' world" (Nash 1997, 33). Stuart Hall (1991), reminds us that a theory is not truth but must be seen as a "set of contested, localized, conjunctural knowledges which have to be debated in a dialogical way" (286). To paraphrase Moore (1997, 91), Indigenous knowledges presented as text or theory do not reside in a fixed, static metaphoric site or space removed from practice, performance, power and process. In fact, the indigenous identity resides within the "situated [political] practices through which identities and places are contested, produced and reworked in particular localities" (Moore 1997, 87). However, indigenous and local struggles cannot be understood exclusively as questions about identity. The recreation of indigenity is linked to the possession of space, land and language, and to the pursuit of politics and economics. Thus, economic, political, symbolic and spiritual considerations need to be taken into account in order to move beyond Eurocentric interpretations of indigenousness. Some of the greatest challenges facing indigenous and local peoples globally are the violations of their knowledges of survival, of their rights to land, to cultures, to traditions and to the maintenance of a connection to the spiritual as well as contemporary material realms of life. In Canada and elsewhere, Native land claim struggles are part of this challenge. Despite the violations of their land claims over the centuries, Native peoples have found the collective and spiritual strength in their integrated connection to the land that has contributed to their survival, resistance and struggle to reclaim their spiritual, material and collective rights. In Africa, colonialism, Western capitalism and global market forces have worked to dispossess families and lineage groups of their communal lands.

Representing Orality in the Academy

Orality is a primary mode of communication in Indigenous and local communities, along with visual representations such as pictographs (paintings on rocks) and petroglyphs (carvings or inscriptions on rocks). One example of a contemporary challenge in bringing indigenous knowledges into the school system is the question of how to best convey spoken words (as narrated in stories, fables, myths and oral accounts of life histories) from another culture. Cruikshank (1992) notes that there are issues of language and cognition with significant pitfalls and implications for understanding Indigenous knowledges. Spoken words as stories, fables, proverbs, myths, folklore and folk songs have long been treated as "objects" to be collected, coded, stored or disseminated. Can cultural knowledge, considered "linguistic expression and material manifestation of ideas," be collected, represented or stored without losing meaning (Cruikshank 1992, 5-6)?

Rosaldo (1980, 91) has argued that we must see oral traditions as texts to be heard not as documents to be stored. Therefore, fluency in the local language is critical to textual representation of the oral. Bearing this in mind two key questions can be posed: What happens to the spoken words when they appear on paper or are "recorded in magnetic or digital codes on tapes, disks or in film or videotape" (Cruikshank 1992, 5) and what are the uses of material artifacts and exhibitions, stories and oral accounts as written texts in [Western] academies? Oral traditions, stories, fables and proverbs collected from Indigenous communities and written as texts in particularly Western academies can become a material manifestation of the colonial encounter (Trigger 1988, cited in Cruikshank 1992, 5). Once located in Western academies, these cultural artefacts become "symbols of cultural oppression" since these institutions are places that have historically participated in colonizing the Other (e.g., the processes of academic imperialism through the establishment of knowledge hierarchies in which certain histories, traditions and values as well as epistemologies prevail) (see also Cruikshank 1992, 8). Spoken words (now viewed as part of material culture) have also become parts of current debates about "cultural/ intellectual property rights" and representations of culture. Since words are said in given contexts/locations, there is a problem of decontextualization when they are produced in print or as texts. Orality can be "frozen" in writing or through the written text.

Moreover, we also need to ask ourselves: What is the socio-political context of gathering spoken words? What are the social conditions under which spoken words are collected, interrogated, produced and used as written texts (see Cole 1985)? Cruikshank (1992, 6) further argues that "physical things and words wrenched from their social and cultural setting become part of another semiotic sphere that cannot be redressed by contextual parading." In other words, cultural artefacts have a continuing life of their own, more so when they are produced as texts. For example, many complexities and nuances of myth making, such as the processes through which myths enter into social life, are integral to the production of Indigenous and local knowledges. When such knowledges are reproduced, myths come to acquire a whole repertoire of social, cultural and political activities relating to their (myths) narration and celebration. It is important, therefore, to be sensitive to the context (i.e., social setting and political situation) in which the spoken word is collected, presented and consumed in written form.

Other questions can help us understand how the receiver/responder is located: What are the processes of framing, interpreting and understanding spoken words before and after they appear on paper/print/text? How do subjectivities and political projects come into play? For example, can text (emerging from the spoken word) be represented and interpreted to expose colonial encounters rather than as the mere glorification of voices/arts (i.e., Western museums and recent controversies)? Furthermore understanding how the oral text was used in a social context of a time or social contexts at different times necessitates the reclaiming of the histories of those places in times so that the texts can be better understood and interpreted. This does not mean that such myths, stories, fables, proverbs, folklore and folk songs will not continue to evolve and have an interpretative place in the social life of a community of the present. What it means is that the historical views/uses over time (past and present) enrich the interpretations and move them from merely being historical objects/artifacts to becoming active social tools in the life of a community.

Cultural Revitalization and Resistance

The cultural revitalization taking place today in many marginalized, Indigenous and local communities is an affirmation and reclamation of a past (and its cultures and traditions) that has been historically demonized by colonizers. More important, this cultural revitalization is a repudiation of European colonization, imperial relations and Western civilization and consumerism (Trask 1993, 188). Indigenous knowledges have generally been excluded from our school systems. Nevertheless, this chapter illustrates the legitimate value of such knowledges in their own right, and their relevance for critically interrogating hegemonic knowledge systems within schools, colleges and universities in different geographical contexts.

Ultimately, we have to consider the role of Indigenous knowledges in school systems as primarily one of resistance to Eurocentrism and the colonizing/colonial order; that is, resistance to the dominance of Eurocentric knowledge as the only valid way of knowing. I interpret resistance as referring to the social actions and practices of subordinate groups (and their allies) that contest hegemonic social formations and knowledges as well as unravel and dislodge strategies of domination (Haynes and Prakash 1991, 3). Kellner (1995, 42) cautions against the "fetishization of resistance." Abu-Lughod (1990) also reminds us of "the tendency to romanticize resistance, to read all forms of resistance as signs of the ineffectiveness of systems of power and the resilience and creativity of the human spirit in its refusal to be dominated" (cited in Moore 1997, 89). My use of resistance is closer to Parry's (1994), who points to Frantz Fanon and Amie Cesaire's work and their "unwillingness to abstract resistance from its moment of performance" (179, cited in Moore 1997, 89). Moore (1997) correctly alludes to the "importance of historical, cultural and geographical specificity to any understanding of resistance" (89). He further understands the limitation of placing the focus on the "intentions" rather than on the consequences of everyday human action and social practice (89).

Moore (1997) holds that we must explore alternative conceptions of resistance "[r]ather than measuring resistance against a yardstick of widespread social and political economic transformation, the micro-politics of tactical manoeuvres... [take] center stage" (90). In other words, we must view resistance in the academy as collective actions and strategies for procedural and incremental change. Resistance starts by using received knowledges to ask critical questions about the nature of the social order. Resistance also means seeing "small acts" as cumulative and significant for social change. As one of my Caribbean-born African graduate students wrote, "I can't tell you how affirming it is to see 'patois' in the books I am evaluating for my thesis. A few years ago, this would never have been possible ... The fact that these languages make their way into texts at all is a phenomenal act of resistance. Of course, I realize that the use of local languages outside their appropriate contexts opens up a whole new set of challenges" (Lawson 1998).

In thinking of Indigenous and local cultural knowledges as "resistance knowledge," we must acknowledge how easy it is to be complicit in the reproduction of hegemonic Eurocentric and colonized knowledges in school settings and educational systems. By failing to speak out about Indigenous and local knowledges, we are complicit in the continued marginalization and negation of such knowledges in the academy. The integration (that is, centering) of Indigenous knowledges into the curricular, instructional and pedagogical practices of schools cannot be an unquestioned exercise. We must consider how power-saturated issues of academic social relations are used to validate different knowledges to serve particular interests.

We must also be wary and critical of the integration of Indigenous and local knowledges into the school system if they are pursued to serve the interests of corporate capital within the modern state. We must be concerned about the exploitative tendencies of institutions of learning in order to affirm the *status quo*. Indigenous knowledges must be critical and oppositional in order to rupture stable knowledge. However, our caution and cynicism should not lead us to claim a separate space for Indigenous and local knowledges inside or outside the school setting, and we must be careful that our academic practice and politics do not feed on the marginality of Indigenous and local cultural knowledges. Maintaining a separate space for Indigenous knowledge feeds on the problematic idea that Indigenous ways of knowing sit outside other bodies of knowledge. As Trask (1993) rightly observes, sometimes because of the power of capital we may not easily understand our own cultural degradation because we are living in it, and "[a]s colonized people[s], we are colonized to the extent that we are unaware of our oppression" (195). We can start to destabilize what constitutes valid academic knowledge by challenging the political economy of knowledge production that accords different costs and privileges to knowledge systems. If scholars fail to recognize the social, political, cultural and personal implications of academic colonization and the erasure of Indigenous and local knowledges, our exercise is futile, indeed, to explore such knowledges within the academy.

There is more that educators, school administrators, and policy-makers can learn from the critical interrogation and application of local communal and Indigenous knowledges. Change must start from within and with what we already know. If educational reform initiatives are to be effective in bringing about desired changes in African schooling and education, educators, administrators and policy workers have to learn from within our communities, our past, histories, cultures and ancestral knowledges as a starting block from which to pursue and promote educational transformation.

Notes:

1.   The institutionalization of post-colonial studies in the academy marks a transformation of the study and analysis of colonialism and world history. Post-colonialism may be defined as "a new designation for critical discourse which thematize issues emerging from colonial relations and their aftermath" (Shohat 1992,101).

2.   This is the Freirian position, in which the dialogue occurs on the ground of the oppressed and not on the ground of the oppressor. Nor can a position be neutral. Otherwise, we support the oppressive regime.

3.   Note the work of Kenyan writer Ngugi wa Thiong'o (1986), who actually retrained himself to write in his native language after having become known as an English writer. The next generation, as he proposes in his text, should not have to go through the difficult process of learning to write in their native language during adulthood. Schools should be building students' bi-, tri- and multi-lingual skills. The academy has much work and learning to do in the area of language learning, maintenance and acquisition from the perspective and needs of speakers of non-European or non-dominant international languages.

4.   As Cruikshank (1992, 8) points out, we must also be aware of the pitfalls of essentialism that attribute "ideas and concepts to the 'Indigenous voice' even when the words are actually being supplied by a Eurocentric ideology."

5.   In *Feminist Poetics*, Threadgold (1997, 20) speaks of the problem of traditional scientific writings not disclosing the process of knowledge creation, including trial and error and the different influences on thinking. Instead knowledge production is presented as abstract, as scientific fact.

6.   By Indigenousness I mean a knowledge consciousness arising locally and in association with a long-term occupancy of a place. Such consciousness emerges

from an awareness of the intellectual agency of local subjects and their capacity to use knowledge to challenge, rupture and resist colonial and imperial relations of domination and, as well, to resuscitate themselves from mental bondage. Indigenousness also accords a broader definition of identity to local subjects.

Chapter 9

CONCLUSION

This book began with a call for education that is culturally and politically relevant as well as socially responsive. Working with the power of local voice, personal and collective identities and the cultural representations of knowledge allows for developing new visions and imaginings of schooling and education. Throughout the text it has been argued that in order to reach the desired goals of responsible and relevant education we must also understand what Ghanaians are doing to reclaim and revitalize their education through articulated responses to reforms emanating from the grassroots community level. As local subjects interrogate the current school system they do so with a hope and desire for an educational system that truly responds to their needs and concerns. I have maintained throughout the text that the on-going educational reforms may offer opportunities for meaningful change provided that educators, students, parents, communities and governments can work in concert to devise measures that address pertinent concerns and needs of local peoples.

In the search for answers there must be some awareness of the existence of countercurrents, which means working with the awareness that local peoples can participate actively in thinking through their own problems and offering solutions. They may not agree with the possible courses of action to follow but the desire to search for their own solutions exist. Such local voices cannot be relegated to the sidelines. These voices must be heard.

The issues of access and equity are fundamental to local peoples' conceptions of relevant education. Educational financing is a huge concern. Education is generally perceived as a privilege rather than a right. However, local subjects question the privilege of those who have the means to education but fail to use it to serve the larger interest of society. Addressing access and equity means placing education at the service of all citizenry. This means addressing the means of education. Local communities, parents, teachers and students have different but overlapping and connecting responsibilities. Obviously there are shared responsibilities to ensure that all can avail themselves of the possibilities and benefits of education. This can be attained to the extent that communities strive to be inclusive entities with shared collective responsibilities. But, as is often times the case, the desire for equal access to education for all is not matched with a reality that shows a denial of access for, not only the poor and rural masses, but also for particular segments of society (e.g., young girls). Educational reforms that fail to highlight and address the needs of rural poor families/communities with a special focus on the status of the poor rural girl child is sowing the seeds of its own failure. In fact approaches to education that do not deal with the fundamental questions of access and relevance is a disaster so far as transformative change is concerned. As the state shirks its responsibility to the larger citizenship either through the failure to provide education to the rural masses, already existing social inequities are only exacerbated. This Ghanaian case study provides us with an important knowledge base from which to interrupt the failings of education and to address current social inequities.

In this chapter I first provide an overview summary of the reforms as critically examined by the participants with a view to making the reforms reflect and work in the interests of student as members of local communities and citizens of the nation. This overview is then followed by recommendations for a broad action plan aimed at addressing these concerns within the context of nation building.

Summary of Participants' Critique and Recommendations for the Reforms:

A. *The Increasing Cost of Education*

Parents complain about the rising cost of education in the country, which is adding to the hardships of ordinary households. Most parents continue to strive to make ends meet under continuing times of harsh economic austerity measures (see also Dei 1993). The deteriorating conditions of most publicly (under)funded local schools and accompanying poor academic test results are forcing those parents who can afford it to rethink the public option and consider enrolling their children in private schools.

B. *The Politics of Reform*

There is genuine concern that educational reform initiatives have been rushed, largely for political reasons. That is, a series of elected governments had the financial backing of the international financial community and wanted to take credit for reforming education without duly considering the implementation aspects of reforms. Educational practitioners argue that they have not been appropriately consulted and that bureaucrats and policy makers have either ignored relevant advice and suggestions or have not fully grasped the harm that the current system is causing to the nation's future.

C. *The Absence of Textbooks, Vocational and Technical Equipment/Materials*

Adequate resource materials are key to developing and providing educational experiences that are of high quality. The absence of textbooks and reading materials for schools has been and continues to be a perennial problem. National political rhetoric to commit state resources to ensure the success of the reforms has not matched concrete action and realities. For example, the intent to provide students with practical skills for maintenance work and to enhance local creativity and resourcefulness is yet to be enacted because vocational and technical institutes still lack the workshops, practical tools and other equipment for teaching technical, vocational and life skills to students. In particular, laboratory equipment for science students and workshop tools for students in technical/vocational areas are minimally available in some schools and non-existent in others.

D. The Duration of Junior Secondary (JSS) and Senior Secondary (SSS) Education

Parents and students, in particular, have concerns about the duration of both the junior and senior secondary school education. In their opinion the reforms excessively reduced the basic education (Junior Secondary School-JSS) and pre-tertiary education (Senior Secondary School - SSS) thereby placing students at risk of being inadequately prepared for post secondary education programs in and outside of Ghana. Throughout the interviews there was an emerging consensus that the pre-tertiary education programs should each be extended from the current three years to a minimum of four years.

E. The Need to Equalize Opportunity for all Students

Current educational reform initiatives do not adequately stress the importance of equalizing opportunity for all students. Within schools, there is a need for program emphasis on reading, writing, speaking and listening skills as well as remedial help for students who fail to meet proficiency levels, particularly in English and mathematics. Some students graduating from JSS and SSS have difficulty expressing themselves in English. It is the common language of instruction but not necessarily the home language. Parents who themselves have minimal educational levels have not learned the English language to the point in which they can assist their children with these language skills. Consequently, their English language and literacy skills may be poor. As English is the dominant language of post-secondary instruction, curriculum and reading materials, such students are placed at a disadvantage. Many parents find themselves in the position of having to send their children to private boarding schools in order for their children to live and be taught in an English language immersion setting. Such private schools charge exorbitant prices. The cumulative effect is the development of a two-tier educational system: public education for the poor and private schools for those from wealthy backgrounds.

F. Placing Emphasis on Ghanaian Languages

Reforms purport to place emphasis on the teaching and learning of Ghanaian languages. At the senior secondary level, educators argue that learning a second Ghanaian language, other than the native regional language, should be one of the core subjects required of all students. Due to the insufficient availability of trained teachers the success of this initiative has been curtailed.

G. In-Service Training and Professional Development

Teachers were not adequately informed and trained to implement the reforms. Educational practitioners have called for the provision of a decentralized in-service training and professional development for teachers to prepare them to apply the required new changes to their practice.

H. The Shortage of Teachers in the Vocational Subjects and Physical Sciences

There is a serious lack of teachers for most subjects. Those available are often inadequately trained. This problem is more acute in science and technology and other newly introduced subject areas.

I. Material Incentives for Teachers

The problem of off-school employment for teachers has had a severe effect on teacher performance and morale and on student respect for authority. Educators maintain that one solution to the problem is the provision of material incentives and compensation to teachers. Public school teachers are thought to be better trained and more qualified. Yet most interviewees held the view that teachers of private schools were better able to sustain a full commitment to students' education because they were better cared for by their proprietors.

J. Problems of Accountability and Transparency

There is a problem with local, regional and national accountability. Many administrators have an unfettered reign with no accountability to students, parents, the local community or the national oversight body, Ghana's Education Service/GES. To this end, qualified, well-trained supervisors should be appointed, nominated or elected for school-based supervision. As Nyalemegbe (1997, 7) argues, "[E]ach school must be inspected at least once a year and the results published for discussion at annual meetings of parents, school management committees and teachers." The issue of accountability is significant. For some educators and parents, variation in accountability structures partly explains why at the primary levels, students in private schools do better academically than their counterparts in some "public" schools. I have placed public in quotation marks because of the costs incurred by parents in schools considered public.

K. Parental Involvement and Control over the Education Process

Many parents complain that schools do not give enough value to parental knowledge. These parents call on schools to view parents as legitimate partners in the delivery of education. They argue that parent, community and student involvement in the school system can be enhanced through the provision of staff resources to support parental involvement. In fact, parent-teacher associations (PTAs) can be strengthened with the establishment of School Councils in each local school/college. The Council would include parents, educators, students and other community members. It would be accessible to students, teachers, parents and parent-teacher associations. Its membership would reflect the diversity of the school and the local community. The Council could have some flexibility to develop structures that meet local needs and circumstances. However, it would generally serve as an advisory board for school administrators and it would also act as the liaison body between the local community and school/college. PTAs have, for the most part, been ineffective partly because of their size and partly because of their inability to co-ordinate the different concerns and interests of parents'. Thus far, parent councils have continually failed to adequately address issues that pertain to students from economically disadvantaged homes and regions.

L. The Importance of Guidance Support

Many students at the senior secondary level make decisions about academic programs without the benefit of expert guidance support. One consequence is that often students take programs based on the interpretation of their school performance records and their academic progress by teachers, administrators and parents. Expert guidance advice is crucial to help students and parents make intelligent, informed choices as to whether the student should pursue university, college, polytechnic education or join the workforce. Providing guidance and support for students to work their way through the different systems, if they have the desire and ability to do so, is particularly critical for those students whose parents have not been through different levels of schooling.

M. *Space/Physical Infrastructure and an Increasing Student Population*

There is concern about the deteriorating physical school infrastructure and the lack of adequate space for learners. Most educators and school administrators complain about inadequate school and classroom facilities, the lack of physical equipment and resources for the different subject areas (i.e. science, physical education, vocational and life skills, the arts). And they complain of the lack of adequate space and facilities for students' accommodation and recreational needs. Because there is not and there may not be a complete transition from the traditional boarding school to that of community schools educating local children, available spaces for accommodation impact greatly on the question of access. Of particular concern was the lack of sufficient spaces and adequate accommodation facilities for girls applying to boarding schools. The increase in the number of girls seeking to enroll in secondary school programs coupled with the lack of accommodation spaces has created an equity/access problem, based on gender. Had the goal of moving towards local community schooling been accompanied by the necessary infrastructures (buildings, teachers, resources and local accountability structures), this basic aspect of gender equity would be less acute.

N. *"Outdoor Education" and Learning Outside the Classroom*

In meeting the contemporary global challenge of knowledge production, dissemination and use, formal school systems could learn from both informal and non-formal learning networks, structures and outlets. Learning experiences and social practices of local communities and groups outside the formal school system could contribute to a meaningful transformation of the educational process in African contexts. Such knowledge is useful in promoting education broadly defined to refer to the options, strategies, processes and structures through which individuals and communities/ groups come to know and understand the world and act within it.

O. The School and Work Connection

Educational reforms were intended to address the issue of finding work upon completion of secondary school for students less inclined towards a more abstract academic environment (e.g., university and college education). The initiative to provide basic hands-on training, practical and vocational skills for students was generally welcome as reform initiatives professed to offer a broad range of options for students. This measure, however, raises the question of whether it is realistic or even appropriate to set the same academic standards for all students. If the initiative is to achieve the desired result of gainful employment for students at the end of each educational cycle, aside from providing the tools for these students to work with, there must be employment opportunities for these graduates. Unfortunately, there is the unpleasant reality that many graduates of SSS do not find immediate employment while opportunities for further education continue to fade.

P. Developing an Effective Apprenticeship Program for Youth

In Ghana there is a very high rate of unemployed, underemployed and undereducated youth. Given this reality, the government must seriously commit itself to the development of a youth apprenticeship program: apprenticeship in technical and vocation skills, which will serve as a workplace-based training program for students or young adults. Youth could spend 80 percent of their time on the job learning skills and the other 20 per cent on in-school training (see discussions in the Canadian contexts contained in a report in *The Toronto Star*, 20 January 1998, A1). This means local and national initiatives that foster the participation of youth in apprenticeship programs would be encouraged and supported: for example, a certification of the apprenticeship program after two years training and a requirement for applicants to have a minimum of two years of Senior Secondary education (SS2). Also, better links between formal schools/colleges and apprenticeship programs in local communities could be established to help train local youth to have access to good jobs at high wages.

Q. Primary and Tertiary Education:

In the face of competition for resources there are bound to be tensions between different levels of the educational system.

Governments have to decide which sector of the educational system need to be prioritized when it comes to the allocation of material support. Traditionally, tertiary education has been viewed as crucial in order to provide skilled human power for professional, managerial and technical vocations which are viewed as the engines of economic growth. But basic/primary education is today seen as a right and essential for the human capacity development of the nation. The case of Ghana is no exception. There is a long standing debate as to where the state ought to devote its resources: primary/basic or tertiary education. In the past, universities and colleges have been heavily subsidised to the detriment of basic/primary education. This trend is still the case and despite current attempts to provide basic education to all children, tertiary education continues to take a lion's share of the national allocation of resources for education. These existing tensions in sectors of the nation's educational system ought to be resolved. For example, the government has committed itself to implementing a Free Compulsory and Universal Basic Education (FCUBE) program but does not have adequate funds to implement the program successfully. One idea is to shift the additional cost of tertiary (and particularly university education) onto students and parents. This idea of shifting cost, supported by the international financial community, is not without opposition and resistance from university students and administrators, and many parents.

Action Plan: What Can the Nation Do?

Based on what has been discussed, a sustained multi-year plan is envisaged to address the magnitude of problems facing the educational system. This plan could be implemented in phases at local, district and regional levels of the "nation." Competent bodies to draw up plans for implementing and executing these ideas and to ensure their eventual success could be appointed by the national government and established through some other agreed upon process.

Research and Development

Further research is needed to study the existing educational system to diagnose problems and find out what is working and what is not working at the primary, secondary and college/university levels. The purpose of research is not simply to know the nature and extent of the problem but to ensure that we hear the concrete voices and concerns of local peoples themselves and use them as a basis to implement a sustained educational plan for educational change. Educational research could solicit ideas at local community gatherings in villages and cities and accord space for parents, students, community workers and others to express their concerns. This body of knowledge allows people to identify and lay claim to the change process. Further research is needed to assess the impact of ongoing educational change to make it possible to learn from mistakes and to recognize what is not working and what needs to be changed or discarded. This research will help to avoid the "reinvention of the wheel" where necessary and avoid the costly duplication of funds and other resources.

Future Directions of Study?

While this particular case study has raised general issues pertaining to educational reforms in Ghana, the study's focus was the south. This gaze may well have to do with why certain issues have emerged as opposed to other issues. Arguably, this observation can be a limitation of the current study. Future work needs to examine this dimension of education as to what gets talked about and what is omitted from discourse about educational delivery. I am engaged in a longer-term study on minority educational and inclusive schooling in Ghana. This study is raising interesting issues about different bodies coming from different regions of the country and how questions of ethnic, cultural, gender, socio-economic, religious, linguistic and regional differences are significant in looking at the structures for teaching, learning and administration of education in the country. We need more work to examine the status of educational institutions in other parts of the country and Africa in general. Are there areas still under-served by current processes of educational reforms? Why is it that there appears to be more students boarding and dislocating to the south of the country? Are Southerners also going to the North of the country for their education? If not, why not? What does this entail for educational reforms? What are the possibilities of addressing such regional imbalances in fostering a sense of country and common citizenship? Some of these questions could guide the direction for future study. Despite attempts by post-colonial governments in Ghana to address the regional disparities in education between the North and South of the country, today more schools are concentrated in the South. The fact that this study was located in the South has implications for any recommendations that are made with regards to rethinking schooling and education in Ghana.

Establishing Effective Structures for Educational Delivery

An approach to decentralization must be encouraged. At the same time, the nation needs a co-coordinated body at various levels to oversee the implementation of policy decisions and to ensure accountability and transparency. Among the suggested administrative structures that should each be headed by a competent body with clear lines of accountability and transparency are: Research and Development; Curriculum Writing; Science and Technology; Arts, Culture, Heritage and Recreation; Language; Primary Education; Secondary Education; College Education; Teacher Training; Teacher Evaluation; Indigenous Philosophies and Local Knowledges; Testing and Assessment; Parents' Council; Students' Council; Community Development; Social Justice and Educational Equity.

The nation must itself have an Officer of Education whose responsibilities rest at the state level and who would co-ordinate activities with the Ghanaian Minister of Education without necessarily being seen to be competing with organizations with conflicting roles and responsibilities.

Addressing Public/Private Split in Education

The public/private split in education is intensifying the disparities among sectors of the community. A way to address this disparity will be to fund public education adequately and to ensure that educators in the public school system receive the resources and material incentives required towards making education effective for Ghanaians.

Making Science and Technology Education a Priority

A policy to make science education a priority and to encourage youth to take science education. Science education must be rooted in local culture, technology, resource and the local environments. The approach should particularly target women.

Adult Education and Literacy Programs

This must also be a priority area to ensure that the talents, resources and knowledges embedded in every citizen of the nation are tapped. Adult education and literacy programs should be set up in every village, town and district in the region to assist adult learners. These programs could cover areas of education, health, social work and service, etc.

Rebuilding the Educational Infrastructure

a. School Buildings

Adequate funding should go into rehabilitation of schools at local, regional and national levels. This applies to rehabilitation of residences, classrooms, administrative buildings, student and staff common halls at the school, college and university levels.

New schools must be built to accommodate the growing population. One approach is to devise a system that will ensure the establishment of schools in each region and district by using the resident population as an index to set up a matching ratio. This ratio should be vigorously pursued as the approach to establishing schools in each regional district/given community. A policy of naming school buildings after philanthropists who finance these buildings could be encouraged.

b. Laboratory Equipment

To make science and technology education a priority, there must be adequate funding to provide the needed physical and material equipment for science and technology laboratories in schools and colleges.

c. Provision of Textbooks

Indigenous publishing of Ghanaian texts and the supply of these texts to schools should be encouraged. While the responsibilities of buying textbooks could rest with parents and guardians, the nation must also have a plan to publish and purchase certain basic textbooks and provide supplies to each school and college.

d. Computers

We live in an age of computers and no school/college in the nation must lack them. The nation must purchase computers, including at least five computers for student use in each school. The distribution of computers must be worked out on a ratio basis determined by the size of the school.

e. School Transportation Vehicles

The nation should embark upon a project to supply every school and college in the district with two buses as gifts from the confederation.

Partnerships with Overseas/International Institutions

All schools and colleges would be encouraged to explore accreditation and ties with external educational institutions. Part of the partnerships could involve the exchange of students and educators and the provision of needed curricular and textual materials to local schools and colleges in Ghana. Ofcourse the challenge will be to ensure that the exchange does not continue to feed into the hegemonization of the dominant Eurocentric educational system, in order for the lauded indigenization of knowledge production to take off.

Addressing Salary/Benefits and Payments issues as Incentives for Teachers/Teaching

A committee must re-examine the salaries and the pay structure of educators are competitive with those offered for comparable expertise in the private sector.

Training and Employment in the Education Sector: The Active Recruitment, Training Retention and Promotion of Educators and Administrative Staff

A body must be set up to co-ordinate the effective recruitment, training, retention and promotion of an educational staff capable of leading the nation to the new millennium. This will require making teaching an attractive vocation. Very early in the educational life cycle learners identified as promising educators and effective teachers can be tapped and routed into the teaching profession. Teaching should not be viewed as an option of last resort for students who cannot find employment elsewhere.

Teaching Local Knowledges, Culture and Languages

The success of any initiatives at educational change depends on the extent to which recipients and beneficiaries of change identify with the goals and aspirations of the purported change.

Education must be rooted in local knowledges, cultures and histories. The nation can take the initiative to ensure that schools in the region teach about local cultures and histories as well as the indigenous knowledges. For example, a scheme to document traditions, cultural and indigenous practices of the nation should be pursued and the accumulated body of knowledge made available to all schools in the region. No learner should 'graduate' from school without a certification of knowledge about local cultures, histories and languages.

Community Schooling

There must be a plan to implement community-based schooling. This means encouraging students to attend schools within their local vicinities and developing a tax support system that sustains such community-based schools. Boarding education must promote students' awareness of their responsibilities to the surrounding communities and national service programs must be tied to this philosophy of student responsibility to their immediate communities.

Vocationalization and Apprenticeship

In order to develop an effective apprenticeship program for youth the nation must commit to the development of an apprenticeship program. This should not be left to individual schools and colleges. Apprenticeship in technical and vocation skills must serve as a work place-based training program for students or young adults. As already noted, youth could spend 80 per cent of their time on the job, learning skills and the other 20 per cent on in-school training (see discussions in the Canadian contexts contained in a report in *The Toronto Star* newspaper, January 20, 1998, A1). National initiatives that foster the participation of youth in apprenticeship should be encouraged and supported. For example, a certification of the apprenticeship program after two years training, and also a requirement for applicants to have a minimum of two years of Senior Secondary education. Links between formal schools/colleges and apprenticeship programs in local communities could be established to help train local youths to have access to good jobs at high wages.

Work-Study Programs for Students as Practical Education

A plan should be encouraged to attach all college students to selected workplaces during the summer holidays with the nation to support employers to finance and benefit the work-study program. Students learn from the practical experience and the involvement can be counted as part of a community service credit course which every student must acquire before graduating from College. The proposal is for a well-planned and supported initiative to provide basic hands-on training, practical and vocational skills for students through a work-study program. Such initiative must aim towards achieving gainful employment for college graduates.

Funding the Initiatives

a. Special Levy/Toll on Citizens

The nation should explore the possibility of instituting an education tax on every income-earning citizen of the land. There must be procedures and mechanisms for discussing the implementation of this toll. Proceeds would go to fund the educational initiatives outlined above. This toll could be separate from any levied for community initiatives such as funerals, road construction, income tax purposes etc. The toll/levy should specifically be named an 'Educational tax' and must be earmarked solely for education. This could complement the current Educational Fund initiative proposed by the government.

b. Contributions by Overseas Nationals

Citizens of the nation today reside in large numbers in foreign countries. The nation should co-ordinate with community organizations in these countries to institute projects to collect funds for educational projects in the nation. Instituting a levy for maintaining citizenry abroad could be explored.

c. The Nation Coffers

Part of the coffers of the nation (e.g., gains from toll lands, holding of customary events, festivals and celebrations such as silver jubilees) should be earmarked for educational projects in the region. In this connection the establishment of the Otumfuo Educational Fund and contributions from diverse group of Ghanaians, non-Ghanaians, community organizations and other governmental and non-governmental agencies to the Fund is indeed heartening.

d. Company Taxation

There are many local and foreign firms and companies operating in the nation. A duty can be levied as educational tax on companies to support educational initiatives.

This book has set out certain theoretical ideas relevant for the pursuit for educational change in Ghana. The ideas presented here can be used as a framework to put in place a system and a structure to support implementing change. It is the responsibility of the larger citizenry ably supported by an effective leadership that can see to the transformation of Ghana's education. Words are no longer enough. Words must be backed by the political and material will to implement and see change through. We cannot be happy with the current state of affairs in the nation's educational system. We owe it to our children and the future generation to ensure that we have in place an educational system that can equip all learners with the tools and resources required to be responsible members and participants in society. We must have a system that truly ensures that all subjects are able citizens participating in a genuine democracy of equal and unfettered access to knowledge and power.

REFERENCES

Abbey, J. S. 1990. "Ghana's Experience with Structural Adjustment: Some Lessons." In *Towards Economic Recovery in sub-Saharan Africa*, edited by H. J. Pickett and H. Singer. London: Routledge.

Abu-Lughod, L. 1990. "The Romance of Resistance: Tracing Transformations of Power Through Bedouin Women." *American Ethnologist* 17(1): 41-55.

Achola, P. W. 1990. *Implementing Educational Policies in Zambia*. Washington, DC: The World Bank.

Adepoju, A. 1993, ed. *The Impact of Structural Adjustment on the Population in Africa*. London: Islington.

African Association for Literacy and Adult Education.1990. *Education for All By a Few: Critique of the Basic Education for All Initiative*. The Association: Jomtien.

Agrawal, A. 1995. "Dismantling the Divide between Indigenous and Scientific Knowledge." *Development and Change* 26: 413-439.

_____. 1995. "Indigenous and Scientific Knowledge: Some Critical Comments." *Indigenous Knowledge and Development Monitor* 3(3):3-5.

Agyakwa, K. 1988. "Intuition, Knowledge and Education." *The Journal of Educational Thought*. 22(3): 161-177.

Alderman, H. 1994. "Ghana's Adjustment's Star Pupil." In Adjusting Policy Failure in African Economies, edited by D. Sahn. Ithaca, NY: Cornell University Press.

Alexander, C. 1996. "Street Credibility and Identity: Some Observations on the Art of Being Black." In *Culture, Identity and Politics,* edited by T. Ranger, Y. Samad, and O. Stuart. Avebury-Ashgate Publishing.

Alexander, N. 1994. "Education and Social Reconstruction: The Case of South Africa." *Africa Development* 19 (4): 35-56.

Altbach, P., ed. 1989. "Symposium: World Bank Report on Education in Sub-Saharan Africa." *Comparative Education Review* 33, 1 (February).

Amadiume, I. 1989. *Male Daughters, Female Husbands*. London: Zed Books.

_____. 1997. *Reinventing Africa: Matriarchy, Religion and Culture*. New York: Zed Books.

Amalric, F. 1998. "Sustainable Livelihoods: Entrepreneurship, Political Strategies and Governance." *Development* 41(3):31C44.

Amin, S. 1989. *Eurocentrism: Critique of an Ideology.* New York: Monthly Review Press.

Anamuah-Mensah, J. 1998. "Native Science Beliefs Among Some Ghanaian Students." *International Journal of Science Education* 20 (1): 115-124.

Anderson-Levitt, K., M. Bloch, and A. M. Soumare. 1998. "Inside Classrooms in Guinea: Girls' Experiences." In *Women and Education in Sub-Saharan Africa: Power, Opportunities and Constraints: Women and Change in the Developing World* edited by M. Bloch, J. A. Beoku-Betts, and B. R. Tabachnick. London: Boulder.

Anderson, M. L., and P. H. Collins. 1992. "Towards Inclusive Thinking Through the Study of Race, Class, and Gender." In. *Race, Class and Gender,* 2nd ed., edited by M. L. Anderson and P. H. Collins. Belmont, CA: Wadsworth Publishing.

Ani, M. 1994. *Yurugu: An African-Centred Critique of European Cultural Thought and Behavior.* Trenton, NJ: African World Press.

Anyinam, C. 1989. "The Social Costs of the International Monetary Fund's Adjustment Programs for Poverty: The Case of Health Care Development in Ghana." *International Journal of Health Services* 19, no. 3: 531-547.

Anzaldúa, G., ed. 1990. *Making Face, Making Soul: Haciendo Caras: Creative and Critical Perspectives by Feminists of Color.* San Francisco: aunt lute books.

Apusigah, A. 2002. *Reconsidering Women, Development, and Education in Ghana: A Critical Transformation.* Unpublished Ph. D. dissertation, Faculty of Education, Queen's University, Ontario, Canada.

Armour, E. T. 1993. *Deconstruction, Feminist Theology, and the Problem of Difference: Subverting the Race/Gender Divide.* Chicago: University of Chicago Press.

Asante, M.K. 1988. *Afrocentricity.* Trenton, NJ: Africa World Press.

_____. 1987. *The Afrocentric Idea.* Philadelphia: Temple University Press.

_____. 1991. "The Afrocentric Idea in Education." *Journal of Negro Education* 60(2):170-180.

Asante, M. K. 1992. "The Afrocentric Curriculum." *Educational Leadership* 49(2): 28-31.

_____, and A. Abarry, eds. 1996. *African Intellectual Heritage.* Philadelphia: Temple University Press.

Ashcroft, B., G. Griffiths, and H. Thiophene, eds. 1995. *The Post-Colonial Studies Reader.* New York: Routledge.

Asobayire, Paul. 1988. "Financing Higher Education in Ghana." *West Africa* (September 5-11): 1625-1628.

Banks, J. 1993. "The Canon Debate, Knowledge Construction and Multicultural Education." *Educational Researcher* 22(5):4-14.

Banks, J., and C. Banks, eds. 1993. *Multicultural Education Issues and Perspectives.* Boston: Allyn and Bacon.

Banya, K. 1991. Economic Decline and the Education System: The Case of Sierra Leone." *Compare* 21(2): 127-142.

_____. 1993. "Illiteracy, Colonial Legacy and Education: The Case of Modern Sierra Leone." *Comparative Education* 29 (2): 159-170.

_____, and J. Elu. 1997. "Implementing Basic Education: An African Experience." *International Review of Education* 43 (5/6): 481-496.

Bernstein, B. B.1975. *Towards a Theory of Educational Transmissions.* London: Routledge and Kegan Paul.

Betts, B., and B. Tabachnick, eds. 1998 . *Women and Education in Sub-Saharan Africa: Power, Opportunities and Constraints.* Boulder, CO.: Lynne Rienner.

Bhabha, H. 1990. *Nation and Narration.* London: Routledge.

_____. 1995. "Signs Taken for Wonders." In *The Post-Colonial Studies Reader,* edited by B. Ashcroft, G. Griffiths, and H. Thiophene: New York: Routledge.

Blakemore, K., and B. Cooksey. 1983. *Education for Africa.* New York: St. Martin Press.

Bledsoe, C. 1992. "The Cultural Transformation of Western Education in Sierra Leone." *Africa* 62 (2):182-201.

Bloch, M., J. A. Beoku-Betts, and R. Tabachnick, eds. 1998. *Women and Education in Sub-Saharan Africa: Power, Opportunities and Constraints.* Boulder, CO: Lynne Rienner.

Bouiya, A. 1994. "Education des Filles: Quelles Perpectives pour l'Afrique subsaharienne au XX1e Siecle? *Africa Development* 19:11-34.

Bracy, W. 1995. "Developing an Inclusive Curriculum: A Model for the Incorporation of Diversity in the Social Work Curriculum." Paper presented at the 41st Annual Program meeting of the Council on Social Work Education.

Bray, M. 1986. "If UPE is the Answer, What is the Question? A Comment on Weaknesses in the Rationale for Universal Primary Education in Less Developed Countries." *International Journal of Educational Development* 6(3):147-58.

_____, P. B. Clarke, and D. Stephens. 1986. *Education and Society in Africa.* London:

Brewer, R. 1993. "Theorizing Race, Class and Gender: The New Scholarship of Black Feminist Intellectuals and Black Women's Labor." In *Theorizing Black Feminisms,* edited by S. James, and A. Busia. New York: Routledge.

Briggs, C. L. 1996. "The Politics of Discursive Authority in Research on the 'Invention of Tradition.'" *Cultural Anthropology* 11(4):435-469.

Brock-Utne, B. 1996. "Reliability and Validity in Qualitative Research Within Education in Africa." *International Review of Education* 42 (6):605-621.

Buchert L. 1994. *Education in the Development of Tanzania 1919-90.* London: Ohio University Press.

Buchert, L., ed. 1998. *Educational Reforms in the South in the 1990s.* Paris: UNESCO.

Burgess, R. G. 1984. *In the Field: An Introduction to Field Research.* London: George Allen and Unwin.

Butler, P. 2000. Principles of Anti-Racism. Class Presentation for SES 1921Y. Delivered at the Department of Sociology and Equity Studies, Ontario Institute for Studies in Education, University of Toronto.

Cabral, A. 1973. *Return to the Source.* New York: Africa Information Service.

Callaway, A. 1973. *Educating Africa's Youth for Rural Development.* The Hague: Bernard van Leer Foundation.

Calliste, A., and G. J. S. Dei, eds. 2000. *Anti-Racism and Critical Race, Gender and Class Studies.* Halifax: Fernwood Publishing.

Campbell, B., and J. Loxley, eds. 1989. *Structural Adjustment in Africa.* London: MacMillan.

Carnoy, M. 1986. "Education for Alternative Development." In *New Approaches to Comparative Education,* edited by P. Altbach and G. Kelly. Chicago: University of Chicago Press.

_____. 1974. *Education as Cultural Imperialism.* New York: D. McKay.

_____, and J. Samoff. 1990. *Education and Social Transition in the Third World.* Princeton University Press.

Castellano, M. B. 2000. "Updating Aboriginal Traditions of Knowledge." In *Indigenous Knowledges in Global Contexts: Multiple Reading of Our World,* edited by G. J. S. Dei, B. Hall, and D. Goldin-Rosenberg. Toronto: University of Toronto Press.

Chabal, P. 1996. "The African Crisis: Context and Intrepretation." In *Postcolonial Identities in Africa,* edited by R. Werbner, and T Ranger. London: Zed Books.

Chandrasekhar, C. P. 2001. "On Rethinking Development Economics." Draft paper prepared for discussion at the United Nations Institute for Social Development (UNRISD) meeting on The Need to Rethink development Economics, 7-8 September, at Cape Town, South Africa.

Chisti, M. 1999. Muslim Women, Intellectual Racism and the Project Towards Solidarity and Alliance Building. Unpublished paper.

Clark, G., and T. Manuh. 1991. "Women Traders in Ghana and the Structural Adjustment Program" In *Structural Adjustment and African Women Farmers,* edited by Christina H. Gladwin.

Clifford, J. 1988. *The Predicament of Culture.* Cambridge, MA: Harvard University Press.

Clifford, J. 1983. "On Ethnographic Authority." *Representations* 1:118-146.

_____, and G. Marcus, eds. 1986. *Writing Culture.* Berkeley, CA: University of California Press. Cole, D. 1985. *Captured Heritage: The Scramble for*

Scramble for Northwest Coast Artifacts. Vancouver; Toronto: Douglas and McIntyre.

Collins, P. 1990. *Black Feminist Thought.* London: Harper Collins.

_____. 1993. "Toward a New Vision: Race, Class and Gender as Categories of Analysis and Connection." *Race, Sex and Class* 1(1): 25B-45.

connelly, c. 1999. Toward a Transformative Pedagogy of Re/Claiming 'Voice/Difference: Inviting/ Supporting Women in Afrikan Contexts. Unpublished paper, Ontario. Institute for Studies in Education/ University of Toronto.

Cooper, R. K. 1997. *Executive EQ: Emotional Intelligence in Leadership and Organizations.* New York: AIT and Essi Systems.

Cornia, G. A., R. Jolly, and F. Stewart. 1990. *Adjustment with a Human Face.* Oxford: Oxford University Press.

Craig, J. 1990. *Comparative African Experiences in Implementing Educational Policies.* Washington: The World Bank.

Crick, M. 1985. "Tracing the Anthropological Self." *Social Analysis* 17:71-92.

Cruikshank, J. 1992. "Oral Tradition and Material Culture: Multiplying Meanings of 'Words' and 'Things.'" *Anthropology Today* 8(3):5-9.

Csete, J. 1998. Beyond the Three Food Groups: Nutrition Education for Women in Africa. In. *Women and Education in Sub-Saharan Africa: Power, Opportunities and Constraints: Women and Change in the Developing World,* edited by M. Bloch, J. A. Beoku-Betts, and B. R. Tabachnick. London: Boulder.

Day, C. 1981. Classroom-Based In-Service Teacher Education: The Development and Evaluation of a Client-Centred Model. *Occasional Paper* (University of Sussex Education Area) Paper 9.

Dean, J. 1997. "Feminist Solidarity, Reflective Solidarity: Theorizing Connections after Identity Politics." *Women and Politics* 18(4):1-25.

Dei, G. 1986. Adaptation and Environmental Stress in a Ghanaian Forest Community. Ph.D. Diss. Department of Anthropology, University of Education, Ann Arbor, MI.

_____. 1988. "Crisis and Adaptation in a Ghanaian Forest Community." *Canadian Journal of African Studies.* 62(1):63-72.

_____. 1992. "The renewal of a Ghanaian Rural Economy." *Canadian Journal of African Studies* 26(1):29-53.

_____.1992. "The World Bank and Education in Africa." *Race and Class* 34 (July—September), 52.

_____. 1993. "Learning in the Time of Structural Adjustment Policies: The Ghanaian Experience." *Canadian and International Education* 22(1):43-65.

_____. 1993. "Indigenous African Knowledge Systems." *Singapore Journal of Tropical Geography* 14(1):28-41.

_____. 1994. "Afrocentricity: A Cornerstone of Pedagogy." *Anthropology and Education Quarterly* 25(1):3-28.

_____. 1994. "The Challenges of Anti-Racist Education and Research in the African Contexts." *Africa Development* 19(3):5-25.

_____. 1996. *Anti-Racism Education: Theory and Practice*. Halifax, NS: Fernwood Publishers.

_____. 1997. "Race and the Production of Identity in the Schooling Experiences of African-Canadian Youth." *Discourse* 18(2):241-257.

_____. 1998. "Interrogating African Development and the Diaspora Reality." *Journal of Black Studies* 29(2):141-153.

_____. 1999. "Educational Reform Efforts in Ghana." *International Journal of Education Reform* 8(3):244-259.

_____. 2000a. "Rethinking the Role of Indigenous Knowledges in the Academy." *International Journal of Inclusive Education* 4(2):111-132.

_____. 2000b. "Local Knowledges and Educational Reforms in Ghana." *Canadian and International Education* 29(1):37-72.

_____. 2000c. "African Development: The Relevance and Implications of 'Indigenousness'." In G. Dei, B. Hall and D. Goldin Rosenberg (eds.). *Indigenous Knowledges in Global Contexts: Multiple Readings of Our World*. Toronto: University of Toronto Press, 70-86.

_____. 2002a. "Spiritual Knowing and Transformative Learning." In *Transformative Learning: Essays on Praxis*, edited by Edmund O'Sullivan. New York: Palgrave/St Martin's Press.

_____. 2002b. "Spirituality in African Education: Issues and Contestations from a Ghanaian Case Study." *International Journal of Children's Spirituality* 7(1):37-56.

_____. 2002c. "Learning Culture, Spirituality and Local Knowledges: Implications for African Schooling." *International Journal of Educational Development* 48, (5):335-360.

_____, B. Hall, and D. Goldin Rosenberg. 2000. "Indigenous Knowledges: An Introduction." In *Indigenous Knowledges in Global Contexts: Multiple Readings of Our World*, edited by G. J. S. Dei, B. Hall, and D. Goldin Rosenberg. Toronto: University of Toronto Press.

_____, and A. Asgharzadeh. 2001. "The Power of Social Theory: The Anti-Colonial Discursive Framework." Journal of Educational Thought. 35(3):297-324.

_____, and C. Connelly. 2000. "Review Essay: Reclaiming African Women's Agency as Actors in Education." In *Women and Education in Sub-Saharan Africa: Power, Opportunities and Constraints: Women and Change in the Developing World*, edited by M. Bloch, M. A. Beoku-betts, and B. R. Tabachnick. London: Boulder. In *Journal of Contemporary African Studies* 18(2):306-309

_____, and S. Razack. 1995. Inclusive Schooling: An Inventory of Contemporary Practices Designed to Meet the Challenge of a Diverse Student Body. Report submitted to the Ontario Ministry of Education and Training, Toronto.

_____, with P. Broomfield, M. Castagna, M. James, J. Mazzuca, and E. McIsaac.1996. Unpacking what works: A critical examination of 'best practices' of inclusive schooling in Ontario. A project funded under the Transfer Grant from the Ontario Ministry of Education and Training to the Ontario Institute for Studies in Education of the University of Toronto.

_____, J. Mazzuca, and J. Zine. 1997. *Reconstructing 'Drop-Out': A Critical Ethnography of the Dynamics of Black Students' Disengagement From School.* Toronto: University of Toronto Press.

_____, and L. L. Karumanchery. 1999. "School Reforms in Ontario: The 'Marketisation of Education' and the Resulting Silence on Equity." *Alberta Journal of Educational Research.* 45(2):111-131.

_____, I. James, L. Karumanchery, S. James-Wilson, and J. Zine. 2000. *Removing the Margins: The Challenges and Possibilities of Inclusive Schooling.* Toronto: Canadian Scholars Press.

_____, S. James-Wilson, and J. Zine. 2002. *Inclusive Schooling: A Teacher's Companion to Removing the Margins.* Toronto: Canadian Scholars Press.

Delamont, S. 1990. *Sex Roles and the School.* London: Routledge.

Dewey, J. 1916. *Democracy and Education: An Introduction to the Philosophy of Education.* New York: Macmillan.

Djokoto, E. D. 2002. Power and Resistance: An Analysis of the State-Owned Enterprises Reform Programme in Ghana. Ph.D. dissertation. Department of Sociology, University of Alberta, Edmonton, AB.

Dore, R. 1976. *The Diploma Disease: Education, Qualification and Development.* London: George Allen and Unwin.

Dove, N. 1998. "African Womanism: An Afrocentric Theory." *Journal of Black Studies* 28(5): 515-539.

Du Bois, W. E. B. 1965 1927. *The Souls of Black Africa.* New York: Avon Books.

_____. [1946] 1965. *The World and Africa.* New York: International Publishers.

Easterly, W. 2001. *The Elusive Quest for Growth.* London: MIT Press.

Ecumenical Coalition for Economic Justice/Canada. 1990. *Recolonization or Liberation: The Bonds of Structural Adjustment and Struggles for Emancipation.* Toronto: Our Times.

Egbo, B. 2000. *Gender, Literacy and Life Chances in Sub-Saharan Africa.* Clevedon, UK: Multilingual Matters.

Elabor-Idemudia, P. 1991. "The Impact of Structural Adjustment Programs on Women and their Households in Bendel and Ogun States, Nigeria." In *Structural Adjustment and African Women Farmers,* edited by C. Gladwin. Grainesville, FL; University of Florida Press.

_____. 1992. Women and Economic Reforms: Development or Burden? Unpublished paper. Department of Sociology in Education, OISE/UT.

_____. 1993. Rural Women Quality of Life Under Structural Adjustment Policy and Programmes: A Nigerian Case Study. Ph.D. diss., University of Toronto.

Elabor-Idemudia, P., and G. J. S. Dei. 1992. "The World Bank and Education: An Alternative View from Under the Sink." *CIDEC Newsletter* 2, (7): 2-4.

Engberg-Pedersen, P., P. Gibbon, P. Raikes, and L. Udsholt, eds. 1996. *Limits of Adjustment in Africa*. London: Villiers Publications.

English, L. 1994. "Financing Education in Africa: Need for Improved Aid Coordination." *Africa Development* 19(4):97-111.

Ermine, W. 1995. Aboriginal Epistemology. In *First Nations Education in Canada: The Circle Unfolds*, edited by M. Battiste, and J. Barman. Vancouver: University of British Columbia Press.

Errington, F., and D. Gewertz. 1989. "Tourism and Anthropology in a Post-Modern World." *Oceania* 60:37-54.

Eshiwani, G. S. 1990. *Implementing Educational Policies in Kenya*. Washington: The World Bank.

Estrada, K., and P. McLaren. 1993. "A Dialogue on Multiculturalism and Democratic Culture." *Educational Researcher* 22(3):27-33.

Etta, F. 1994. "Gender Issues in Contemporary African Education." *African Development* 19:57-84.

Fafunwa, A. B. 1982. "African Education in Perspective." In *Education in Africa: A Comparative Study*, edited by A. B. Fafunwa, and J. Aisiku. London: George Allen & Unwin.

Fals-Borda, O. 1980. *Science and the Common People*. Yugoslavia.

_____, and M. A. Rahman. 1991. "Some Basic Ingredients." In *Action and Knowledge: Breaking the Monopoly with Participatory Action-Research*, edited by O. Fals-Borda, and M.A. Rahman. New York: The Apex Press.

Fanon, F. 1963. *The Wretched of the Earth*. New York: Grove Weidenfeld.

Fine, M. 1991. *Framing Dropouts: Notes on the Politics of an Urban Public High School*. Albany, NY: State University of New York Press.

_____, L. Powell, L. Weis, and L. M. Wong. 1997. "Preface." In *Off White: Readings on Race, Power and Society*, edited by M. Fine, L. Weis, L. Powell, l and L. Mun Wong. New York: Routledge.

Folson, R. B. 1995. *The Contribution of Formal Education to Economic Development and Economic Underdevelopment: Ghana As a Case Study*. Frankfurt am Main: Peter Lang.

Foster, P. 1965. *Education and Social Change in Ghana*. London: Routledge and Kegan Paul.

Foucault, M. 1980. *Power/Knowledge: Selected Interviews and Other Writings, 1972-1977*. New York: Pantheon Books.

_____. 1983. "The Subject and Power." In *Michel Foucault: Beyond Structuralism and Hermeneutics*, edited by H. Dreyfus, and P. Rabinow. Chicago: University of Chicago Press.

Frankenberg, R. 1993. *The Social Construction of Whiteness: White Women, Race Matters*. Minneapolis, MI: University of Minnesota Press.

Friedman, J. 1992. "The Past in the Future: History and the Politics of Identity." *American Anthropologist* 94(4):845-854.

Freire, P., and D. Macedo. 1987. *Literacy: Reading the Word and the World*. Boston: Bergin & Garvey.

Galabawa, C. J. 1990. *Implementing Education Policies in Tanzania*. Washington: The World Bank.

Gandy, O. H., Jr. 1998. "A Critical Research Agenda." In *Communication and Race: A Structural Perspective*. London: Arnold.

Garvey, A. J., ed. 1986 1923. *Philosophy and Opinions of Marcus Garvey*. New York: Atheneum Press.

George, B. S. 1976. *Education in Ghana*. Washington: U.S. Government Printing Office.

Ghana Statistical Service. 1987. *1984 Population Census of Ghana: Demographic and Economic Characteristics, Total Country*. Accra: The Service.

Ghana Statistical Service.1991. *Quarterly Digest of Statistics* 9, no. 1.

Ginsburg, F. 1994. "Embedded Aesthetics: Creating Discursive Space for Indigenous Media," *Cultural Anthropology* 9 (3):365-382.

Glewwe, Paul. 1991. *Schooling, Skills, and the Returns to Government Investment in Education: An Exploration Using Data from Ghana*. Washington: The World Bank

Gordon, A., D. Nkwe, and M. Graven 1998. "Gender and Education in Rural South Africa." In *Women and Education in Sub-Saharan Africa: Power, Opportunities and Constraints*, edited by M. Bloch, J. Bekou-Betts, and R. Tabachnick. Boulder, CO: Lynne Rienner.

Groome, T. H. 1999. "Infuse Education with Spiritual Values." Reprint, from the *Christian Science Monitor*, 10 February, 1998.

Guba, E., and Y. Lincoln. 1994. "Competing Paradigms in Qualitative Research." In *Handbook of Qualitative Research*, edited by N. K. Denzin, and Y. S. Lincoln. Beverly Hill, CA.: Sage.

Gyekye, K. 1995. *African Philosophical Thought*. Philadelphia: Temple University Press.

Gyimah-Boadi, E., ed. 1991. *The Political Economy of Recovery*. Boulder; London: Lynne Rienner.

Hall, B. 1993. "Re-Centering Adult Education Research: Whose World is First?" *Studies in Continuing Education* 15(2):149-161.

──────. 2001. Mwalimu Julius Nyerere: A Critical Review of His Contributions to Adult Education and Postcolonial Theory. Draft Paper, Department of Adult Education, Community Development and Counselling Psychology,. Ontario Institute for Studies in Education of the University of Toronto.

Hall, S. 1991. "Old and New Identities: Old and New Ethnicities." In. *Culture, Globalization and the World System*, edited by A. King. New York: State University Press.

_____. 1996. "Politics of Identity." In *Culture, Identity and Politics*, edited by T. Ranger, Y. Samad, and O. Stuart. Avebury-Ashgate Publishing.

Handler, R. 1986. "Authenticity." *Anthropology Today* 2(1):2-4.

Hanson, A. 1989. "The Making of the Maori: Culture Invention and Its Logic." *American Anthropologist* 93:449-450.

Harding, S. 1998. "Gender, Modernity, Knowledge: Postcolonial Standpoints." In *Is Science Multicultural? Postcolonialisms, Feminisms, Epistemologies*. Bloomington, IN: Indiana University Press.

_____. 1998. "The Curious Coincidence of Feminine and African Moralities." *Afrikan Mothers*. New York: Statue University of New York Press.

Harris, C. 1993. "Whiteness as Property." *Harvard Law Review* 106(8):1707-1791.

Hatcher, R. 1998. "Social Justice and the Politics of School Effectiveness and Improvement." *Race, Ethnicity and Education* 1(2):267-289.

Haynes, D., and G. Prakash. 1991. "Introduction: The Entanglement of Power and Resistance." In *Contesting Power: Resistance and Everyday Social Relations in South Asia*, edited by D. Haynes, and G. Prakash. Delhi: Oxford University Press.

Heller, P. 1979. "The Underfunding of Recurrent Development Costs." *Finance and Development* (March).

Henry, A., 1991. Taking Back Control: Toward a Black Woman's Afrocentric Standpoint on the Education of Black Children. Ph.D. diss., Department of Curriculum, Ontario Institute for Studies in Education, Toronto, Canada.

Herman, C., and S. Bunwaree, eds. 1999. *Gender, Education and Development*. London: Zed Books.

Herman, H. 1995. "School-Leaving Examinations, Selection and Equity in Higher Education in South Africa." *Comparative Education* 31(2):261-274.

Herzfeld, E. 1988. "Changing the Future." *West Africa,* 19-25 August.1364-1375.

Hicking-Dyson, A. 1994. "The Environment as Radical Politics: Can 'Third World' Education Rise to the Challenge?" *International Review of Education* 40(1):19-36.

Higginbotham, E., 1990. "Designing an Inclusive Curriculum: Bringing all Women into the Core." *Women's Studies Quarterly* 1:7-23.

Hilliard, A. 1992. "Why We Must Pluralize the Curriculum." *Educational Leadership* 49(4):12-15.

Hobsbawn, E., and T. Ranger, eds. 1983. *The Invention of Tradition*. Cambridge, UK: Cambridge University Press.

Hoffman, D. 1995. "Models of Self and Culture in Teaching and Learning: An Anthropological Perspective on Japanese and American Education." *Educational Foundations* 9(3):19-42.

_____. 1999. Spirit, Self, and Culture: Individuality in the Japanese Educational Tradition. Paper presented at the Annual meeting of the Comparative and International Education Society, Ontario Institute for Studies in Education of the University of Toronto, 15-18, Toronto.

Holmes, L. 1999. "Heart Knowledge, Blood Memory and the Voice of the Land: Implications of Research among Hawaiian Elders." In *Indigenous Knowledges in Global Contexts: Multiple Readings of Our World*, edited by G. Dei, B. Hall, and D. Goldin Rosenberg. Toronto: University of Toronto Press.

Hooper, J. 1990. Structural Adjustment Policies in Ghana, 1983-1990: Sustainable Development? Paper presented at the Annual Conference of the Canadian Association of African Studies, Dalhousie University; 9-12, May, Halifax, NS.

Horton, R. 1967. "African traditional thought and Western Science." *Africa* 37:155-187.

Hough, J. R. 1989. "Inefficiency in Education: The Case of Mali." *Comparative Education* 25(1):77-86.

Hutchful, E. 1989. "From Revolution to Monetarism: The Economics and Politics of the Adjustment Program In Ghana." In *Structural Adjustment in Africa,* edited by B. Campbell, and J. Loxley. London: Macmillan.

_____. 1990. *The IMF and Ghana: The Confidential Record*. London: Zed Books.

_____. 1995. "Adjustment in Africa and the Fifty Years of the Bretton Woods Institutions: Change or Consolidation?" *Canadian Journal of Development Studies* 16(3):331-417.

_____. 1996. "Ghana: 1983-1994." In *Limits of Adjustment in Africa*, edited by P. Engberg-Pedersen, P. Gibbon, P. Raikes, and L. Udsholt. London: Villiers Publications.

Hussain, I.,. and R. Furuqee, eds. 1994. *Adjustment in Africa: Lessons from Country Case Studies.* Washington: The World Bank

Ibrahim, A. 1997. Becoming Black: Race, Language, Culture and the Politics of Identity: African Students in a Franco-Ontarian High School. Ph.D diss., Ontario Institute for Studies in Education of the University of Toronto.

Itwaru, A. 1999. Creativity, Resistance, Transformation: An Instance in the Life of an Othered Other. Public Lecture presented at Department of Sociology and Equity Studies in Education, Ontario Institute for Studies in Education of the University of Toronto.

James, S., and A. Busia, eds. 1993. *Theorizing Black Feminisms*. New York: Routledge.

Jegede, O. 1994. "African Cultural Perspectives and the Teaching of Science." In *STS Education: International Perspectives on Reform*, edited by J. Solomon, and G. Aikenhead. New York: Teachers College Press.

_____. 1997. "School Science and the Development of Scientific Culture: A Review of Contemporary Science Education in Africa." *International Journal of Science Education* 19:1-20.

Jespersen, E. 1992. "External Shocks, Adjustment Policies and Economic and Social Performance." In *From Adjustment Development in Africa*, edited by G. Cornia, G. A., G. van der Hoeven, and T. Mkandawire. London: MacMillam.

Johnson, D. 1995. "Introduction: The Challenges of Educational Reconstruction and Transformation in South Africa." *Comparative Education* 31(2):131-140.

Jolly, R. 1969. *Planning Education for African Development*. Kampala: Makerere Institute for Social Research.

Jones, P. W. 1988. *International Policies of Third World Education*. London: Hutchinson.

_____. 1992. *World Bank Financing of Education*. New York: Routledge.

_____. 1997. "The World Bank and the Literacy Question: Orthodoxy, Heresy and Ideology." *International Review of Education* 43(4):367-375.

_____. 1997. Review of *Policies and Strategies for Education: A World Bank Review. Comparative Education* 33(1): 117-130.

_____. 1998. "Globalisation and Internationalism: Democratic Prospects for World Education." *Comparative Education* 34(2): 143-155.

Kaduri, R.C. 1997. Experiences of Wazizi (TAPA) Schools. Paper presented at the Conference on the Quality of Education in Tanzania. organized by the Faculty of Education of the University of Dar es Salaam in collaboration with the Ministry of Education and Culture.

Kalu, A. 1996. "Women and the Social Construction of Gender in African Development." *Africa Today* 43:269-288.

Kankwenda, M. 1994. "'Marabouts' and Merchants of Development in Africa.." *CODESRIA Bulletin* 3:9-15.

Kelly, G. 1989. "Achieving Equality in Education: Prospects and Realities." In *International Handbook on Women's Education*, edited by G. Kelly. New York: Greenwood Press.

Keesing, R. M. 1989. "Creating the Past: Custom and Identity in the Contemporary Pacific." *The Contemporary Pacific* 1(1/2):19-42.

_____. 1991. "Reply to Trask." *The Contemporary Pacific* 3(spring, 1):168-171.

Kellner, D. 1995. *Media Culture: Cultural Studies, Identity and Politics Between the Modern and the Postmodern*. New York: Routledge.

Kincheloe, J. L., and P. L. McLaren. 1994. "Rethinking Critical Theory and Qualitative Research." In Handbook of Qualitative Research, edited by N. K. Denzin, and Y. S. Lincoln. Beverly Hills, CA: Sage.

Kinyanjui, K. 1993. "Enhancing Women's Participation in the Science-Based Curriculum: The Case of Kenya." In *The Politics of Women's Education: Perspectives from Asia, Africa and Latin America*, edited by J. K. Conway, and S. C. Bourque. Ann Arbor, MI:Michigan University Press.

Kiluva-Ndunda, M. 2000. *Women's Agency and Educational Policy: The Experiences of the Women of Kilome, Kenya.* New York: State University of New York Press.

Kwapong, A. 1992. Capacity Building for People-Centred Development, With Special Reference to Africa. Paper delivered to the British Columbia Council for Internal Co-operation, 1 February, Vancouver, BC.

_____, and B. Lesser, eds. 1989. *Capacity Building and Human Resource Development in Africa.* Halifax, NS: Lester Pearson Institute for International Development.

Lattas, A. 1993. "Essentialism, Memory and Resistance: Aboriginality and the Politics of Authenticity." *Oceania* 63:2-67.

Lawson, E. 1998. Conversation with the author. Department of Sociology and Equity Studies in Education, Ontario Institute for Studies in Education of the University of Toronto.

Lawuyi, T. 1991. Conversation with the author on "Maintaining the Infrastructure of Development for Africa." Received at the Annual Conference of the Canadian Association of African Studies, 16-18 May, York University, Toronto.

Lee, E. 1985. *Letters to Marcia: A Teacher's Guide to Anti-Racist Education.* Toronto: Cross-Cultural Communication Centre.

_____. 1991. "An Interview with Educator Enid Lee: Taking Multicultural, Anti-Racist Education Seriously." *Rethinking Schools* 69 (October-November):1-4.

Leechor, C. 1994. "Ghana: Frontrunner in Adjustment." In *Adjustment in Africa: Lessons from Country Case Studies,* edited by I. Hussain, and R. Furuqee. Washington: The World Bank.

Lemon, A. 1995. "Education in Post-Apartheid South Africa: Some Lessons from Zimbabwe." *Comparative Education* 31(1):101-114.

Levira, M. 2000. Instructional Resources as a Factor in Educational Performance: A Case Study in Tanzania. Ph.D diss., Department of Education, Concordia University, Montreal, Quebec.

Limón, J. 1991. "Representation, Ethnicity and Precursory Ethnography: Notes of a Native Anhropologist." In *Recapturing Anthropology*, edited by R. Fox.. Santa Fe, NM.: School of American Research.

Lincoln, S., and E. G. Guba. 1985. *Naturalistic Inquiry.* Beverley Hills, CA.: Sage.

Lindsay, B. 1989. "Redefining the Educational and Cultural Milieu of Tanzanian Teachers: A Case Study in Development or Dependency." *Comparative Education* 25(1):87-96.

Linnekin, J. 1992. "On the Theory and Politics of Cultural Construction in the Pacific." *Oceania* 62:249-263.

_____. 1991. "Texts Bites and the R-Word: The Politics of Representing Scholarship." The Contemporary Pacific (spring):171-176.

Lipatu, M. A. Experiences from the Community Education Fund (CEF). Paper presented at the Conference on the Quality of Education in Tanzania organized by the Faculty of Education of the University of Dar es Salaam in collaboration with the Ministry of Education and Culture.

Lockheed, M., and A. Verspoor. 1990. Improving Primary Education in Developing Countries: A Review of Policy Options (Draft). Washington: The World Bank.

Loxley, J. 1988. *Ghana: Economic Crisis and the Long Road to Recovery.* Ottawa: The North-South Institute.

Maclure, R. 1994. "Misplaced Assumptions of Decentralization and Participation in Rural Communities: Primary School Reform in Burkina Faso." *Comparative Education* 30(3):239-254.

Makang, J. M. 1997. "Of the Good Use of Tradition: Keeping the Critical Perspective in African Philosophy." In *Postcolonial African Philosophy: A Critical Reader*, edited by E.C. Eze. Cambridge, MA: Blackwell Publishers.

Malekela, G. A. 1983. Access to Secondary Education in Sub-Saharan Africa: the Tanzania Experiment. Ph.D. dissertaion, University of Chicago, Illinois.

Maravanyika, O. E. 1990. *Implementing Educational Policies in Zimbabwe.* Washington: The World Bank.

Mazama, A. 1998. "The Eurocentric Discourse on Writing: An Exercise in Self-Glorification." *Journal of Black Studies* 29(1):3-16.

Mazrui, A. 1975. "The African University as a Multinational Corporation: Problems of Penetration and Dependency." In. *Education and Colonialism*, edited by P. Altbach, and G. Kelly. New York: Longman.

Mbilinyi, M. 1998. "Searching for Utopia: The Politics of Gender and Education in Tanzania." In *Women and Education in Sub-Saharan Africa: Power, Opportunities and Constraints*, edited by M. Bloch, M. Bekou-Betts, and R. Tabachnick. Boulder, CO.: Lynne Rienner.

Mbilinyi, M, P. Mbuguni, R. Meana, R, and P. Ole Kambaine. 1991. Education in Tanzania with Gender. Report submitted to SIDA, Dar es Salaam.

Mbiti, J. S. 1969. *African Religions and Philosophy.* London: Heinemann.

McCarthy, C., and W. Crichlow, eds. 1993. *Race, Identity and Representation in Education.* New York: Routledge.

McLeod, K., and E. Krugly-Smolska. 1997. *Multicultural Education: A Place to Start: Guidelines for Classroom, Schools and Communities.* Toronto: Canadian Association of Second Language Teachers.

Memmi, A. 1969. *The Colonizer and the Colonized*. Boston: Beacon Press.

Miller, R. 1989. "Two Hundred Years of Holistic Education." *Holistic Education Review* 1(1):5-12.

Miller, R. 1997. *What are Schools for?: Holistic Education in American Culture*. Brandon, VT.: Holistic Education Press.

Miller, R. 1999. Transcripts of "Holistic Education and the Emerging Culture."

Minh-ha, T. 1989. *Woman, Native, Other: Writing Postcoloniality and Feminism*. Bloomington, IN: Indiana University Press.

Ghana. Ministry of Education. 1974. *The New Structure and Content of Education for Ghana*. Accra: The Ministry.

_____. 1990. Keynote Address by Mrs. Vida Yeboah, Deputy Secretary for Education at National Seminars on the Education Reform Programme, January, Accra..

_____. 1990. The Senior Secondary School Programme and 2nd Phase of the Education Reform Programme. Address delivered by Mrs. Vida Yeboah, Deputy Secretary for Education at National Seminars on the Education Reform Programme, January, Accra.

Mitchell, T. 1990. "Everyday Metaphors of Power." *Theory and Society* 19:545-577.

Mlambo, A. S. 1995. "Towards an Analysis of IMF Structural Adjustment Programmes in Sub-Saharan Africa (SSA): The Case of Zimbabwe." *Africa Development* 20(2):77-98.

Mohanty, C. 1990. "On Race and Voice: Challenges of Liberal Education in the 90's." *Cultural Critique* 14:179-208.

_____. 1991. "Under Western Eyes: Feminist Scholarship and Colonial Discourses." In *Third World Women and the Politics of Feminism*, edited by C. Mohanty, A. Russo, and L. Torres. .Indiana University Press.

_____. 1995. "Feminist Encounters: Locating the Politics of Experience." In *Social postmodernism: Beyond Identity Politics*, edited by L. Nicholson, and S. Seidman. New York: Cambridge University Press.

Moock, P., and W. Harbison. 1988. *Education in Sub-Saharan Africa: Policies for Adjustment, Revitalization, and Expansion*. Washington: The World Bank.

Moore, D. S. 1997. "Marxism, Culture and Political Ecology: Environmental Struggles in Zimbabwe Highlands." In *Liberation ecologies: Environment, development, social movements*, edited by R. Peet, and M. Watts. London: Routledge.

Motala, S. 1995. "Surviving the System: A Critical Appraisal of Some Conventional Wisdoms in Primary Education in South Africa." *Comparative Education* 31(2):161-180.

Mulugu, M. 1999. Obstacles to Women's Participation in Post-Colonial Education in Tanzania: What is to be Done? Ph.D diss., Department of Interdisciplinary Studies, Concordia University, Montreal, Quebec.

Munck, R. 1999. "Deconstructing Development Discourses: Of Impasses, Alternatives and Politics." In. *Critical Development Theory: Contributions to the New Paradigm*, edited by R. Munck, and D. O'Hearn. London: Zed Books.

Muteshi, J. 1996. Women, Law and Engendering Resistance: A Pedagogical Project. Ph.D. diss., Department of Education, University of Toronto, Toronto, ON..

Mundy, K. 1992. The Case for Universal Primary Education Revisited: The Tanzanian and Zimbabwean Experience in Comparative and International Perspective. Course paper, Ontario Institute for Studies in Education.

Muwanga, N. 2000. The Politics of Primary Education in Uganda. Parental Participation and National Reforms. Ph.D. diss., Department of Political Science, University of Toronto, ON.

Mwingira, A. C., and S. Pratt. 1967. *The Process of Educational Planning in Tanzania*. Paris: UNESCO.

Myers, L. J. 1993. *Understanding an Afrocentric World View: Introduction to an Optimal Psychology*. Dubuque, IA: Kendall/Hunt Publishing

Nash, J. 1997. "The Reassertion of Indigenous Identity: Mayan Responses to State Intervention in Chiapas." *Latin American Research Review*:7-41.

Ndulu, B., K. Gyekye, A. Mbembe, O. Aboyade, and B. Ouattara. 1998. "Toward Defining a New Vision of Africa for the 21st Century." CODESRIA Bulletin 1:4-10.

Ngomo, P., and J. Oenham, eds. 1989. "Adjusting Education to Economic Crisis." *Institute of Development Studies Bulletin* (January).

Ninsin, K. A. 1991. "The PNDC and the Problems of Legitimacy." In *Ghana: The Political Economy of Recovery*, edited by D. Rothchild. Boulder, CO: Lynne Reinner.

Nkrumah, K. 1970. *Consciencism: Philosophy and Ideology for Decolonization*. London: Panaf.

Nsiah-Peprah, Y. 1998. "Ghana's Educational Reform." *Ghana Review International* 052(June): 8-9.

Ntiri, D. W. 1993. "Africa's Educational Dilemma: Roadblocks to Universal Literacy for Social Integration and Change." *International Review of Education* 39(5):357-372.

Nwagwu, C. C. 1997. "The Environment of Crises in the Nigerian Education System." *Comparative Education* 33(1):87-96.

Nyalemegbe, K. 1997. "The Educational Reforms So Far." *Daily Graphic*, 26 February, 7.

Nyerere, J. 1974. *Man and Development*. New York: Oxford University Press.

_____. 1979. "Adult Education and Development." In *Education for Liberation and Development: The Tanzanian Experience*, edited by M. Hinzell, and C. H. Hundsdorfer. Paris: UNESCO.

_____. 1985. "Education in Tanzania." *Harvard Educational Review* 55(1):45-
52.

Obanya, P. 1989. "Going Beyond the Educational Reform Document."
Prospects 19(3):33-47.

_____. 1995. "Case Studies of Curriculum Innovations." *International Review
of Education* 41(5):315-336.

Obenga, T. 1992. *Ancient Egypt & Black Africa: A Student's Handbook for the
Study of Ancient Egypt in Philosophy, Linguistics and Gender Relations.*
Translated by Amon Saba Saakana, ed. London: Karnak House.

Obbo, C. 1980. *African Women: The Struggle for Economic Independence.*
London: Zed Press.

Odaet, C. F. 1990. *Implementing Educational Policies in Uganda.* Washington: The
World Bank.

O'Hearn, D., 1999. "Tigers and Transnational Corporations: Pathways from
the Periphery." In *Critical Development Theory: Contributions to the New
Paradigm,* edited by R. Munck, and D. O'Hearn. London: Zed Books.

Okeke, P. 1994. Patriarchal Continuities and Contradictions in African
Women's Education and Socio-Economic Status. Ph.D diss.,
Department of Education, Halifax, NS.

Olukoshi, A 2001. Towards Development Democracy: A Note. Draft paper
prepared for discussion at the United Nations Institute for Social
Development (UNRISD) meeting on The Need to Rethink
development Economics, 7-8 September, Cape Town, South Africa.

Okolie, A. 2000. "Regulating the World Economy as if Africa Mattered."
Africa Quarterly 40: 41-79.

_____. 2001. Producing Knowledge for Sustainable Development in Africa:
Implications for Higher Education. Paper presented at the Annual
Conference of the Association for the Study of Higher Education, 15-
18 November, Richmond, VA.

_____. 2002. Personal communication with the author. Department of
Sociology and Equity Studies in Education, Ontario Institute for Studies
in Education of the University of Toronto. Toronto, February 22.

Omi, W., and H. Winant. 1993. "On the Theoretical Concept of Race." In
Race, Identity and Representation in Education, edited by C. McCarthy, and
H. Crichlow. New York: Routledge.

_____. 1997. "Behind Blue Eyes: Whiteness and Contemporary U.S. Radical
Politics." In *Off White: Readings on Race, Power and Society,* edited by M.
Fine, L. Weis, L. Powell, and L. Mun Wong. New York: Routledge.

Otunga, R. 1997. "School Participation by Gender: Implications for
Occupational Activities in Kenya." *Africa Development* 22(1):39-64.

Palmer, P. 1999. "The Grace of Great Things Recovering the Sacred in
Knowing, Teaching and Learning." Transcripts, Parker Palmer.

Panford, K. 2001. *IMF-World Bank and Labor's Burden in Africa: Ghana's
Experience.* Westport, CT: Praeger.

Parpart, J. 1995. "Is Africa a Postmodern Invention?" *Issue: A Journal of Opinion* 23(1):16-18.

Parry, B. 1994. "Resistance Theory/Theorising Resistance, or Two Cheers for Nativism." In *Colonial Discourse/Postcolonial Theory*, edited by F. Barker, P. Hulme, and M. Iversen. Manchester, UK: Manchester University Press.

_____. 1995. "Problems in Current Theories of Colonial Discourse." In *The Post-Colonial Studies Reader*, edited by B. Ashcroft, G. Griffiths, and H. Thiophene. New York: Routledge.

Passi, F. O. 1990. "Planning for the Supply and Demand of Qualified Teachers in Uganda." *International Review of Education* 36(4):441-452.

Philip, M. Nourbese. 1989. *She Tries Her Tongue, Her Silence Softly Breaks.* Charlottetown, PEI.: Ragweed.

Pickett, J., and H. Singer, eds. 1990. *Towards Economic Recovery in Sub-Saharan Africa.* London: Routledge.

Prah, K. 1997. "Accusing the Victims - In My Father's House." Review of *In My Father's House* by Kwame Anthony Appiah. *CODESRIA Bulletin*, no.1:14-22.

Prakash, G. 1995. "Introduction: After Colonialism." In *After Colonialism: Imperial Histories and Postcolonial Displacements*, edited by G. Prakash. Princeton, NJ: Princeton University Press.

_____. 1992. "Can the Subaltern Ride?: A Reply to O'Hanlon and Washbrook." *Comparative Studies in Society and History* 34(1):168-184.

Price, E. 1993. Multiculturalism: A Critique. Paper presented in Department of Sociology and Equity Studies, Ontario Institute for Studies in Education of the University of Toronto.

_____. 1998. First Thoughts Toward a Thesis Proposal. Paper presented in Department of Sociology and Equity Studies in Education, Ontario Institute for Studies in Education of the University of Toronto.

Psacharopoulos, G. 1989. "Why Educational Reforms Fail: A Comparative Analysis." *International Review of Education* 35 (2):179-195.

_____. 1990. *Why Educational Policies Can Fail: An Overview of Selected African Experiences.* Washington: The World Bank.

Psacharopoulos, G., J.P. Tan and E. Jimenez. 1986. *Financing of Education in Developing Countries: An Exploration of Policy Options.* Washington, D.C.

Purcell, T. W. 1998. "Indigenous Knowledge and Applied Anthropology: Question of Definition and Direction." *Human Organization* 57(3):258-272.

Quist, H. 1994. Illiteracy, Education and National Development in Postcolonial West Africa: A Re-Appraisal." *Africa Development* 19:127-145.

Raftopoulos, B. 1986. "Human Resources Development and the Problems of Labor Utilization." In *Zimbabwe: The Political Economy of Transition*, edited by I. Mandaza. Dakar: CODESRIA.

Ragwanja, P. M. 1997. "Post-Industrialism and Knowledge Production: African Intellectuals in the New International Division Labor." *CODESRIA Bulletin* 3:5-11.

Rahnema, M. 1995. "Participation." In *Development Dictionary: A Guide to Knowledge as Power.* London: Zed Books.

Razack, S. 1998. *Looking White People in the Eye.* Toronto: University of Toronto Press.

Riddell, Barry. 1992. "Things Fall Apart Again: Structural Adjustment Programmes in Sub-Saharan Africa." *The Journal of Modern African Studies* 30, (1):53-68.

Roberts, H. 1998. "Indigenous Knowledges and Western Science: Perspectives from the Pacific." In *Science and Technology Education and Ethnicity: An Aotearoa/New Zealand Perspective,* edited by D. Hodson. Conference Proceedings of the Royal Society of New Zealand, Thorndon, Wellington, 7-8 May, 1996.

Rodney, W. 1972. *How Europe Underdeveloped Africa.* Washington: Howard University Press.

Rosaldo, R. 1980. "Doing Oral History." *Social Analysis* 4:89-99.

Rothchild, D., ed. 1991. *Ghana: The Political Economy of Recovery.* Boulder, CO.: Lynne Reinner.

Rothenberg, P. 1998. "The Social Construction of Race, Class, Gender and Sexuality." In *Race, Class, and Gender in the United States,* edited by P. Rothenberg. New York: St Martin's Press.

Russo, A. 1991. "We Cannot Live Without Our Lives." In *Third World Women and The Politics of Identity,* edited by C. Mohanty, A. Russo, and L. Torres.

Sahn, D., ed. *Adjusting Policy Failure in African Economies.* Ithaca, NY: Cornell University Press.

Said, E. 1979. *Orientalism.* New York: Vintage Books.

_____. 1993. *Culture and Imperialism.* New York: Vintage Books.

Salmi. J. 1992. "The Higher Education Crisis in Developing Countries: Issues, Problems, Constraints and Reforms." *International Review of Education* 38(1):19-33.

Samoff, J. 1990. "Educational Reform in Tanzania: Schools, Skills and Social Transformation." In *Education: From Poverty to Liberty,* edited by B. Nasson, and J. Samuels. South Africa: David Phillip Publishers.

_____. 1992. "The Intellectual/Financial Complex of Foreign Aid." *Review of African Political Economy* 53:60-75.

_____. 1993. "The Reconstruction of Schooling in Africa." *Comparative Education Review* 37 (2):181-222.

_____. 1996. "African Education and Development: Crises, Triumphalism, Research, Loss of Vision." *Alberta Journal of Educational Research* 42:121-147.

Samuels, J. 1991. The Sound of Silence: Racism in Contemporary Feminist Theory. Master's thesis, Department of Sociology and Anthropology, University of Windsor.

Sandbrook, R. 1989. Economic Crisis, Structural Adjustment and the State in Sub-Saharan Africa. Paper read at the Annual Conference of the Canadian Association of African Studies, 10-13 May, Carleton University, Ottawa.

Sandbrook, R. 1993. *The Politics of Africa's Economic Recovery.* Cambridge: Cambridge University Press.

Sardar, Z. 1999. "Development and the Location of Eurocentrism." In *Critical Development Theory: Contributions to the New Paradigm,* edited by R. Munck, and D. O'Hearn. London: Zed Books.

Scanlon, D. 1964. *Traditions of African Education.* New York: Columbia University Press.

Scheurich, J., and M. Young. 1997. "Coloring Epistemologies: Are Our Research Epistemologies Racially Biased?" Educational Researcher 22(8):5-16.

Seidman, S. 1994. *Contested Knowledge: Social Theory in the Postmodern Era.* Oxford: Blackwell Publishers.

Shohat, E. 1992. "Notes on the 'Post-Colonial." *Social Text* 31/32:99-113.

Shujaa, M. J. 1994. *Too Much Schooling, Too Little Education: a Paradox of Black Life in White Societies.* Trenton, NJ: Africa World Press.

Shaw, T. 1988. "Africa in the 1990's: From Economic Crisis to Structural Readjustment." *Dalhousie Review* 68:37-69.

Shepard, M. 1988. "Spirituality and the Jewish School: Models and Meanings." Religious Education 83(1):101-115.

Shields, J. 1999. The Spiritual Foundations of Japanese Education. Paper presented at the Annual meeting of the Comparative and International Education Society, 15-18 April, Ontario Institute for Studies in Education of the University of Toronto.

Sicherman, C. 1995. "Ngugi's Colonial Education: The Subversion of the African Mind." *African Studies Review* 38(3):11-41.

Sifuna, D. N. 1992. "Diversifying the Secondary School Curriculum: The African Experience." *International Review of Education* 38(1):5-20.

Sklar, R. L. 1993. "The African Frontier for Political Science." In *Africa and the Disciplines,* edited by R. Bates et al. Chicago: University of Chicago Press.

Slemon, S. 1995. "The Scramble for Post-Colonialism." In *The Post-Colonial Studies Reader,* edited by B. Ashcroft et al. New York: Routledge.

Smith, L. 1999. *Decolonizing Methodologies.* London: Zed Books.

Sowah, N. K. 1993. "Ghana." In *The Impact of Structural Adjustment on the Population in Africa,* edited by A. Adepoju. London: Islington.

Srivastava, S. 1999. Discourses of Anti-Racist Change in Feminist Organizations: At Crossroads or Cross-Purposes? Paper presented at the Congress meeting of the Canadian Sociology and Anthropology Association, 6-9 June, Bishop's University, Lennoxville, QUEBEC.

Stanfield, J. H. 1995. "Methodological Reflections." In *Race and Ethnicity in Research Methods*, edited by Stanfield and R. M. Dennis. Sage.

Steady, F.C., ed. 1990. *The Black Woman Cross-Culturally*. Rochester, NY: Schenkman Books.

Stiglitz, J. E. 2001. "An Agenda for the New Development Economics. Draft paper prepared for discussion at the United Nations Institute for Social Development meeting on The Need to Rethink Development Economics, 7-8 September, Cape Town, South Africa.

Stromquist, N. 1998. "Agents in Women's Education: Some Trends in the African context." In *Women and Education in Sub-Saharan Africa: Power, Opportunities and Constraints: Women and Change in the Developing World*, edited by M. Bloch, J. A. Beoku-Betts, and B. R. Tabachnick. London: Boulder.

Suleri, S. 1992. *The Rhetoric of English India*. Chicago: Chicago University Press.

Tabulawa, R. 1998. "Teachers' Perspectives on Classroom Practice in Botswana: Implications for Pedagogical Change." *International Journal of Qualitative Studies in Education* 11(2):249-268.

Tedla, E. 1995. *Sankofa: African Thought and Education*. New York: Peter Lang.

Thakur, D. S. 1991. "Implementing Educational Policies in Sub-Saharan Africa: Review Essay." *Economics of Education Review* 10(4):385-390.

Thielen-Wilson, L. 1999. Notes on Class Presentation. Unpublished paper, Department of Sociology and Equity Studies, OISE/UT.

_____. 1999. Whiteness as Dominance, Multiple Subjectivity and Freirean Critical Pedagogy. Unpublished paper, Department of Sociology and Equity Studies, OISE/UT.

Thiophene, H. 1995. "Post-Colonial Literatures and Counter-Discourse." In *The Post-Colonial Studies Reader*. New York: Routledge, 95-98.

Thisen, J. K. 1993. "The Development and Utilization of Science and Technology in Productive Sectors: Case of Developing Africa." *Africa Development* 18(4):5-36.

Thomas, B. 1984. "Principles of Anti-Racist Education." *Currents* 2(2):20-24.

Thompson, A. R. 1984. *Education and Development in Africa*. New York: St. Martin's Press.

Tobin, J. 1992. "Japanese Preschools and the Pedagogy of Self." In *Japanese Sense of Self*, edited by N. Rosenberger, N. New York: Cambridge University Press.

Toh, S. H. 1993. "Bringing the World into the Classroom: Global Literacy and the Question of Paradigms." *Global Literacy* 1(1):9-17.

Trask, H. K. 1991. "Natives and Anthropologists: The Colonial Struggle." *The Contemporary Pacific* 3(1):159-167.

Threadgold, T. 1997. *Feminist Poetics: Poiesis, Performance, Histories*. London: New York: Routledge.

_____. 1993. In *From a Native Daughter: Colonialism and Sovereignty in Hawai'i*, edited by H. K Trask. Monroe, ME: Common Courage Press.

Trigger, B. 1988. "A Present of their Past? Anthropologists, Native People and their Heritage." *Culture* VIII (1):71-79.

Troyna, B., and P. Forster.1988. "Conceptual and Ethical Dilemmas of Collaborative Research: Reflections on a Case Study." *Educational Review* 40(3):289-300.

Tucker, V. 1999. "The Myth of Development: A Critique of Eurocentric Discourse." In *Critical Development Theory: Contributions to the New Paradigm*, edited by R. Munck, and D. O'Hearn. London: Zed Books.

Turner, I. 1999. Changing the Subject: Objectivity, Nanaboozhoo and the Western Academy. Master's thesis, Department of Sociology and Equity Studies in Education, OISE/UT.

Uchendu, C. V. 1979. *Education and Politics in Tropical Africa*. London: Heineman.

Ungerleider, C. 1996. Immigration, Multiculturalism and Citizenship: The Evolution of Canadian Multiculturalism. Paper presented at the Learned Societies meeting of the Canadian Society for the Study of Education, 4 June, Brock University, St. Catharines, ON.

Walcott, R. 1990. "Theorising Anti-Racist Education." Western Canadian Anthropologist 7(2): 109-120.

Warren, D., M. L. J. Slikkerveer, and D. Brokensha, eds. 1995. *The Cultural Dimension of Development*. Exeter, UK: Intermediate Technology Publications.

wa Thiong'o, N. 1986. *Decolonising the Mind*. London: James Carrey.

Weismann, S. R. 1990. "Structural Adjustment in Africa: Insights from the Experiences of Ghana and Senegal." *World Development* 18(12):1621-1634.

White, B. 1996. "Talk About School: Education and the Colonial Project in French and British West Africa." *Comparative Education*. 32(1):9-20.

Wilson-Tagoe, N. 1997. "Reading Towards a Theorization of African Women's Writing: African Women Writers with Feminist Gynocriticism." In *Writing African Women: Gender, Popular Culture and Literature in West Africa*, edited by S. Newell. London: Zed Books.

Wisner, Ben. 1992. What Are Human Beings For? Rethinking Basic Human Needs, Sustainble Development and the Rio Summit. Paper presented at the Annual Conference of the Society for Applied Anthropology, 25-29 March, Memphis, TN.

World Bank. 1988. *Education in Sub-Saharan Africa: Adjustment, Revitalization and Expansion*. Washington: The World Bank.

_____. 1989. *Sub-Saharan Africa: From Crisis to Sustainable Development*. Washington: The World Bank.

_____. 1989. *Basis Education for Self-Employment and Rural Development: West Africa Region.* Washington: The World Bank.

_____. 1991. *World Development Report.* Washington: The World Bank.

_____. 1992. *The Third Report on Adjustment Lending: Private and Public Resources for Growth.* Washington: The World Bank.

Yuval-Davies, A. 1994. "Women, Ethnicity and Empowerment." *Feminism and Psychology* 4(1): 179-197.

Zeleza, T. 1997. "Fictions of the Postcolonial: A Review Article." *CODESRIA Bulletin* 2:15-19.

Zymelman, M. 1990. *Science Education and Development in Sub-Saharan Africa* (World Bank Technical Paper, no. 4). Washington: The World Bank.

APPENDIX

Family codes with subcodes

Class:	Career:	Community:	Curriculum:
access, cost, poverty, privilege, unequal, visible, study habits	motivation, history, path, goal, role profession, accountant, business, engineer	school/ community relations (S/C rel.), admission, church, distance, local economy	economics, math, music, phys ed, science, social studies, standard, subject, technology, extra curricular, exam
Demography: diverse, male/female (MF), religion, numbers, enrolment, outcome	**Dropout:** ability, afford, behaviour, employment, expectation, label, family, rural, school, sexuality, study habits, teacher/student resources	**Ed finance:** expenses, inequity, joint fund, public fund, research, facilities, cost, loans, scholarship	**Ed/value:** citizen, certification, contribute, employment, good life international, literacy, respect, security
Gender: behavior, access, divorce/ married, equal/same, equity, dress, harassment, math/science, parent, attitude, relations, role, segregate, standpoint, stereotype, teacher, tradition, treatment, rural differences, same, representation	**Local:** culture, geography, history, language, science, texts, value	**Parent/Child Relations (PC rel)** communication, home conflict, parent/authority	**Parent Involve[4]:** aspiration, parent, daily care, fee, guide, homework, monitor, parent/teacher rel, parented, role model, study help, teacher help time

PTA: mandate, obstacles, participation, procedures, projects	Peer: friends, pressure, proverb, school help, sports, youth problems	Priv/public[1]: expectations, outcomes, primary/secondary, private teachers, resources	Reform: assessment, critique, curricular, duration, FCUBE[2] hist/ed, implement, outcomes, political economy, resources, rural, science, subject, syllabus, textbook, training/practical
Regional: allowance, conflict, culture, difference/same, disparity, ethnicity, north/south, preference (discriminate), tribes, rural/urban	Religion: history, indigenous, interfaith relations, moral, policies, population, practice	School evaluation: academic rep, discipline, environment, equipped, facilities, food, grading, program teacher/student relations(T/S rel), reputation, schedules(shift)	Spiritual[3]: faith, interfaith
Student: ability, access, difference/same, ethnicity, minority, study habit	Student life: accommodation, conflict, day/board, discipline, fee, grading, grievance, home, inclusive, social, student governance, study, study groups, representation, work	Study program: field, goal,T/S rel, syllabus, resources	Success: academic, applied assessment, improvement, social, think
Teacher: approach, career history, career goal, collegial, dedicated	Teacher Practice: applied, approach, assessment	Teacher Training: certification, duration, evaluation	Text: authorship, availability, content, cost, publication

diversity, efficient, evaluation, female/male, good teacher, guide, harassment, incentives, listener, parent/teacher relations (P/T rel), punctual, qualifications renumeration represention role model, status, understand, work conditions, vocation	discipline, diverse, holistic, improvise, inclusive, innovative, integrative, listener, mixed ability, philosophy, structured, teacher authority, teacher/student relations	observation, incentives, practical, sponsorship, supports	technology

The following codes did not have subcodes:

Boundary	Early Childhood Education /ECE:	English	Fears	Future
Knowledge	Power[5]	Silence:	Special Needs	

Code Notes:

1. With regards to private schools and teaching , there is much in the transcripts under the codes related to teacher practices and working conditions in terms of evaluation, conditions of work and expectations.

2. FCUBE: Free Compulsory Basic Education.

3. Spirituality as a response to an independent question framed in that way has not elicited much discussion. However, by listening to the tapes and reading the transcripts it comes through in the context of discussions on religious practices but more so in discussions of local cultures, languages and ways of being in and seeing the world.

4. This theme comes up in the students', parents' and teachers' views on school involvement.

5. This issue as a general theme posed similar possibilities as theme of power (see note below).

6. Power was also identified as a parent code in some places. But it cuts across many relational topics discussed : parent/teacher relations, government reform processes (i.e., inadequate consultation), student governance, teacher/student relations, school community relations, parent/child relations, gender relations, issues of access in terms of class, rural and others, issues of discipline etc. It therefore has possibilities as a theme if examining this issue through the various other themes in which it emerges. However this poses a problem coding and then selecting the excerpts by code. Investigation of the issues of power and knowledge can be brought up as they emerge in the themes discussed or can be examined comprehensively as a topic of research across the various relevant themes.

Index

Key Concepts and Themes

Authors